Côte d'Ivoire

WORLD BIBLIOGRAPHICAL SERIES

General Editors:
Robert G. Neville (Executive Editor)
John J. Horton

Robert A. Myers   Hans H. Wellisch
Ian Wallace   Ralph Lee Woodward, Jr.

John J. Horton is Deputy Librarian of the University of Bradford and was formerly Chairman of its Academic Board of Studies in Social Sciences. He has maintained a longstanding interest in the discipline of area studies and its associated bibliographical problems, with special reference to European Studies. In particular he has published in the field of Icelandic and of Yugoslav studies, including the two relevant volumes in the World Bibliographical Series.

Robert A. Myers is Associate Professor of Anthropology in the Division of Social Sciences and Director of Study Abroad Programs at Alfred University, Alfred, New York. He has studied post-colonial island nations of the Caribbean and has spent two years in Nigeria on a Fulbright Lectureship. His interests include international public health, historical anthropology and developing societies. In addition to *Amerindians of the Lesser Antilles: a bibliography* (1981), *A Resource Guide to Dominica, 1493-1986* (1987) and numerous articles, he has compiled the World Bibliographical Series volumes on *Dominica* (1987), *Nigeria* (1989) and *Ghana* (1991).

Ian Wallace is Professor of German at the University of Bath. A graduate of Oxford in French and German, he also studied in Tübingen, Heidelberg and Lausanne before taking teaching posts at universities in the USA, Scotland and England. He specializes in contemporary German affairs, especially literature and culture, on which he has published numerous articles and books. In 1979 he founded the journal *GDR Monitor*, which he continues to edit under its new title *German Monitor*.

Hans H. Wellisch is Professor emeritus at the College of Library and Information Services, University of Maryland. He was President of the American Society of Indexers and was a member of the International Federation for Documentation. He is the author of numerous articles and several books on indexing and abstracting, and has published *The Conversion of Scripts and Indexing and Abstracting: an International Bibliography*, and *Indexing from A to Z*. He also contributes frequently to *Journal of the American Society for Information Science*, *The Indexer* and other professional journals.

Ralph Lee Woodward, Jr. is Professor of History at Tulane University, New Orleans. He is the author of *Central America, a Nation Divided*, 2nd ed. (1985), as well as several monographs and more than seventy scholarly articles on modern Latin America. He has also compiled volumes in the World Bibliographical Series on *Belize* (1980), *El Salvador* (1988), *Guatemala* (Rev. Ed.) (1992) and *Nicaragua* (Rev. Ed.) (1994). Dr. Woodward edited the Central American section of the *Research Guide to Central America and the Caribbean* (1985) and is currently associate editor of Scribner's *Encyclopedia of Latin American History*.

VOLUME 131

Côte d'Ivoire

Morna Daniels

Compiler

CLIO PRESS

OXFORD, ENGLAND · SANTA BARBARA, CALIFORNIA
DENVER, COLORADO

British Library Cataloguing in Publication Data
Daniels, Morna
Côte d'Ivoire – (World bibliographical series; v. 131)
1. Côte d'Ivoire – Bibliography
I. Title
016.9'6668

ISBN 1–85109–120–3

ABC-CLIO Ltd.,
Old Clarendon Ironworks,
35A Great Clarendon Street,
Oxford OX2 6AT, England.

———————

ABC-CLIO Inc.,
130 Cremona Drive,
Santa Barbara,
CA 93116, USA.

Designed by Bernard Crossland.
Typeset by Columns Design and Production Services Ltd., Reading, England.
Printed and bound in Great Britain by Bookcraft (Bath) Ltd., Midsomer Norton.

THE WORLD BIBLIOGRAPHICAL SERIES

This series, which is principally designed for the English speaker, will eventually cover every country (and many of the world's principal regions), each in a separate volume comprising annotated entries on works dealing with its history, geography, economy and politics; and with its people, their culture, customs, religion and social organization. Attention will also be paid to current living conditions – housing, education, newspapers, clothing, etc. – that are all too often ignored in standard bibliographies; and to those particular aspects relevant to individual countries. Each volume seeks to achieve, by use of careful selectivity and critical assessment of the literature, an expression of the country and an appreciation of its nature and national aspirations, to guide the reader towards an understanding of its importance. The keynote of the series is to provide, in a uniform format, an interpretation of each country that will express its culture, its place in the world, and the qualities and background that make it unique. The views expressed in individual volumes, however, are not necessarily those of the publisher.

VOLUMES IN THE SERIES

*To my mother, on whose 80th birthday
I was completing the text.*

Contents

Contents

Contents

Introduction

The Côte d'Ivoire lies on the West African Atlantic coast between 4° and 11° latitude north and 3° and 8° longitude west, and covers an area of 322,463 square kilometres (124,503 square miles). Its name became officially accepted in the French form in 1986, to avoid confusion over translations into various languages of 'Ivory Coast'. Ivory was an important early export, and an elephant's head features in the country's crest, but the declining elephant population is prey to poachers. Its neighbours are Ghana to the east, Burkina Faso and Mali in the north and Guinea and Liberia to the west. Its largest city and former capital is the port of Abidjan with an estimated population of two and a half million. The official administrative capital was moved to Yamoussoukro, the home town of President Houphouët-Boigny, in 1983. It grew rapidly, and a huge Roman Catholic basilica, a larger copy of St. Peter's in Rome, was consecrated by Pope John Paul II in 1990.

The Côte d'Ivoire is a country of great social contrasts, between the air-conditioned sky-scrapers in Abidjan, where land values are among the highest in Sub-Saharan Africa and office work is computerized, and agricultural villages to which the same office workers return in order to renew their links with their ethnic group. Here many believe in animism and the power of sorcerors and take part in traditional ceremonies and funerals, often wearing body-enveloping masks.

The country's four main rivers, which flow north–south into the Atlantic, are (from west to east): the Cavally, the Sassandra, the Bandama, which has been dammed to form Lake Kossou and to produce hydro-electricity, and the Comoé.

The coastline of the Côte d'Ivoire has deterred traders throughout history because of 'la barre', a heavy surf and strong currents caused by on-shore winds. Access was easier in the eastern half, where the coastline is penetrated by sandy lagoons and trading posts such as Grand-Lahou and Jacqueville (called Grand Jack until colonization by the French in the late nineteenth century) and Grand-Bassam became established. The general physical relief of the country is formed by a sloping plateau rising from the coastal plain to an average of 300-400 metres above sea level in the north. The only mountainous area is in the extreme north-west adjoining Guinea, where the Dan and Toura mountains reach 1,300 metres at their highest point. Mount Nimba, the country's highest mountain at 1,752 metres, is at the point where the borders of Guinea, Liberia and the Côte d'Ivoire meet.

Half the country is covered by rainforest, which is thickest in the south-west, although it has been cleared for agriculture to such an extent that environmental programmes are under way to preserve what forest remains and to re-plant some areas. The centre of the country is an area of transition to the humid grassland savannah of the north, which becomes drier and less wooded towards the northern border.

Rainfall varies widely over the country. It is heaviest in the mountainous Man region, and along the coast at the eastern and western ends, and lightest in the north-east of the country. The climate of the southern part of the country is humid equatorial. Annual rainfall in Abidjan, on the coast, averages 2,000 mm. It falls in about 140 days of the year, June being by far the wettest month, followed by July. April, May, September and October are also fairly wet. Humidity here can top 90 per cent while average annual temperatures range only between 25° and 28° centigrade. In the west of the country, the rainy season is from July to September, and the climate is a little cooler and less humid. In the north-east annual rainfall averages 1,000 mm. Tropical showers fall between June and October and a long and very hot dry period lasts from November to May, up to 40° centigrade in the day, but with cool nights. In December and January the harmattan winds blow sand and dust from the desert.

The 1991 population estimate is 14 million, with foreigners numbering over 2 million, since there are no restrictions on immigration. Most of the immigrants are from Burkina Faso, Guinea, Ghana and Mali, with smaller numbers from Mauretania and Senegal. There is a Syrian–Lebanese commercial community of about 120,000 and officially about 30,000 French people (the true figure is probably nearly twice that) though, as a result of Ivoirization campaigns, only 1,600 were working in 1989. Such large numbers of immigrants seeking work have caused friction and even riots in times of economic hardship. Average population growth between 1975 and 1988 was 3.8 per cent, with an increase in the annual rate of immigration of 6 per cent; 45 per cent of Ivoirians were under fifteen.

Population density is only 34 inhabitants per square kilometre, so a projected population of over 20 million by 2005 does not alarm the authorities. They are concerned, however, with urban over-population which has led to slums in Abidjan and San Pedro. Average life expectancy at birth was 56 in 1988, but infant and child mortality are still high. The population of Abidjan is about 2.5 million. The alarming spread of AIDS and other infections such as TB which prey on HIV-positive patients, is placing a strain on health and welfare services, since even the non-infected children of infected parents may become orphaned. The 9th AIDS Conference in 1993 heard that about 11 per cent of adults in Abidjan were HIV-positive. Malaria may also be resisting existing drug treatments, and a high proportion of the population is affected.

The native population falls into four large ethnic clusters, or five if one follows the theory that the Lagoon cluster is not Akan. Each of these clusters is present in neighbouring countries. These larger clusters are further divided into over sixty ethnic groups, who speak different dialects, though many within one cluster may be related.

The Mande people stretch from Senegal across Africa. The Southern Mande are among the oldest settlers of the Côte d'Ivoire, and are found in the forest region. They include the Dan, the Guro and the Toura and the Gagou. These groups were pushed towards the south and west by the Northern Mande or Manding, who occupy the north-west and who migrated from Mali from the end of the fifteenth to the seventeenth centuries. They are mostly Muslim and include the Malinké and the Diula.

The north-east and north-centre of the country form only a corner of the territory occupied by the Voltaic group, who inhabit Burkina Faso, Northern Ghana and Benin. These include the Senufo, among the oldest inhabitants of the Côte d'Ivoire, who once covered a wide area, but retreated under pressure from the Malinké from the west and the Baule in the south to their present still-extensive area in the north-centre of the country. The Kulango, also long established in the country, were compressed into their present position in the north-east in the eighteenth century by other Voltaic groups, the Lobi and Birifor, who now occupy the extreme north-east of the country.

The Kru group extends into Liberia. They moved into their present position in the south-west of the country in the fourteenth and fifteenth centuries under pressure from the Northern Mande to the north, and the Akan in the east. They are very fragmented, and include the Dida, the Godié, the Bété, the Bakwé, the Kru proper, and the Wè, formerly considered to be two groups, the Guéré and the Wobe.

The Akan cluster are distributed throughout southern Ghana. Waves of immigrants entered the Côte d'Ivoire from there. The Abron settled in the Bondoukou area in the fifteenth century, and they established their kingdom there in the seventeenth century. The Agni settled along the eastern border of the country, and the Baule in the forested savannah east of the centre, where they have become the dominant ethnic group of the country, especially as President Houphouët-Boigny and his successor Henri Konan Bédié are both Baule. The Lagoon peoples may be early Akan settlers, or may be a distinct cluster, but they have fragmented into about thirteen small groups along the coast.

Numerically, the Baule form the largest group (23 per cent), followed by the Bété (18 per cent), the Senufo (15 per cent), and the Malinké (11 per cent). Migration towards the town and plantations of the south has lead to a complete ethnic mix in the towns. French is the official language of the country, and the language of education, particularly secondary education. Diula is spoken by many as a language for trade, and many also use pidgin French.

About 25 per cent of the country is Muslim and 15 per cent Christian, mainly Roman Catholic. The latter group includes much of the ruling élite. Most other people follow syncretic cults loosely based on Islam or Christianity (which leads to considerable variations in the statistics quoted for these religions), or are animist, and many official members of Western religions also hold to animist beliefs and practices.

President Houphouët-Boigny was born in 1905 (or even earlier) and elected President at independence in 1960, when he was already Prime Minister. He retained his position until his death on 7 December 1993, when he was succeeded by his chosen candidate Henri Konan Bédié. He was strongly pro-Western, retaining close ties with France and welcoming foreign investment. He achieved an era of peace, stability and prosperity rare in Africa, and even when he was forced to allow other political parties than his own to enter politics and contest the elections, he retained his position. The rapid economic growth after independence was hailed as the 'African miracle', although the economy has faltered since the mid-1980s.

Eighty per cent of the labour force is employed in agriculture. The Côte d'Ivoire is the world's largest producer of cocoa, and cocoa accounts for about 34 per cent of the country's exports. The government tried to resist the world decline in cocoa prices in 1988, by stockpiling cocoa and subsidizing its growers, but was forced to sell eventually, largely in block sales, and to reduce guaranteed prices for growers by half by 1990. From 1991 the government has been able to sell the crop forward, and after the devaluation of the CFA (Communauté Financière Africaine) franc was able to increase the producer price from 200 CFA francs per kilogram to 240 CFA francs for 1993/4 and 290 CFA francs for 1994/5. Prospects for increases in production and prices are good. Coffee, of which the Côte d'Ivoire is the third-largest producer, forms about 7 per cent of exports. Plans were announced in 1994 for a programme to renew neglected plants. Timber is an important export, at about 8 per cent of the total, but supplies are becoming exhausted. Other commercial crops in order of significance are palm oil, cotton, sugar, pineapples, bananas and rubber. It is hoped to expand rubber production. Food crops are yams, cassava, plantains, rice and maize. Meat animals are goats, cattle and poultry, who supply only 40 per cent of requirements, the rest being imported from the European Union or Sahel countries.

France is the country's main trading partner, taking 15 per cent of exports, and supplying about 32 per cent of imports. Germany, the Netherlands, Italy and the United States are next in importance as receivers of exports. After international donors and the European Union, France is the major provider of development assistance, at 356.6 million dollars in 1991. There is also aid from Japan, West Germany and the United States.

Oil production started in 1980, but output has proved disappointing. Large amounts of crude oil are imported for refining at the Vridi refinery at Abidjan, and much of it is re-exported. Most electricity was produced by hydro-electric power, but after the droughts of 1983-84, thermal sources were increasingly used, and now provide over 40 per cent of requirements. There are diamond mines at Tortiya and Séguéla, and gold is mined at Ity in the west, and at Aniuri.

The currency of the country is the CFA (Communauté Financière Africaine) franc, which had a fixed exchange rate with the French franc of 50 CFA francs to 1 French franc until 11 January 1994, when it was devalued by 50 per cent. The CFA is shared by other members of the West African Monetary Union (Union Monétaire de l'Afrique de l'Ouest): Senegal, Mali, Niger, Burkina Faso, Togo and Benin.

The country is governed by a president, and, since 1990, a prime minister, an innovation which was designed to allow the elderly president Houphouët-Boigny to relinquish the day-to-day running of affairs and to avoid a vacuum on his death. There are 175 members in the National Assembly, elected every five years. The country is divided into 50 départements, 185 sub-prefectures and 132 communes, administered by prefects, sub-prefects and mayors, respectively. Traditional customs have been suppressed by law in the interest of unity and development, to encourage the nuclear family and to advance the rights of women. Polygamy, traditional matrilineal rules of inheritance, whereby property may not descend to a couple's children but may pass to the spouse's male relatives, and the payment of dowries are abolished in law, but continue in fact. Female circumcision also persists.

History

Tradition claims that the earliest inhabitants of the Côte d'Ivoire were pygmies, and the Gagou, who are certainly among the oldest inhabitants of the country, are their descendants. From Neolithic times the Bété occupied an area between the Cavally and Sassandra rivers to the north-east of their present territory, but were displaced from the eighth to eleventh centuries by invading Dan across the Sassandra to settle between Soubré and Guibéroua. The Senufo have probably occupied the north of the country from prehistoric times.

By the tenth century Lohron, later known as the Kulango, were established in the savannah regions of the North. The Senufo, who originally occupied a large area, were pushed north by the Baoulé. In the twelfth century Kong was founded as a trading centre by the Senufo.

The fourteenth and fifteenth centuries saw the first Manding migrations into the Côte d'Ivoire from the north. From 1490 to 1510 a second wave of Manding immigrants arrived from the north, the most important group in this wave being the Kamara or Diomandé. Europeans, in particular the Portuguese and Dutch, began to trade with native boats, from what they called the Côte des Dents [teeth], referring to the ivory which they bought. The country was also known as the Côte des Mal-Gens, because of the fearsome appearance of the natives, and the belief that they were cannibals.

In the sixteenth century the Malinké began moving into the north-west of the country and the Lohron moved into the north-east. The Kru settled the western coastal area. In this and the next century the Abron migrated from the Gold Coast to the Bondoukou area.

In the middle of the sixteenth century the kingdom of Gbona, or as the French transcribed it, Bouna was founded, traditionally by a ruler named Boukani, among the Lohron, to whom he gave the name Kulango, or 'loyal vassals', the name by which they are now better known. The kingdom expanded greatly, and the Lobi, to the north, became its vassals. The seventeenth century also saw Malinké and Peul immigration into the Odienné region in the north-west. During the seventeenth and eighteenth centuries there was also a limited slave trade by Europeans.

The French attempted to settle Assinie in 1637. Of five Capuchin missionaries, three soon died and the other two fled to the Portuguese Axim, now Ghana. In 1670 the Nzima from the Gold Coast conquered the coastal area. In 1687 the Frenchmen Damon and Ducasse signed an agreement at Assinie with the Essouma kingdom to allow the establishment of a Dominican mission, but Father Cerizier died a few years later, and Father Gonzalvès retreated to Dahomey. In 1688 two Ivoirians, Banga and Anaiba from Assinie, were taken to visit the court of Louis XIV and entered royal service for a time. They returned to the Côte d'Ivoire in 1695 and 1701 respectively. In 1690 the ancient Abron kingdom of Gyaman was created, which included the Senufo, Mande, Abron and Agni.

Between 1700 and 1750 the Baule migrated from the Gold Coast into the centre of the country under their princess Abla Pokou and established a kingdom in the Bouaké area where they searched for gold.

The eighteenth century saw the main immigration of the Akan from the Gold Coast, pushed west by the Ashanti, though some may have migrated into the east of the Côte d'Ivoire in the previous two centuries, and some historians believe the Lagoon people of the coast were originally Akan who migrated from the east earlier. The Guro began to be pushed out of the area now occupied by the Bété, Baule and Malinké to their present territory.

In 1701 Damon brought more French ships and missionaries to establish a fort called Saint-Louis at Assinie. In 1702 the fort was attacked and the attack repulsed, but the discouraged French abandoned the fort in 1704. Sékou Ouattara founded the Diula Kong empire in 1705, in order to protect trade in ivory, cotton, gold, iron and wool. Kong became one of the great towns of Islamic Africa, and the empire occupied the north-east of the country and stretched into Mali. In 1725, during one of the many wars between Bouna and Bondoukou, Bouna was captured and burned by the Abron king Adingra Panyin. Further raids occurred in 1750 and 1790.

From 1730 to 1850 Agni groups migrated into the Côte d'Ivoire from the Gold Coast, and in the mid-18th century established the independent kingdoms of Moronou and Indénié (or N'dényé). There is still an Agni monarch today. In 1740 the Ashanti conquered the kingdom of Gyaman and maintained their domination until 1875 in spite of many Abron revolts.

Eighteenth-century Bondoukou grew as the trading centre of the Gyaman kingdom, a point of exchange between Diula and Ashanti traders. It also became a Muslim academic and religious centre.

In 1760 Bambara people, sent by King Ségou to help the Malinké of Odienné, seized territory for themselves and, allied with the

Diomandé, created the small kingdom of Nafana on the present north-west border of the Côte d'Ivoire.

Bouna was sacked by the Abron in 1815. Abu Bakr al Siddiq, a scholar from Timbuktu, was captured and taken into slavery by the Abron. From 1819 Catholic missions penetrated West Africa. The Fathers of the Holy Spirit settled in the Côte d'Ivoire. In about 1820 the Muslim state of Kabadougou was founded in north-west, and organized from 1830 by Vacaba Touré, a Diula, who invaded Guinea and created a large territory centred on Odienné. His son extended his conquests into Mali. Further attacks on Bouna occurred in 1825, 1853 and 1875 but the kingdom of Bouna survived because of its trading activities and its reputations as an centre of Islamic learning.

In 1843, Fleuriot de Langle, under the orders of the Frenchman Bouët-Villaumez, occupied Assinie and Bassam. He signed a treaty with Chief Amatifou in accordance with which he placed his lands under the authority of King Louis-Philippe, in exchange for help from the sailors in their fight against the Ebrié. A block-house, Fort-Joinville, was established, but after two deaths it was abandoned by 1844. In 1843, after a treaty was signed with local chiefs, a fort was established at Dabou to control the Ebrié lagoon and to protect trade.

From 1843 to 1858 the Etablissements Régis Aîné of Marseille traded at Assinie and Grand-Bassam and in 1854 installed themselves at Dabou. The French attacked the Abure of Bassam in 1849, and in 1853 a revolt against the French posts along the Ebrié lagoon was crushed. In 1858 Arthur Verdier took over the trading-post at Grand-Bassam when Régis left and in 1860 he created the Compagnie de Kong, a private trading company. In 1871 French posts in the Côte d'Ivoire were temporarily evacuated as a result of France's defeat at home by Germany, but they were officially re-occupied in 1883. The first cocoa plantation was established in 1880, and in 1881 the first coffee trees were planted at Elima, on the east bank of the Aby lagoon, and the first mahogany logs shipped out by Arthur Verdier.

In 1888 Louis-Gustave Binger and Marcel Treich-Laplène, who had been leading separate explorations from the coast, met in Bondoukou and signed a protectorate treaty with the Abron king Adjumani. They also visited Kong and then travelled to the coast where they arrived in 1889, having signed numerous treaties of alliance.Their explorations were a result of the plan to fulfil the conditions of the 1885 Congress of Berlin which laid down that territories should be occupied by the European powers which claimed them.

In 1889 Samori (or Samory) Touré, a Malinké, who from 1880 had established a large empire in the countries to the north and west of the Côte d'Ivoire, entered the Côte d'Ivoire itself and expanded his conquests and destruction. In 1892 Binger and the English Major Lang travelled inland from the coast on the eastern border of the country to draw up a frontier between the Côte d'Ivoire and the Gold Coast. The campaign against Samori intensified. A decree issued on 10 March 1893 established French colonial government. Louis-Gustave Binger was named first governor, with his headquarters at Grand-Bassam, a post he filled until 1895. He used military force to occupy the western part of the country, including Sassandra, Grand-Béréby, Tabou and Bliéron, and established Cavally as the most western town. Although he was himself a Protestant, he encouraged the establishment of the Missionaries of Lyon. In 1893 the Baule began their resistance to the French and in the ensuing war Tiassalé was captured by Captain Marchand. The Guro fought Samori who invaded their territory.

The Baule revolt flared up again in 1895 and continued until 1911. The Agni too offered protracted resistance to French conquest. The struggle with Samori continued. In 1896 his son Saranké Mori sacked Bouna because of its European bias. The Guro inflicted a defeat on Samori himself. In 1897 Bondoukou was overrun by Samori but later re-established. Kong was captured and destroyed. Captian Braulot and his detachment were killed in the Bouna area by Mori.

The French steadily increased their domination. They occupied Odienné in the north-west, a centre of the Kabadougou kingdom, after having been called in to help in internal struggles. Conquest was not steady, however. In 1898 a revolt occurred at Bouaké against increasing demands for forced labour to build the railway. The Guro also engaged in a bitter struggle with the French invaders, which continued until 1913. They were never totally subdued. Bouna in the north-east was captured by the French in 1898, but French attempts to conquer the Dan and occupy the Man region in the west failed. The Dan were not conquered until 1921. In 1899 the Ngban and Ouarébo of Toumodi rose against the French who burned Toumodi. The French at last defeated Samori and on 29 September 1898 captured him near Guélémou and sent him into exile in Gabon, where he died in 1900.

In 1899 Grand-Bassam was decimated by yellow fever and the next year the capital was transferred to the more salubrious Bingerville.

Imposition of a head tax in 1900 was resisted by the native population and enforced only after bitter battles. There was a military occupation of the Baule region. The revolts of various ethnic groups and their suppression continued until 1911. The population was disarmed and fined, and regrouped into a uniform administration, many of the chiefs having been exiled.

Gabriel Angoulvant became governor in 1908 until 1915. He imposed an authoritarian rule with a strict administrative hierarchy and the centralization of the administration in urban centres. He began the cultivation of cash crops. In 1910 he faced a great revolt of the Abbé who lived in the forest area of Agboville, on the railway line. It was caused by colonial interference in their local affairs, by tax increases and increased forced labour, and by religious objections to the railway. They were subdued by the end of the year. Military recruitment caused discontent throughout the native population.

From 1913 to 1915, the missionary William Wade Harris (who came from Liberia) gained a great number of converts to his version of Christianity. He was expelled in 1915.

In 1914 many tribesmen volunteered to fight in the Great War in the hope of booty, but by 1917 forest-dwelling tribes were fleeing from military recruitment, and the Agni of Assinie went to the Gold Coast. Increased demands for agricultural products and rubber for the war effort increased discontent. Even after the war forced labour continued for both public projects and private plantations. The French plantation owners were paid the market price for their crops, while the African planters were paid artificially low prices while providing their own labour.

In 1919 Senegal, Mauretania, Guinea, Niger, Dahomey and the Côte d'Ivoire were all incorporated into French West Africa. The Upper Volta (now Burkina Faso) became a separate colony but in 1932 it was dismembered and divided between the French Sudan (now Mali), Niger and the Côte d'Ivoire. This did not, however, bring the expected economic benefits to the Côte d'Ivoire. The capital was transferred from Bingerville to Abidjan in 1934, and in 1937 a decree granted French citizenship to a very few Africans who fulfilled eleven conditions. The Upper Volta became a separate administrative unit. It later reverted to its previous status as a separate colony – in 1947.

At the beginning of the Second World War many Africans were sympathetic to the French cause in Europe as they abhorred Hitler's racism. Volunteers served with French forces, and a resistance movement arose against the Vichy government of French West Africa. In 1941 the king of Bondoukou, his son Prince Kouamé Adingra and ten thousand of his subjects migrated to the Gold Coast to serve with the Free French.

The Federation of French colonies in West Africa was created in 1944, with its capital in Dakar, Senegal. In the same year the Brazzaville Declaration called for the end of forced labour and reforms in administration. Félix Houphouët-Boigny began his political career by campaigning for fairer cocoa prices for African farmers in 1932, and in 1944 formed the African Agricultural Union to combat forced labour and obtain equal treatment for African planters.

In November 1945 Houphouët-Boigny was elected to the French National Assembly, and he remained a member until 1959. On 9 April 1946, he founded the Parti Démocratique de Côte d'Ivoire, and achieved a great triumph in April when, at his urging, the French Assemblée Nationale abolished forced labour. In October he helped found the Rassemblement Démocratique Africain, a pan-African movement, and the PDCI became its local branch. The French settlers struggled to retain their rights, and used *agents provocateurs* to create disturbances for which PDCI leaders were imprisoned. The settlers also got rid of the liberal governor André Latrille. In 1949 the PDCI, prompted by the French Communist Party, became involved in a series of strikes, boycotts and demonstrations. A warrant was issued for the arrest of Houphouët-Boigny on 24 January 1950, but his membership of the French National Assembly protected him from arrest. On 30 January troops shot 13 protesters at Dimbroko. Houphouët-Boigny decided to end his party's affiliation with the French Communist Party and in the next year aligned himself with the Socialists.

The Vridi Canal was opened in 1950 to allow better access to Abidjan from the sea.

In 1956 reforms were passed in the French National Assembly to introduce universal suffrage and local government for overseas France. The PDCI won seven seats in the January elections and Houphouët-Boigny was made a French cabinet minister. He continued to hold ministerial posts in Paris until 1959 and favoured close ties with France rather than a West African Federation with its capital at Dakar.

Riots against immigrants in 1958 led to the expulsion of 18,000 African foreigners. A referendum on 28 September decided in favour of independence. The Federation of French colonies in West Africa was disbanded but the Côte d'Ivoire voted for membership of the French Community.

Houphouët-Boigny became Prime Minster of Côte d'Ivoire in April 1959, but retained his French ministry. On 6 May the Conseil de l'Entente, a political and economic confederation was created, at the instigation of the Côte d'Ivoire, to include the Côte d'Ivoire, Dahomey, the Upper Volta and Niger. On 9 June the Côte d'Ivoire, Dahomey, Senegal, Mali, Mauretania and Niger created a customs union for West Africa, the Union Douanière des Etats de l'Afrique de l'Ouest.

On 6 August 1960 the Independence Agreement was signed and in the evening Houphouët-Boigny proclaimed in parliament that the Côte d'Ivoire would be independent from midnight. Independence is celebrated annually on 7 August. On 27 November Houphouët-Boigny was elected President.

In 1963 a foiled coup against Houphouët-Boigny was reported. The chief of internal security, Henry Goba, uncovered a 'plot' against the government. The Presidents of the National Assembly and the Supreme Court, ministers and members of parliament, and Ahmadou Koné, a writer, were arrested or confined to house arrest, accused at a show trial of leading a 'communist plot'. The President of the Supreme Court, Ernest Boka, died in detention, officially suicide. Those condemned had their death sentences commuted.

Another plot against the government was discovered in 1964, but by the end of the year the opposition had been suppressed. Legislation was passed to prohibit polygamy, the payment of a bride-price and matrilineal inheritance, but they still continue. In 1966 three former ministers and nearly a hundred political detainees were released and returned exiles pardoned. In 1967 Kraghé Gnagbé, an opponent of the President, created a 'Parti Nationaliste'. He was arrested, and rumoured to have been imprisoned in a lunatic asylum, but was later exiled to his village in the Gagnoa sub-prefecture.

In 1968 Houphouët-Boigny declared national mourning and an amnesty for political prisoners on the death of his mother. He admitted there had never been a plot against him, but that he had been misled by his chief of security, who had since died.

On 24 May 1969 the President ordered the closure of Abidjan University after an outbreak of student unrest. Public 'dialogues' were held with students. In 1970 Gnagbé was the focus of unrest among the Bété in the Gagnoa region where he organized a strike. The army suppressed the movement and rumours suggested that between 3,000 and 4,000 people may have been killed. Gnagbé was not seen again.

The oil crisis of 1973 had a grave effect on the economy as the Côte d'Ivoire has few mineral resources. Twelve young army officers were tried and convicted for planning a coup that was to have taken place on 7 August. They were imprisoned, but all except Sio Koulahou were released some years later. In the late 1970s the government borrowed heavily to finance ambitious projects, and the high cost of servicing the debt has been one of the factors leading to a recession since 1981. In 1977 three senior ministers were purged, amid allegations of corruption, as the country faced economic problems. Among them was Henri Konan Bédié, who lost his post as

Finance Minister but served as an adviser to the World Bank until 1980, when he returned to the Côte d'Ivoire and became President of the National Assembly.

In 1980 there were rumours of a coup attempt by Oulaï Zoumana, the police chief.

In the face of recession, the government imposed austerity measures in January 1981, and the first structural adjustment loan was made by the International Monetary Fund. In February there was a cabinet re-shuffle to appoint younger, more technically proficient members. The worsening economic conditions nearly led to a general strike. A drought in 1982-84 caused hardships which were alleviated by good harvests in 1985-86.

In 1982 students went on strike; the University was closed and grants suspended. Laurent Gbagbo, a Bété from Gagnoa, and the leader of one of the main opposition parties, the Front Populaire Ivoirien, went into exile. The next year saw a teachers' strike, and they were followed by doctors and pharmacists. The President sacked the Minister of Education and ordered the teachers back to work.

Houphouët-Boigny was re-elected as President in 1985. He restored diplomatic links with Israel and the Soviet Union. The Pope visited Côte d'Ivoire and consecrated a new cathedral in Abidjan. The President successfully mediated an end to the Christmas border war between Burkina Faso and Mali. Relations with Burkina were strained while the radical Captain Thomas Sankara was head of state, but after he was overthrown and assassinated in 1987, and succeeded by Blaise Compaoré, whose wife was a niece of the President, relations improved. In April 1986 the President announced that the country would officially be called Côte d'Ivoire and not the translated name of Ivory Coast. In 1987 a Bété, Robert Gbai Tagro, called a congress of his 'Parti Républicain de Côte d'Ivoire', but it was banned and its leaders imprisoned.

In 1987 the fall in coffee and cocoa prices and the outflow of capital led to an annual balance of payments deficit of $970 million. The country's foreign debt was over $8 billion and the government suspended debt repayments. Backed by French aid, the President placed an embargo on cocoa exports in an attempt to maintain prices in the face of speculation, but in 1989 he had to lower the guaranteed price of cocoa to producers. The balance-of-payments deficit continued to worsen. During the 1980s the government re-negotiated agreements with the London Club (of commercial bank creditors), and the Paris Club (of Western Bank creditors), and received three structural adjustment loans from the World Bank. The government reduced state expenditure and abolished some of the inefficient state organizations for the sale of agricultural commodities. In September 1989 the $14 billion debt was re-scheduled by the Paris Club of Western government creditors over 14 years, and new loans were received from the IMF and the World Bank. The government promised austerity measures.

In 1988 construction began on a huge Roman Catholic basilica at Yamoussoukro. Its official cost was 40 billion CFA francs, but it may have cost twice that (about $200 million). Houphouët-Boigny insisted the money came from himself and his family. It was accepted by the Pope, after some misgivings at the expense, in 1989, and consecrated by His Holiness in September 1990.

In September 1988 Laurent Gbagbo returned from exile to lead the opposition to the government. A business acquaintance, Kobena Innocent Anaky, was tried and given a twenty-year prison sentence for financial crimes, though it was suspected that his real 'crime' was to finance the Front Populaire Ivoirien. From February to May 1990 there were protests and strikes in the public sector against government plans to lower public service pay and increase taxes at the urging of the World Bank. Army mutineers even seized the airport for a day. The government gave way and relaxed the austerity measures. After anti-government street demonstrations, and strikes and disturbances among students, Houphouët-Boigny announced in May the installation of a multi-party system after 30 years of single-party rule. Nine opposition parties were approved.

In October Houphouët-Boigny won an overwhelming victory (82 per cent of the vote) in the first multi-party elections, and was elected for a seventh five-year term as president, though there were accusations of vote-rigging. The PDCI also won the parliamentary elections, with 163 out of the 175 seats. Under the new constitution, a Prime Minister, Alassane Ouattara, was appointed, to run the country on a day-to-day basis, while Houphouët-Boigny retained his symbolic powers. Ouattara was born in Burkina Faso and has a Burkinabè father, and great support among Burkinabè immigrants and the Muslim population of the north. In April he had been appointed President of the Inter-ministerial Coordination Committee for the economic recovery programme and he announced a new programme in June. He eventually gave notice to 7,000 government officials and sold off government vehicles.

In 1991 Prime Minister Ouattara conducted tough negotiations with the IMF over a structural adjustment programme and introduced reforms in public and private financial management, in taxation and the Stock Exchange. He also began a programme of privatizing public companies. On the 20 June Ouattara ordered the dissolution of the student federation after the death of a student in a riot. Further strikes and demonstrations followed, including a demonstration of 10,000 people in Abidjan calling for the resignation of the government. A report issued the following year condemned the army for indulging in torture and rape, but no one was punished, and further riots took place, followed by arrests, including that of the student leader Martial Ahipeaud and the opposition leader Laurent Gbagbo. Gbagbo and others were fined and sentenced to two years in prison, under legislation which had been rushed through, making leaders responsible for the actions of their followers. They were released six months later. It was also in 1992 that the Côte d'Ivoire's external debt reached $20 billion, and the IMF suspended payments on the grounds that financial reforms were not being implemented. As a result of the Liberian civil war, begun in December 1989, 250,000 refugees had entered the Côte d'Ivoire. Doctors announced that the numbers of AIDS cases had tripled in a year, with 10,000 cases and 500,000 people HIV-positive.

On 7 December 1993 Houphouët-Boigny died at Yamoussoukro. Henri Konan Bédié succeeded as President in spite of a challenge from Prime Minister Ouattara. He designated Daniel Kablan Duncan, an economist considered to be apart from political struggles, as Prime Minister.

On 11 January 1994 the heads of state of the Franc Zone met at Dakar and devalued the CFA franc by 50 per cent from midnight of that day. The Ivoirian government cushioned the effect by announcing price increases of 20 per cent for coffee and 45 per cent for cocoa, the lowering of some taxes and duties, freezing of most prices, and slight increases in public salaries. As the year progressed, the Côte d'Ivoire suffered less than other francophone countries, as exports increased at rising prices. Prices within the country rose about 40 per cent. Farmers switched to producing food for domestic consumption, and yams, bananas and manioc flour replaced imported foods. Money sent abroad before the devaluation flooded back to be available for investment, and new petrol deposits were announced. The gold-mines at Afema and Ity produced over two tons of gold.

In January 1994 a new agreement was signed with the IMF which included 281 billion CFA francs in aid over three years. In February the World Bank agreed aid of 260 billion CFA francs for 1994, and in March the European Union offered 28.5 million écus for development and the Paris Club re-scheduled debts on condition of government savings. In May and June Switzerland and Canada also wrote off part of the debts owed to them. On 7 February 1994 the funeral of Houphouet-Boigny took place in the basilica at Yamoussoukro. In

April Laurent Gbagbo protested at the arrest of his second-in-command Abou Dramane Sangaré as the result of an article he wrote inciting civil resistance. In September agreements were signed with American companies to explore off-shore gas. In October the international community pledged over $2 million to fight AIDS and 10,000 people attended a rally organized by the Rassemblement des Républicains, a splinter of the PDCI formed in June. In November legislation was announced to deprive non-Ivoirians of their right to vote, and to insist that both parents of any presidential candidates should be Ivoirian, which was seen as a move against the main presidential rival Alassane Ouattara.

In spite of a boycott by the opposition parties and public disorders in the preceding months, presidential elections were held on 22 October 1995. Henri Konan Bédié was re-elected. Only 1.72 million votes were cast although there are 3.8 million registered voters.

Notes on arrangement, transcriptions and sources

The arrangement of this bibliography is alphabetical, by title, except for the sections on the ethnic groups, languages and part of the arts section where it seemed more helpful to arrange items by ethnic group; and the history section, where a chronological arrangement seemed more appropriate. Transcription of ethnic names varies in the literature. One of the main problems is caused by the transcription of the 'oo' sound by 'ou' in French and 'u' in English. I have preferred the spelling Baule, for example, to Baoulé, as it is commonly found in English works. This cannot be a comprehensive bibliography, and preference has been given to recent material, comprehensible to the general reader, which may still be in print, and preferably in English. The study of the countries of Africa still falls along colonial lines, however, and the Côte d'Ivoire is relatively ignored by English-language students of Africa, and even by English tourists, while remaining one of France's most important African partners and tourist destinations. It is inevitable that, since French is also the language of government and education in the Côte d'Ivoire, the majority of publications about the country are in French. Books and periodicals have been obtained from the British Library, and from the School of Oriental and African Studies at London University. Citations in the health section are selected from recent years, and more up-to-date citations may be traced through medical databases available either on-line, or on CD-ROMs which are available in many libraries. In all fields, on-line databases provide invaluable citations, but CD-ROMs now provide cheaper access.

The Country and Its People

1 **Abidjan. Un grand livre-reportage en couleurs de 200 pages et 300 photos.** (Abidjan. A big colour guide with 200 pages and 300 photographs.)
Fraternité Matin newspaper. Abidjan: Fraternité Matin, 1982. 212p.
A report on the life of the capital, written by the staff of the newspaper of the PDCI, the one party legal at the time. It includes some history, reports on the different regions of the city, and emphasizes the positive aspects of Abidjan.

2 **Africa south of the Sahara. 1994.**
London: Europa Publications, 1993. 23rd ed. 1012p. bibliog.
A useful annual reference book. In its section on the Côte d'Ivoire, this issue includes an article on recent history by Pierre Englebert, an article on the economy (with statistics) by Edith Hodgkinson and the usual directory of government, political and trade organizations, together with addresses of embassies.

3 **L'Afrique noire politique et économique.** (Political and economic Black Africa.)
Paris: Ediafric – La Documentation Africaine, 1983. 5th ed.
(Pages numbered in several sequences).
This reference work, which is re-issued every few years, contains 52 pages packed with information and statistics on the economic situation, agriculture, industry, energy, transport, foreign trade and mining industry of the Côte d'Ivoire. There is also a list of government ministers, an outline of government policy, and extracts from the president's speeches.

4   **Aspects des départements et des sous-préfectures.** (Aspects of departments and sub-prefectures.)
Ministère de l'Information, Sous-Direction de la Documentation Générale.   Abidjan: Le Ministère, 1968. 159p. 6 maps.

A compilation of information on each sub-prefecture, its history, geography, population and economic activities. The sub-prefectures are grouped into the six departments of the country, and maps indicate the extent of each department.

5   **The Cambridge encyclopedia of Africa.**
Edited by Roland Oliver, Michael Crowder.   Cambridge: Cambridge University Press, 1981. 492p. maps. bibliog.

The index entry 'Ivory Coast' leads to numerous references to the economic and political life of the country, its foreign relations and arts. The history of the Côte d'Ivoire is related briefly, and references are included in the general historical sections.

6   **Côte d'Ivoire.**
Compiled by the Librairie Pociello, Abidjan, in collaboration with the Bureau d'Informations Touristiques de la Côte d'Ivoire, Paris.
Boulogne, France: Delroisse, 1973. 144p. map.

An album of coloured photographs with brief explanatory texts.

7   **La Côte d'Ivoire.**
Gabriel Rougerie.   Paris: Presses Universitaires de France, 1982. 128p. 5th ed. 5 maps. bibliog. (Que sais-je? no. 1137).

A volume in a well-known series which gives a general introduction to the geography, history and peoples of the Côte d'Ivoire. Despite being the fifth edition, it does not show much sign of being updated; there is only a brief mention of recent developments in the last few pages and no new items in the bibliography.

8   **Côte d'Ivoire, post report.**
United States Department of State.   Washington, DC: Superintendent of Documents, US Government Printing Office, 1990. 20p. map. bibliog. (Sudocs. no. S1. 127:C82/2).

The post report consists of notes on the country for the guidance of Americans. The first part gives a brief outline of the country, while the second part covers the American Embassy and notes for travellers. The work is available in the general microfilm series of American official publications, and is traceable by the Sudocs. number. Updates will be found through the indexes to the monthly catalogue of United States government publications. A previous post report was included in volume one of *Cities of the world*, edited by Margaret Walsh Young and Susan L. Stetler (Detroit, Michigan: Gale Publications, 1985).

9   **Côte d'Ivoire contrastes.** (Côte d'Ivoire contrasts.)
     Photographs by Maurice Ascani, text by Yacouba Konaté.   Abidjan:
     Edipresse, 1991. [110p.].
This volume of lively photographs, with a short text in English and French, gives a
general view of the country today.

10   **Côte d'Ivoire 1892-1982. Timbres-poste.** (Côte d'Ivoire 1892-1982.
     Postage stamps.)
     Michel Nédélec.   Abidjan: CEDA, 1983. 141p.
Most of the stamps illustrated in colour in this album were produced after
independence, and provide illustrations of every aspect of life in the Côte d'Ivoire.
The accompanying text decribes the flora and fauna of the country, its agriculture,
arts, music, party organization and sports. The historical section features famous
figures from colonial history.

11   **La Côte d'Ivoire. Economie et société.** (The Côte d'Ivoire. Economy
     and society.)
     Henri Bourgoin, Philippe Guilhaume.   Paris: Stock, 1979. 333p.
     14 maps. bibliog.
The authors provide a comprehensive account of the country, its economy, resources,
social services and transport. Detailed maps are included.

12   **Côte d'Ivoire, ou les racines de la sagesse.** (The Côte d'Ivoire, or the
     roots of wisdom.)
     Text by Arthur Conte, photographs by Michael and Aubine Kirtley.
     Paris: Jeune Afrique, 1981. 186p. map. (Grands Livres).
A collection of lavish photographs by the Kirtleys is accompanied by travel sketches
by Arthur Conte.

13   **Country Profile, Côte d'Ivoire, Mali.**
     London: Economist Intelligence Unit, 1993- . annual. map. bibliog.
     (Profile, no. 20).
A concise and fact-filled overview of the country, with an emphasis on economic
conditions. It is available on microfilm from World Microfilms Publications Ltd, 2-6
Foscote Mews, London W9 2HH. The profile for the Côte d'Ivoire was previously
published on its own, and before 1988 the term Ivory Coast was used.

14   **Country Report. Côte d'Ivoire.**
     London: Economist Intelligence Unit, 1986- . quarterly. (Country
     Report, no. 73).
A detailed analysis of political events and economic conditions in the previous
quarter, including statistics on economic activity and trade. Available on microfilm
from the same address as the Country Profile (item no. 13). From 1986 to 1988, it was
issued under the title *Country report. Ivory Coast,* and before that similar information
was included in the *Quarterly Economic Review of Ivory Coast.*

15 **Les élites ivoiriennes. Who's who in the Ivory Coast.**
Paris: Ediafric, 1976. 178p. (Special issue of the *Bulletin de l'Afrique Noire*).

This volume contains 1,500 brief biographies (in French) of the country's leaders. A second edition was published in 1978 with 235 pages, and a third edition in 1982 with 209 pages.

16 **Encyclopedia of the Third World.**
Edited by George Thomas Kurian.   New York; Oxford: Facts on File, 1992. 4th ed. 3 vols. maps. bibliog.

In volume 2 the section on the 'Ivory Coast' is found on pages 915-32. A very useful summary of facts and basic statistics is provided, with a short history of the country, and a plan to illustrate the structure of the government. The previous edition appeared in 1987.

17 **Etonnante Côte d'Ivoire.** (Astonishing Côte d'Ivoire.)
Attilio Gaudio, Patrick Van Roekeghem.   Paris: Karthala, 1984. 266p. bibliog.

A popular introduction to the country, throwing into contrast the modern capital with the luxuriant tropical forest and traditional village life so closely surrounding it. There are sketches of different peoples and their arts and way of life, as well as a look at questions of ecology and conservation.

18 **Ghana and the Ivory Coast. Perspectives on modernization.**
Edited by Philip Foster, Aristide R. Zolberg.   Chicago, Illinois; London: University of Chicago Press, 1971. 303p.

Contributions from various authors cover political development in the Ivory Coast from independence, the administration of the country; attempts to modernize its laws; economic development; and the development of education.

19 **Le grand dictionnaire encyclopédique de la Côte d'Ivoire.**
(The great encyclopaedic dictionary of the Côte d'Ivoire.)
Raymond Borremans.   Abidjan: Nouvelles Editions Africaines, 1986- .

Only four volumes (A-M) of this comprehensive guide to the country have appeared at the time of writing – the last having appeared in 1988 – but six are projected. It contains many illustrations, some in colour. Since most of the articles have bibliographies, this work includes what is probably the fullest available bibliographical guide to the country.

20 **The Ivory Coast: African success story.**
Michael Kirtley, Aubine Kirtley.   *National Geographic,* vol. 162, no. 1 (July 1982), p. 94-125. map.

This article on the 'miracle of Africa', with 'no coups, no mass rioting, no tribal wars' and 'the highest standard of living in Black Africa', was written before the economic crisis had begun to bite, although the falling coffee prices were already causing concern. The authors describe a panther ceremony among the Wè (Guéré) in the West, and visit the Senufo in the north. The life of the villages is contrasted with a Western style of life for some in the capital.

21   **Ivory Coast [Côte d'Ivoire] in pictures.**
[Albert Rosellini].   Minneapolis, Minnesota: Lerner Publications,
1988. 64p. maps. (Visual Geography Series).

Despite its title, this text-book provides a considerable amount of text to accompany
the photographs, giving a general outline of the country, its history, geography, ethnic
groups and economic conditions. Many of the pictures are in colour. This is a new
edition of a work previously published by Sterling Publishing in 1976, although the
new edition is 'based on' Rosellini whose name does not appear prominently.

Geography and Geology

General

22   **A propos des changements de climat récents en Afrique de l'Ouest.**
(Concerning the recent climatic changes in West Africa.)
Jean Tricart.   *Journal des Africanistes,* vol. 63, fasc. 1 (1993),
p. 73-81. map.

A look at the history of the climate of West Africa, and the recent changes which have been observed. Between 1955 and 1965 forest was cut down east of Pimbokro in order to grow cocoa, but the loss of forest which had previously sheltered the area from the drying harmattan wind, opened the crops to wind desiccation and they fell prey to diseases.

23   **The climatology of West Africa.**
Derek F. Hayward, Julius S. Oguntoyinbo.   London: Hutchinson, 1987.
271p. maps. bibliog.

A detailed study, including many maps and statistics, of the climate of the area. Fourteen observing stations were used in the Côte d'Ivoire. Studies were made of the effects on human comfort, housing, transport and food storage of such a hot climate, and some resulting practical advice is given. There is also a section on the human impact on the climate.

24   **A comprehensive geography of West Africa.**
Reuben K. Udo.   Ibadan, Nigeria; London: Heinemann Educational
Books, 1978. 304p. maps. bibliog.

The first half of the book covers the geography of the whole region, its relief, vegetation, climate, peoples, agriculture, minerals and transport. The second half covers the same topics for each country of the region, Chapter 22 being devoted to the Côte d'Ivoire.

25 **Ground water in North and West Africa.**
United Nations, Department of Technical Co-operation for
Development and Economic Commission for Africa. New York:
United Nations, 1988. 405p. 6 maps. bibliog. (ST/TCD/5) (Sales no.
E.87.11.a.8).

Pages 135 to 146 are devoted to the Côte d'Ivoire, giving details of the climate, rivers, and geology and the use and potential of ground water, which appears sufficient for the needs of the rural population and much of the urban population as well.

26 **West Africa.**
W. B. Morgan, J. C. Pugh. London: Methuen, 1969. 788p. maps.

A weighty regional study covering climate, geology, agriculture, and the environment. There is also material on the historical geography of the area, including the impact made by Europeans, a history of population and settlement, and of the development of transport.

27 **West Africa. A study of the environment and of man's use of it.**
R. J. Harrison Church. London: Longmans, 1980. 8th ed. 526p. maps.
(Geographies for Advanced Study).

An account of the climate, vegetation, resources and transport facilities of the region. Pages 340-54 are devoted specifically to the Côte d'Ivoire and give a short history as well as information on climate, trade, vegetation and crops. Exports are of coffee, cocoa, bananas, pineapples, palm oil and timber. Earlier editions appeared in 1957, 1960, 1961, 1963, 1966, 1968, 1974 and 1980.

Regional

28 **Kong et sa région.** (Kong and its region.)
Edmond Bernus. *Etudes Eburnéennes,* vol. 8 (1960), p. 239-323.
3 maps. bibliog.

A study of the city and the surrounding villages, their history, social life, population, structure, housing and agriculture.

29 **Kossou aujourd'hui et demain.** (Kossou today and tomorrow.)
Abidjan: Autorité pour l'Aménagement de la Vallée du Bandama, 1972.
(Pages not numbered). map.

A short guide to the creation of the lake and the dam, and to the development prospects for the region. This planning body proved not to be efficient.

30 **Le milieu naturel de la Côte d'Ivoire.** (The natural environment of the
    Côte d'Ivoire.)
    J. M. Avenard (et al.).   Paris: ORSTOM, 1971. 391p. maps. bibliogs.
    (Mémoires ORSTOM, no. 50).

This detailed and technical survey includes sections on geomorphology, climate, the
river system, vegetation and soils.

31 **Le régime de l'Atlantique près d'Abidjan (Côte d'Ivoire). Essai
    d'océanographie littorale.** (The Atlantic regime near Abidjan.
    An essay in coastal oceanography.)
    F. Varlet.   *Etudes Eburnéennes,* vol. 7 (1958), p. 97-222. bibliog.

A study of temperatures, currents, salinity and dissolved oxygen content in the sea off
the coast. The first chapter covers surface waters, the second deeper regions, and the
third the tides and shifting sands of the coast.

Geology

32 **Afrique de l'Ouest. Introduction géologique et termes
    stratigraphiques.** (West Africa. Geological introduction and
    stratigraphical terms.)
    J. M. Bertrand (et al.), edited by J. Fabre.   Oxford: Pergamon, 1983.
    (Lexique Stratigraphique International. Nouvelle Série, no. 1.
    International Union of Geological Sciences, Stratigraphic Commission).

A collection of articles on the geology of the region, only one of which is on the Côte
d'Ivoire. Only two of the contributions are in English, one being an outline of the
geology of West Africa. The second half of the book is an encyclopaedia of named
formations, and is almost entirely in French.

33 **Aplanissements cuirassés et enrichissement des gisements de
    manganèse dans quelques régions d'Afrique de l'Ouest.**
    (Encrusted peneplanations and the enrichment of manganese deposits
    in West Africa.)
    Georges Grandin.   Paris: ORSTOM, 1976. 275p. maps. bibliog.
    (Mémoires ORSTOM, no. 82).

A technical study, comparing various manganese deposits, particularly in the Côte
d'Ivoire.

34 **Atlas des minéraux en grains. Identification par photographies en couleurs.** (Atlas of minerals in grains. Identification by colour photographs.)
Jacques Broche, Roger Casanova, Gustave Loup. Abidjan: SODEMI, 1977. 173p. map. bibliog.

A collection of magnified photographs of grains of minerals found in the Côte d'Ivoire, with geological details in French, German, English, Spanish and Russian. The introductory articles are in the same languages.

35 **Bibliographie de la géologie et de la recherche minière en Côte d'Ivoire. (1885-1983).** (Bibliography of geology and mining research in the Côte d'Ivoire, 1885-1983.)
H. Madon. Abidjan: SODEMI, 1985. 2 vols.

This is a very full bibliography. The first volume (of 300 pages), lists items in alphabetical order. The second classes them by geographical location and by mineral.

36 **Carte au 1/2,000,000 et catalogue des gîtes et principaux indices minéraux de la Côte d'Ivoire.** (Map of scale 1/2,000,000 and catalogue of deposits and principal mineral indices of the Côte d'Ivoire.)
B. Tagini. Abidjan: SODEMI (Société pour le Développement Minier de la Côte d'Ivoire), 1981. 72p. 4 maps. bibliog. (SODEMI. Rapport, no. 469).

The four sheets of maps each cover the whole country but show different details of geology and the mineral deposits. The text consists of a detailed catalogue of minerals and their location in the country.

37 **Carte géologique de la Côte d'Ivoire.** (Geological map of the Côte d'Ivoire.)
E. Bagarre, B. Tagini. Abidjan: Direction des Mines et de la Géologie du Gouvernement de la Côte d'Ivoire, 1965. 1 map, 90 × 72cm. Scale 1:1,000,000.

A very detailed geological map of the Côte d'Ivoire.

38 **Carte pédologique de la Côte d'Ivoire au 1-2.000.000.** (Pedological [soil] map of the Côte d'Ivoire.)
B. Dabin, N. Leneuf, G. Riou. Abidjan: Secretariat d'Etat à l'Agriculture, Direction des Sols, 1960. 1 sheet 52 × 52 cm. and 30p. booklet. bibliog. Scale 1:2,000,000.

The booklet provides detailed analysis of the soils of Côte d'Ivoire.

39　**Classement des sables des formations quaternaires du littoral ivoirien d'après le résidu lourd.** (The classification of sands of Quaternary formations on the Ivoirian coast, based on the heavy minerals.)
René Pomel, Henri Pelletier.　*Annales de l'Université d'Abidjan, Série G, Géographie*, vol. 7 (1977), p. 190-233. map. bibliog.
An analysis of sand samples taken from along the coast, prefaced by a geological description of the coast.

40　**Contribution à l'étude géomorphologique du bassin sédimentaire et des régions littorales de Côte d'Ivoire.** (A contribution to the geomorphological study of the coastal regions of the Côte d'Ivoire.)
P. Le Bourdiec.　*Etudes Eburnéennes*, vol. 7 (1958), p. 7-102. bibliog.
A look at the geological history and present relief of the coastal area and the shifting coastline.

41　**Etude morphologique du bassin français de la Bia et des régions littorales de la lagune Aby (Basse Côte d'Ivoire orientale).**
(Morphological study of the French basin of the Bia and the coastal regions of the Aby lagoon, lower eastern Côte d'Ivoire.)
Gabriel Rougerie.　*Etudes Eburnéennes*, vol. 2 (1951), p. 7-108.
2 maps. bibliog.
A geological study of the region in the south-east corner of the country around the Aby lagoon and the Bia river which drains into it, with detailed maps, diagrams and photographs.

42　**Geology and mineral resources of West Africa.**
J. B. Wright.　London: Allen & Unwin, 1985. 187p. 24 maps. bibliogs.
A detailed study of the geology of the area, with many diagrams and details of valuable minerals. Besides editing the volume, J. B. Wright is the principal author.

43　**Les gisements aurifères de la Côte de l'Or Française. Côte d'Ivoire.**
(Gold-bearing strata of the French Gold Coast. Côte d'Ivoire.)
Henry Bondonneau.　Paris: The author, [1902]. 47p. 4 maps.
A geographical and geological description of the Sanwi region, in the south-east corner of the country, with a reminder that the coastal region was formerly known as the French Gold Coast. The mining industry is described and compared with that of the Transvaal.

44   **Morphologie, sédimentologie et paléogéographie au quaternaire récent du plateau continental ivoirien.** (Morphology, sedimentology and palaeogeography in the recent Quaternary of the Ivoirian continental shelf.)
     Louis Martin.   Paris: ORSTOM, 1977. 265p. maps. bibliog. (Travaux et Documents de l'ORSTOM, no. 61).

A report of studies of the continental shelf off the coast of the Côte d'Ivoire made between 1967 and 1973 in the oceanic centre of Abidjan.

45   **Le 'V' Baoulé (Côte d'Ivoire centrale). Héritage géomorphologique et paléoclimatique dans le tracé du contact forêt–savane.** (The Baulé 'V', central Côte d'Ivoire. The geomorphological and palaeoclimatic heritage in the record of forest–savannah contact.)
     P. [Pierre] Peltre.   Paris: ORSTOM, 1977. 198p. map. (Travaux et Documents de l'ORSTOM, no. 80).

A study of the geological evolution, the prehistoric climate and the development of soils in this central area. Originally presented as a thesis, it elucidates the problem of why savannah developed as an anomaly in an area of tropical forest. There is a summary in English.

Maps and atlases

46   **Abidjan. Guide-plan de la ville et des communes.** (Abidjan. Guide-plan of the city and its districts.)
     Atelier Art 7.   Abidjan: Edition Publicité, 1985. 184p. maps.

A detailed street plan of the city, with lists of public and private services, giving their grid references on the plans. There is an introductory article on Abidjan in both English and French.

47   **Africa West. World travel map.**
     London: Bartholomew, 1993. 1 sheet. Scale 1:3,500,000.

A fairly basic map of the region.

48   **Atlas de la Côte d'Ivoire.** (Atlas of the Côte d'Ivoire.)
     Office de la Recherche Scientifique et Technique Outre-Mer and Institut de Géographie Tropicale, Université d'Abidjan.   Abidjan: Ministère du Plan, 1975. 1 loose-leaf atlas, 44 × 59 cm.

This atlas contains 43 sheets of maps, some sheets being full-page maps, and others figuring several smaller maps grouped together to illustrate some aspect of the life and economy of the Côte d'Ivoire. With each map sheet are one or two sheets of information and statistics. Subjects covered include geology, climate, urban settlement, transport, agriculture, raw materials and industry, ethnic groups, health services and educational services.

49 **Atlas de la Côte d'Ivoire.**
Edited by Pierre Vennetier. Paris: Editions Jeune Afrique, 1978.
72p. (Les Atlas Jeune Afrique).

A compact and useful atlas with maps and articles illustrating every aspect of the
geography, including the economic and social geography of the country. A second
edition was brought out by the same publisher in 1983.

50 **Carte internationale du monde. Abidjan.** (International map of the
world. Abidjan.)
Paris: Institut Géographique National, 1967. 1 sheet (NB 29/30). Scale
1/1,000,000.

A map indicating roads, rivers and relief. The Abidjan sheet covers the southern part
of the country, while the northern half is covered by the sheet entitled Bobo-
Dioulasso, NC 29/30, published in 1968.

51 **Côte d'Ivoire. Carte routière et touristique.** (Côte d'Ivoire. Tourist
and road map.)
Paris: Michelin, 1993. 1 sheet. Scale 1/800,000. 1 cm : 8 km. (Africa
with Michelin Maps, no. 957).

A road map, with indications as to the conditions of the roads, and explanatory notes
in English and French. A plan of Abidjan figures on the corner of the sheet. Michelin
re-issue and update the map periodically.

52 **L'expression cartographique régionale. Journées d'étude d'Abidjan
13-15 décembre 1970.** (Regional mapping. Study days at Abidjan,
13-15 December 1970.)
Cahiers d'ORSTOM Sciences Humaines, vol. 9, no. 2 (1972), maps.
bibliogs.

Several papers deal with the mapping of the Côte d'Ivoire and there is an introduction
to a new atlas of the country, including two sample pages of maps of population
density and agricultural crops. There is also an article on the geographical distribution
of crops.

53 **République de Côte d'Ivoire.** (The Republic of Côte d'Ivoire.)
Paris: Institut Géographique National, 1970. 1 sheet. Scale 1/1,000,000.

A general map with major roads, rivers and relief.

54 **République de Côte d'Ivoire.**
Paris: Institut Géographique National in collaboration with Abidjan:
Direction de l'Institut Géographique, 1973- . Scale 1/200,000.

This is being published region by region, with 12 maps available at the time of writing.

55 **République de Côte d'Ivoire.**
Abidjan: Institut Géographique, 1973- . Sheets 56 × 55 cm. Scale:1/50,000.

A very detailed map series in progress, beginning with a sheet covering Abidjan.

Travel Guides

56   **Backpacker's Africa. A guide to West and Central Africa for walkers and overland travellers.**
David Else.   Chalfont St Peter, England: Bradt Publications (distributed USA by Hunter Publishing, Edison, New Jersey), 1988. 248p. maps.

Practical advice for the budget traveller. Chapter 15, pages 155-61, covers the Côte d'Ivoire and its main towns, and includes a simple map and plan of Abidjan.

57   **Côte d'Ivoire.**
Anne Arvel.   Paris: Arthaud, 1989. 218p. maps. bibliog. (Guide Arthaud).

A handy pocket-sized guide of mainly practical information, with some historical and cultural background material.

58   **Côte d'Ivoire.**
Geneva: Nagel, 1985. 320p. 16 maps. (Encyclopédie du Voyage).

This very detailed guide, with no named author, contains a considerable amount of historical and geographical information. The two chapters by G. Niangoran Bouah – 'Les hommes' p. 91-104 and 'La culture' p. 105-32 – are among the best surveys in print of the peoples of the Ivory Coast, their religions and customs. The book considers each region and provides maps for several cities and towns, with a larger folding map covering the Ivory Coast's major motorways. This is a particularly good book for its descriptions of some of the smaller towns and the local religious festivals and customs.

13

59 **La Côte d'Ivoire aujourd'hui.** (The Ivory Coast today.)
Mylène Rémy, photographs by Guy Philippart de Foy. Paris: Editions
Jeune Afrique, 1983. 4th ed. 255p. 14 maps.

A guide-book with 92 pages of colour photographs. It has more emphasis on
understanding the Ivoirian way of life than on practical information, but it does list
hotels.

60 **En Côte d'Ivoire.** (In the Ivory Coast.)
Françoise Bussang, Gilles Leblanc. Paris: Hachette, 1990. 165p.
4 maps. bibliog. (Hachette Guides Visa).

A practical, illustrated guide-book, with information on the history and customs of the
country, as well as the usual itineraries, hotels and information on transport. Earlier
editions were published in 1979, 1982 and 1986.

61 **Le guide du routard. 1990/91. Afrique noire.** (Hitch-hiker's guide.
1990/91. Black Africa). Paris: Hachette, 1990. 260p.

The section on the Côte d'Ivoire has a detailed map of the country, a plan of Abidjan,
and practical suggestions on transport and accommodation in all parts of the country.

62 **Guide du voyageur en Afrique de l'Ouest.** (A guide for the use of the
traveller in West Africa.)
Edited by Sylvie Glaser. Paris: Ahmed Afif ben Yedder, Ediafric,
1984. 271p. maps.

The chapter on the Côte d'Ivoire gives addresses and telephone numbers of hotels and
restaurants, a map of the country, a plan of Abidjan, and notes on other towns.

63 **Ivory Coast.**
Regina Fuchs. Chalfont St Peter, England: Bradt Publications; Raritan
Center Parkway, New Jersey: Hunter Publishing, 1991. 106p. 6 maps.

Originally published in German by Conrad Stein of Kiel, this is a practical guide-book
to the country, with some general history and information and full descriptions of
regional attractions and transport.

64 **Mali, Côte d'Ivoire, Sénégal.**
Mylène Rémy. Paris: Flammarion, 1985. 381p. maps. (Collection des
Guides Delta).

The first part of this guide covers the history, religion, social structures and arts of all
three countries, together with practical information on transport and accommodation.
There follows a short A-Z of information concerning all three countries. The second
half of the guide covers each country individually, with practical advice, maps and
some history.

65 **Traveller's guide to West Africa.**
[Anon]. London: IC Publications, 1988. 7th ed. 274p. maps.

This guide includes a brief section on the Côte d'Ivoire, with practical travel tips.

66   **West Africa. A travel survival kit.**
     Alex Newton.   Hawthorn, Australia: Lonely Planet Publications, 1992.
     2nd ed. 800p.

Pages 204-64 cover the Côte d'Ivoire in considerable detail, with city plans and plenty of practical information. The first edition was published in 1988.

67   **West Africa. The rough guide.**
     Jim Hudgens, Richard Trillo.   London: Harrap-Columbus, 1990.
     1232p. maps.

Pages 732-804 of this guide cover the Côte d'Ivoire. Several pages are given to the history of the country, and there is a very full account of travel and accommodation within Côte d'Ivoire, including town plans and a guide to costs.

Travellers' Accounts

68 **Aux temps héroïques de la Côte d'Ivoire. Des lagunes au Pays de l'Or et aux forêts vierges.** (In the heroic era of the Côte d'Ivoire. From the lagoons to the 'Gold Country' and virgin forests.)
A. Brétignère. Paris: Pierre Roger, 1931. 251p. 2 maps.

A presentation of the diaries of Amédée Brétignère (1856-90), who explored the interior of the country as the representative of the Arthur Verdier Company, also known as the Compagnie de Kong. He visited King Amatifou and did a reconnaissance from 1881 to 1883 on the gold concessions the King had made over to the Verdier Company. Brétignère describes the explorations of Treich-Laplène and work on the boundary commission. The diaries also record a mission in 1889 to inspect the coffee plantation he had established in 1882 at Elima, and struggles with the government over customs duties.

69 **La Côte-d'Ivoire.**
Philippe David. Paris: Karthala, 1986. 223p. 5 maps. (Méridiens).

A book of travel impressions. The author provides a picture of life in the capital and around the country. Some of the illustrations are in colour.

70 **De la Côte d'Ivoire au Soudan et la Guinée.** (From the Côte d'Ivoire to Soudan and Guinea.)
Capitaine D'Olonne. Paris: Hachette, 1901. 313p. 2 maps.

The Hostains-D'Olonne mission, led by the two officers named, sailed west along the coast of the Côte d'Ivoire from Grand-Bassam in December 1898. They then struck inland from Bérébi in February 1899 to follow the Cavally river and set up the post of Fort Binger, now Patokla, at the junction of the Hana and Cavally rivers. They visited areas in this borderland with Liberia not previously explored by Europeans. The mission was attacked, and captured villages in retaliation. They proceeded to Guinea and the coast, proving that the Côte d'Ivoire was accessible from the north, through forest which had previously been thought impenetrable.

71 **Du Niger au Golfe de Guinée par le pays de Kong et le Mossi.**
(From Niger to the Gulf of Guinea through Kong and Mossi territory.)
Louis-Gustave Binger. Paris: Hachette, 1892. 2 vols. 7 maps.

A diary of the travels of Captain Binger, who signed protectorate treaties in order to consolidate the claims of France to the country as a colony. He travelled through 'Upper Niger', now Mali and Burkina Faso, and the north of the Côte d'Ivoire, meeting Marcel Treich-Laplène, who had travelled inland from the coast, in the then great city of Kong, which was to be destroyed by Samori in 1897. Binger also visited Bondoukou and travelled down the Comoé river on the east side of the country to Grand-Bassam and the coast where he describes the coastal trading-posts. His fascinating experiences are illustrated by lively woodcuts, and appendices give information on the climate, fauna, history and ethnic groups of the region. Binger became the first governor of the colony from 1893 to 1895.

72 **Finding the centre.**
V. S. Naipaul. Harmondsworth, England: Penguin Books, 1985. 159p.

The second of these two autobiographical sketches, 'The crocodiles of Yamoussoukro', is an account of a visit to the Côte d'Ivoire in 1983. The crocodiles are those of the presidential palace. The well-known writer records his meetings with expatriates and Ivoirians. The book was first published by in 1984 by André Deutsch in London and A. Knopf in New York.

73 **France noire (Côte d'Ivoire et Soudan). Mission Binger.**
(Black France. Côte d'Ivoire and Soudan. The Binger mission.)
Marcel Monnier. Paris: Plon, 1894. 298p. map.

An account of the second expedition by Captain Binger in 1892. After some time in the coastal region, with a visit to the King of Krinjabo, they travelled with a British team, in a joint project to mark the border between the Côte d'Ivoire and the Gold Coast, to Kong in the north of the country. There they renewed contacts with chiefs made by Binger on his first journey in 1889. There is a description of Bondoukou, a Muslim capital in an animist country, and the town of Kong, which then had 15,000 inhabitants, but which was destroyed in 1897. The party returned to the coast down the River Komoé. The author describes the country vividly and provides sympathetic portraits and interesting photographs of the people he met.

74 **Les frontières de la Côte d'Ivoire, de la Côte d'Or et du Soudan.**
(The frontiers of the Côte d'Ivoire, of the Gold Coast and of the Sudan.)
Maurice Delafosse. Paris: Masson, 1908. 256p. map.

The diary of a joint Anglo-French expedition made in 1901-3 to mark out the boundary between the Côte d'Ivoire, the French colony of the Soudan (now Burkina Faso, and nothing to do with the area now called the Sudan) and the Gold Coast. The border was decided in principle between the French and British governments in 1893. The party travelled to 11° North, but spent some time in Bondoukou, a town of 3,000 inhabitants, of whom 2,700 were Muslim and 300 pagan. The colourful street life is described, and there are small photographs. Celebrations of the 14 July at the smaller town of Bouna included a race for women carrying water-pots on their heads, donkey races and a beauty contest, in which the prize was diplomatically awarded to the sister of the king.

75 **Jours de Guinée.** (Guinea days.)
   Pierre d'Espagnat.   Paris: Perrin, 1899. 344p.

A lively account of travels and encounters from 1895 to 1896 in the Côte d'Ivoire, which the writer calls the Guinea Coast. The author travelled up the Comoé river and explored the falls of Malamalasso and met the King of Bettié, Bénié Kouamé. He spent some time in Assinie and Grand-Bassam, where some of the Europeans he met had been reduced to hollow-eyed, yellow skeletons after a mere four months in the country. He also explored the Aboisso region adjoining the Gold Coast and met Aka Simandou, King of Sanwi at Krinjabo. Returning to the Côte d'Ivoire several years later, he died near Bingerville.

76 **Six mois dans l'Attié (un Transvaal français).** (Six months in the Attié, a French Transvaal.)
   Camille Dreyfus.   Paris: L. Henry May, [1899]. 319p. 4 maps.

An account of travels and encounters in the territory of the Attié (or Akyé), an area north-east of modern Abidjan. The author also spent some time in the coastal ports where he met traders. He gives information on rubber production and on the prospecting done with a view to the construction of a railway. The book includes thirty-five attractive line-drawings.

77 **Une vie d'explorateur. Souvenirs extraits des carnets de route ou notés sous la dictée par son fils Jacques Binger.** (An explorer's life. Memories from travel notes or notes dictated to his son Jacques Binger.)
   L.-G. [Louis-Gustave] Binger, annotated by René Bouvier, Pierre Deloncle.   Paris: Fernand Sorlot, 1938. 287p. map.

These reminiscences from Binger's life include his explorations of Côte d'Ivoire in 1887-89 and 1889-92, and notes on his governorship of the new colony from 1893 to 1895. He also describes some events, such as the capture of Samori. He made another brief visit in 1927.

78 **Voyage au Dahomey et à Côte d'Ivoire.** (Voyage to Dahomey and Côte d'Ivoire.)
   René Le Hérissé.   Paris: Henri Charles-Lavauzelle, 1903. 268p.

A member of the Conseil Supérieur des Colonies writes about his visit to Dahomey (Benin) and the Côte d'Ivoire. He describes the newly created administrative capital of Bingerville, the Ebrié lagoon, Dabou, Jacqueville, Grand-Bassam, which had recently been devastated yet again by yellow fever, and the gold mines. He also includes a chapter on the customs of the Alladians. Photographs are included in the text.

Flora and Fauna

Flora

79 **Etudes sur les fôrets des plaines et plateaux de la Côte d'Ivoire.**
(Studies on the forests of the plains and plateaux of the Côte d'Ivoire.)
Georges Mangenot. *Etudes Eburnéennes*, vol. 4 (1955), p. 5-61. bibliog.
The soils, climate and species of various types of forest in the Côte d'Ivoire.
Immediately following in the same issue of this periodical is an article by Jacques
Miège, 'Les savanes et forêts claires de Côte d'Ivoire' (The savannah and open forests
of Côte d'Ivoire), on pages 62-81. That too includes a bibliography, in which forest
areas are described and species listed.

80 **Flora of West Tropical Africa.**
J. Hutchinson, J. M. Dalziel, second edition revised by R. W. J. Keay.
London: Crown Agents, 1954-72. 4 vols. map.
In this comprehensive work prepared at Kew, the fullest possible details of plants are
given, along with citations of specimens found.

81 **Medicinal plants in tropical West Africa.**
Bep Oliver-Bever.   Cambridge: Cambridge University Press, 1986.
375p. bibliog.
An extemely detailed analysis of the pharmaceutical uses of many plants, with over 80
pages of bibliography.

82 **Medicinal plants of West Africa.**
Edward S. Ayensu.   Algonac, Michigan: Reference Publications, Inc.,
1978. 330p. map. bibliog.
An illustrated listing of useful plants, with names given in the many languages of the
Côte d'Ivoire in addition to the medicinal uses of each plant. An index leads from
medical problems to medicinal plants.

83 **Plant ecology in West Africa. Systems and processes.**
Edited by George W. Lawson. Chichester, England; New York: John
Wiley & Sons, 1986. 357p. maps. bibliogs.

Articles on the various types of vegetation in West Africa: forest, savannah, coastal
and aquatic. There are studies both of changes in vegetation since prehistoric times
and of problems of conservation.

84 **Plantes médicinales de la Côte d'Ivoire.** (Medicinal plants of Côte
d'Ivoire.)
A. [Armand] Bouquet, M. [Maurice] Debray. Paris: ORSTOM, 1974.
231p. bibliog. (Travaux et Documents, no. 32).

A detailed botanical reference work, with many illustrations, some in colour. An index
gives local names.

85 **The useful plants of west tropical Africa.**
H. M. Burkill. Kew, London: Royal Botanic Gardens, 1985- .

This is a revision of a work of the same name published by J. M. Dalziel in 1937, and
is published as a supplement to the second edition of his *Flora of West Tropical Africa*
(1954-72). It is in progress at the time of writing. Very full descriptions are given of
plants, as are their vernacular names and their uses in the countries of West Africa.
Bibliographical references are included for each plant. There is a listing of plant
species by usage and an index from vernacular names to Latin ones.

86 **Végétation et flore de la région montagneuse du Nimba (Afrique
occidentale française).** (Vegetation and flora of the mountainous region
of Nimba. French West Africa.)
R. Schnell. Dakar: IFAN, 1952. 598p. bibliog. (Mémoire de l'Institut
Français d'Afrique Noire, no. 22).

A very detailed study of the soils and vegetation of the mountainous area around
Mount Nimba, where the borders of Guinea, Liberia and the Côte d'Ivoire meet.
A catalogue of plant species is included.

87 **West African lilies and orchids.**
J. K. Morton. London: Longman, 1961. 71p. (West African Nature
Handbooks).

A short guide for the layman, illustrated in colour.

88 **West African trees.**
D. Gledhill. London: Longman, 1972. 72p. (West African Nature
Handbooks).

A description of sixty-four of the more easily recognizable trees of West Africa, with
colour illustrations and line-drawings of distinctive features. Mention is made of some
industrial and local uses.

Fauna

89　African insect life.
S. H. Skaife, revised by John Ledger, photographs by Anthony Bannister.　London: Country Life (distributed by Hamlyn), 1979. rev. ed. 279p.

A guide for the general reader, profusely illustrated with many striking colour photographs. This edition includes spiders and scorpions.

90　Annales de l'Université d'Abidjan. Série E. Ecologie. (Annals of the University of Abidjan. Series E. Ecology.)
Abidjan: Université d'Abidjan, 1968- . annual. (3 fascs a year in opening years.)

Most of the articles in this periodical concern the fauna of the country and are specialist zoological studies, but some botanical studies are also published in the series.

91　The atlas of Africa's principal mammals.
Stephen J. Smith.　Fourways, South Africa: Natural History Books, 1985. 241p. maps.

The author gives brief details of 121 species, together with a silhouette, a footprint, and a map of Africa showing distribution within the continent.

92　An avifaunal survey of Taï National Park, Ivory Coast. 28 January – 11 April 1989.
M. E. Gartshore.　Cambridge: International Council for Bird Preservation, 1989. 67p. 9 maps. bibliog. (Study Report, no. 39).

The Taï Park is in the south-west corner of the country, east of the Cavally River which forms the border with Liberia, and west of the Sassandra River, within the rainforest area. A total of 207 species were documented and are listed, including many rare ones. The author discusses problems of detection and identification, and survey methods.

93　The bats of West Africa.
D. R. [Donovan Reginald] Rosevear.　London: Trustees of the British Museum (Natural History), 1965. 418p. map.

An exhaustive study with detailed descriptions, based on specimens in the Natural History Museum.

94　The behaviour guide to African mammals.
Richard Despard Estes, illustrated by Daniel Otte.　Berkeley, California: University of California Press, 1991. 661p. maps. bibliog.

The author, a behavioural biologist who has worked in Africa for twenty years, provides detailed studies of African animals and their behaviour. Distribution maps are included.

95 **Birds of the West African town and garden.**
John H. Elgood. London: Longman, 1960. 66p. (West African Nature Handbooks).

This handbook, with coloured illustrations, is for the general reader. It gives a description and notes on habitats and calls, and also includes a brief note on distribution.

96 **Birds of West Central and Western Africa.**
C. W. Mackworth-Praed, C. H. B. Grant. London: Longman, 1970, 1973. 2 vols. maps. (African Handbook of Birds. Series III).

A very full guide to species in West Africa, giving descriptions, and details of habits and recorded breeding. It also includes a small map to indicate the distribution of each bird. The illustrations are in colour.

97 **Birdwatching in the Ivory Coast.**
David Leesley. Douglas, Isle of Man: D. Leesley, 1983. 37p.

A short practical guide to birdwatching based on the author's experiences, with practical advice on contacts, travel and health. The author lists the species seen.

98 **The carnivores of West Africa.**
D. R. [Donovan Reginald] Rosevear. London: Trustees of the British Museum (Natural History), 1974. 584p. bibliog.

This weighty tome gives detailed descriptions of the animals, based on specimens preserved in the Natural History Museum. There is also as much information about the animals as the author could gather from all recorded sources.

99 **Essai de zoogéographie d'un milieu naturel protégé. Le Parc national de la Comoé.** (An outline of the zoogeography of a protected natural environment. The National Park of the Comoé.)
Francis Laginie, Gérard Sournia. *Annales de l'Université d'Abidjan, Série G, Géographie*, vol. 7 (1977), p. 145-88. 7 maps. bibliog.

The Comoé National Park covers a large area in the north-east of the country. After a brief history of the park, the article describes its geography and climate; its vegetation (briefly); the species of animals and birds found in the park; and problems of the control of poaching. A list of birds observed in the park is found at the end of the article.

100 **A field guide to the birds of West Africa.**
William Serle, Gérard J. Morel. London: Collins, 1977. 1992 printing. 371p. map. (Collins Field Guide).

An illustrated guide, with some of the illustrations in colour, to the birds of West Africa, including also descriptions and notes on habitat. Five hundred species are fully described and illustrated, and 200 allied species described more briefly. At the back of the volume are the names in Latin, English, French, Spanish and German.

101   **A field guide to the mammals of Africa including Madagascar.**
Theodore Haltenorth, Helmut Diller.   London: Collins; Boston,
Massachusetts: Houghton Mifflin, 1980. 400p. maps. bibliog.

A compact but comprehensive guide, with concise detailed descriptions and
information on distribution and habitats. Tiny maps indicate distribution. The work
was originally published in German.

102   **Malimbus. Journal of the West African Ornithological Society.**
Huntingdon, England: West African Ornithological Society,
1978- . bi-annual.

Volumes 7 (p. 1-59), 10 (p. 201-6) and 12 (p. 61-86) are devoted to the birds of the
Côte d'Ivoire, but there are references to the Côte d'Ivoire in other issues, and articles
on birds in adjoining countries which may be of interest. Although some articles are in
French, the ones on the Côte d'Ivoire are in English.

103   **Les parcs nationaux.** (The national parks.)
Documentation Générale et de la Presse du Ministère de l'Information.
Abidjan: Imprimerie Nationale, 1975. 24p.

A short illustrated brochure on the Comoé, Marahoué and Taï national parks.

104   **Poissons de mer de l'Ouest africain tropical.** (Sea fish from tropical
West Africa.)
Bernard Seret, illustrated by Pierre Opic.   Paris: ORSTOM, 1986.
2nd ed. bibliog. (Initiations-Documentations Techniques, no. 49).

A very full and detailed guide, without being too technical. The illustrations are large,
and some are in colour.

105   **La réserve naturelle intégrale du Mont Nimba.** (The complete
natural reserve of Mount Nimba.)
[Various authors].   Dakar: IFAN, 1952-63. 5 fascs. bibliogs.
(Mémoires de l'Institut Français [later renamed Fondamental]
d'Afrique Noire, nos. 19 (1952), 40 (1954), 43 (1955), 53 (1958),
66 (1963)).

A detailed zoological survey of a biologically rich mountainous area on the border of
the Côte d'Ivoire, Guinea and Liberia.

106   **The rodents of West Africa.**
D. R. [Donovan Reginald] Rosevear.   London: Trustees of the British
Museum (Natural History), 1969. 604p. bibliog.

An exhaustive illustrated study, based on specimens in the Natural History Museum,
and including previously collected information and records of the specimens.

107   **Les serpents de l'Ouest africain.** (The snakes of West Africa.)
A Villiers.   Dakar: Nouvelles Editions Africaines, 1975. 195p. bibliog.

An illustrated classification and guide, with a general introduction.

108 **Small mammals of West Africa.**
A. H. Booth. London: Longman, 1960. 68p. map. (West African Nature Handbooks).

An illustrated and lively guide for the layman. The author ends many entries with information on how to keep the animal as a pet, or, at the other end of the spectrum, comments on how the animal has become a pest and might be controlled.

109 **West African butterflies and moths.**
John Boorman. London: Longman, 1970. 79p. (West African Nature Handbooks).

A short guide, with many illustrations in colour.

110 **West African insects.**
John Boorman. London: Longman, 1981. 88p. bibliog. (West African Nature Handbooks).

A short guide to some of the insects of West Africa, excluding butterflies and moths. It is illustrated with photographs and line-drawings.

111 **West African snakes.**
G. S. Cansdale. London: Longman, 1961. 74p. (West African Nature Handbooks).

An illustrated, non-technical guide, with a short general introduction on snakes.

112 **Wildlife resources of the West African savanna.**
Sde Bie. Wageningen, Netherlands: Wageningen Agricultural University, 1991. 266p. maps. bibliog. (Wageningen Agricultural University Papers, no. 91-2, 1991).

An intensive study of the 'Boucle du Baoulé' reserve in Mali (the River Baoulé flows from the Côte d'Ivoire into Mali). Much of the book, however, provides more general information on the ecology and fauna of the West African savannah. The ranges of some mammals are shown on maps.

Prehistory and Archaeology

113 **Contribution à la connaissance de l'archéologie préhistorique et protohistorique ivoiriennes.** (Contribution to the knowledge of prehistoric and protohistoric Ivoirian archaeology.) Raymond Mauny. *Annales de l'Université d'Abidjan, Série I, Histoire*, vol. 1 (1972), p. 11-32. 2 maps. bibliog.

In this account of archaeological studies of the Côte d'Ivoire up to 1969 Mauny includes a summary of their findings.

114 **Contribution à l'élaboration de la carte archéologique du Worodugu: la région de Mankono (nord-ouest de la Côte d'Ivoire).** (Contribution to the enrichment of the archaeological map of Worodugu: the region of Mankono (north-west of Côte d'Ivoire.) Lémassou Fofana. *Annales de l'Université d'Abidjan, Série I, Histoire*, vol. 17 (1989), p. 9-30. 2 maps. bibliog.

An account of recent excavations around Mankono, a savannah Mande region in the north-west of the country. It was settled from prehistoric times to the end of the nineteenth century.

115 **Etude de la collection des industries lithiques (paléolithiques et néolithiques) du Musée national d'Abidjan.** (A study of the collection of stone artefacts, Palaeolithic and Neolithic, from the National Museum at Abidjan.) Y. Guédé. *Annales de l'Université d'Abidjan, Série I, Histoire*, vol. 15 (1987), p. 37-73. bibliog.

A study of the artefacts in the museum, illustrated by drawings of the stone tools. The objects come from the whole of the area formerly known as French West Africa.

116 **Ivory Coast prehistory: recent developments.**
Robert Chenorkian. *African Archaeological Review*, vol. 1 (1983),
p. 127-42. map. bibliog.
An illustrated summary of the archaeological work of the last ten years, during which
the first systematic excavations have taken place, and the Institut d'Histoire, d'Art et
d'Archéologie Africaines (Institute of African History, Art and Archaeology) of
Abidjan University has come into being. Palaeolithic material has been discovered in
quarries at Attinguié and Anyama. Work on shell middens is noted, and recently
discovered Neolithic tools described and illustrated. There is a table of radio-carbon
dates established in the last ten years.

117 **Recherches préhistoriques dans le nord-ouest de la Côte d'Ivoire.
Mission 1983.** (Prehistoric researches in the north-west of the Côte
d'Ivoire. 1983 survey.)
R. de Bayle des Hermens, Colette Faucquez-Tao, Ginette Galli.
Anthropologie (Paris), vol. 87, no. 2 (1983), p. 241-7.
The report of a systematic ground survey of the north-west of the Côte d'Ivoire, where
no previous prehistoric research has been done. The presence of both pre-Acheulean
and Acheulean remains has been established, together with traces of quartz industries,
but no chronology of the sites has yet been possible. Neolithic civilization also
developed in the Côte d'Ivoire independently of the Sahel, but there remains a great
deal of excavation still to be done.

118 **West Africa before the Europeans. Archaeology and prehistory.**
Oliver Davies.   London: Methuen, 1967. 363p. bibliog. maps.
(Methuen's Handbooks of Archaeology.)
This survey of the prehistory of West Africa works through the Palaeolithic, the
Neolithic and the Iron Ages to the arrival of the Europeans. There is an index of sites
including some in the Côte d'Ivoire and many line-drawings of scrapers and tools.

History of West Africa.
See item no. 120.

A thousand years of West African history.
See item no. 121.

Sites littoraux du pays Alladian. (Coastal sites of the Alladian region.)
See item no. 232.

History

General history of West Africa

119 Africa. Endurance and change south of the Sahara.
Catherine Coquery-Vidrovitch, translated by David Maisel. Berkeley, California: University of California Press, 1988. 403p. bibliog.
A social and demographic history of Africa, with references to demographic trends in the Côte d'Ivoire, the effects of colonization, and labour history.

120 History of West Africa.
Edited by J. F. A. Ajayi, Michael Crowder. London: Longman, 1985-87. 3rd ed. 2 vols. maps.
A very full and scholarly survey of West African history, including a long chapter on prehistory.

121 A thousand years of West African history. A handbook for teachers and students.
Edited by J. F. Ade Ajayi, Ian Espie. London: Nelson; Ibadan: Ibadan University Press, 1965. 543p. maps. bibliog.
A general history from prehistoric times, with one chapter on the colonial phase of French West Africa and another on the nationalist movements of the 1950s.

122 A history of West Africa. 1000-1965.
Roger Truelove. Nairobi: East African Publishing House, 1975. 274p. bibliog.
This school text-book gives a general history of the region. Illustrations accompany and amplify the text.

123   **A history of West Africa (A.D. 1000-1984).**
Toyin Falola, A. G. Adebayo.   Lagos: Paico, 1985. maps.
This history for schools was written in Nigeria and contains information on the early
history of the area derived from oral tradition and an African perspective on colonial
rule. The emphasis is on the former English colonies.

124   **West African food in the Middle Ages according to Arabic sources.**
Tadeusz Lewicki, Marion Johnson.   Cambridge: Cambridge
University Press, 1974. 262p. bibliog.
An interesting survey of food plants. Because the sources are Arabic there is more
information on the northern part and on the Mande and their crops and animals.

125   **History of West Africa since 1800.**
Elizabeth Isichei.   New York: Africana Publishing, 1977.
380p. 31 maps. bibliog.
A general history for schools: a clear and readable introduction to the subject.

126   **Main currents of West African history, 1940-1978.**
Frank Pedler.   London: Macmillan, 1979. 301p. 5 maps.
This work includes chapters on the Federation of French West Africa, 1940-46, the
French colonies in the early 1950s, and one on the Côte d'Ivoire from 1950 to 1975.

General history of Côte d'Ivoire

127   **The African bourgeoisie. Capitalist development in Nigeria,
Kenya, and the Ivory Coast.**
Edited by Paul M. Lubeck.   Boulder, Colorado: Lynne Rienner, 1987.
414p. bibliog.
A collection of studies on the emergence of a middle class in these three African
countries. There are three contributions on the Côte d'Ivoire: one on commercial
agriculture and social transformation in Assikasso from 1880 to 1940 by David H.
Groff, another on the State and capitalist development from 1960 to 1980 by Bonnie
Campbell, and one on the development of the agrarian capitalist classes from 1945 to
1975 by Peter Anyang' Nyong'o.

128   **Bibliographie de l'histoire de Côte d'Ivoire (1960-1980).**
(Bibliography of the history of the Côte d'Ivoire, 1960-80.)
Jean-Noël Loucou.   Abidjan: Université d'Abidjan, Faculté des
Lettres et Sciences Humaines, 1982. 133p.
A comprehensive bibliography with indexes.

129 **Croissance d'une capitale africaine: Abidjan.** (Growth of an African capital: Abidjan.)
Claude Fluchard. *Revue Belge de Geographie,* fasc. 42 (new series), 113rd year, no. 1 (1989), p. 3-12. 4 maps. bibliog.
A short history of Abidjan, including a description of the city in 1989.

130 **Grand-Bassam and les comptoirs de la côte.** (Grand-Bassam and the warehouses of the coast.)
Georges Courrèges. [Clermont-Ferrand, France]: L'Instant Durable, 1987. [96]p.
A lavishly illustrated history of the coastal region and its trading-posts. There are several studies of the history of the Côte d'Ivoire's external trade in *Commerce et commerçants en Afrique de l'Ouest. La Côte d'Ivoire* (Trade and traders in West Africa. The Côte d'Ivoire), edited by Leonhard Harding and Pierre Kipré (Paris: L'Harmattan, 1992. 327p. Collection Racines du Présent).

131 **Histoire de la Côte d'Ivoire.** (A history of the Côte d'Ivoire.)
Jean-Noël Loucou. Abidjan: CEDA, 1984- . maps. bibliog.
At the time of writing, only Volume one, covering the formation and migration of ethnic groups, had appeared. Volume two is to cover African civilization, and Volume three the colonial period.

132 **Historical dictionary of the Ivory Coast.**
Robert J. Mundt. Metuchen, New Jersey: Scarecrow Press, 1987. 246p. 2 maps. bibliog.
This historical encyclopaedia is prefaced by a short chronology and general survey of the country, some statistics, and a listing of ethnic groups. Nearly half the volume is taken up by a bibliography classed by subject. The volume begins with a chronology and a list of ethnic groups.

Pre-colonial period

133 **Cannibales et bons sauvages: stéréotypes européens concernant les habitants de la Côte d'Ivoire.** (Cannibals and noble savages: European stereotypes of the inhabitants of the Côte d'Ivoire.)
Adam Jones. In: *Images de l'Africain de l'antiquité au XXe siècle. Images of the African from antiquity to the 20th century.* Edited by Daniel Droixhe, Klaus H. Kiefer. Frankfurt am Main: Peter Lang, 1987, p. 33-44. bibliog. (Bayreuther Beiträge zur Literaturwissenschaft, no. 10).
Before 1750 Europeans believed the people of the Côte d'Ivoire were cannibals, because of their pointed, filed teeth and their red-daubed faces. These fears, together

with the difficulties of landing, prevented the growth of trade, including the slave trade. With eighteenth-century ideas of the 'noble savage', the fear of the Europeans diminished, and trade, including the slave trade, increased. As the Ivoirians were sometimes abducted to be slaves, they also feared the Europeans.

134 **Semper aliquid veteris: printed sources for the history of the Ivory and Gold Coasts, 1500-1750.**
Adam Jones. *Journal of African History,* vol. 27, no. 2 (1986), p. 215-35. bibliog.

An annotated bibliography of early sources is preceded by a discussion of their use and value, including plagiarism and inter-borrowing between authors. Only a few are first-hand accounts. The early ones are mainly in Dutch or German. Only in the eighteenth century did English become the major language in publications, to be followed later by French. Another survey of original source materials on precolonial West Africa is *A guide to original sources for pre-colonial western Africa, published in European languages*, by John D. Fage (Madison, Wisconsin: University of Madison, 1987. 192p.). It is arranged in roughly chronological order and includes indexes by author and by geographical area.

135 **La côte Ouest-Africaine du Sénégal à la Côte d'Ivoire. Géographie, sociétés, histoire, 1500-1800.** (The West African coast from Senegal to the Côte d'Ivoire. Geography, societies, history, 1500-1800.)
Christophe Wondji. Paris: L'Harmattan, 1985. 163p. 6 maps. bibliog.

A history of the peoples of the coast, their trade and migrations, including information on the coastal kingdoms of the Côte d'Ivoire. The two pages of bibliography on the Côte d'Ivoire cite mainly theses and articles from local journals. A guide to the first maps of West Africa and the original names of its settlements is to be found in 'The historical evidence in old maps and charts of Africa with special reference to West Africa' by René Baesjou, *History of Africa*, vol. 15 (1988), p. 1-83. 11 maps.

136 **Bouna, royaume de la savane ivoirienne.** (Bouna, an Ivoirian savannah kingdom.)
Jean-Louis Boutillier. Paris: Karthala, 1993. 396p. map. bibliog.

Bouna is a dry, savannah region in the north-east corner of the Côte d'Ivoire where a multilingual and multi-ethnic kingdom was created in the early seventeenth century, based on trading caravans passing from the Sahel to the coast. The people of the area, who became known as the Kulango and the Lobi, were ruled by a dynasty founded by Bunkani. This work describes their clan and political structures, their economic activities and their trading links. The kingdom was often attacked by the Abron of Bondoukou. At the end of the nineteenth century, the kingdom's trading links were destroyed in three ways during the Samori wars: by an attack by Saranké Mori, by colonial penetration, and by the dispute between the English and French. As it was so far from the new coffee and cocoa plantations, the kingdom decayed.

137 **Le royaume de Kong des origines à 1897.** (The kingdom of Kong
from its origins to 1897.)
N. G. Kodjo. *Annales de l'Université d'Abidjan, Série I, Histoire*,
vol. 14 (1986), p. 120-31.
A brief account of the kingdom and of sources for its history. It was created at a
trading cross-roads, and reached its peak in the eighteenth century, only to be
destroyed by Samori at the end of the nineteenth century. There is a short summary in
English.

138 **Table ronde sur les origines de Kong.** (Round table on the origins of
Kong.)
Edited by M. J. Derive. *Annales de l'Université d'Abidjan, Série J,
Traditions Orales,* vol. 1 (1977). 504p.
The whole volume of this periodical is taken up with a report of this conference, held
in November 1975 in Kong. The proceedings consisted of recitations in Diula of oral
traditions concerning the history of Kong. These are set out, with translations into
French on the opposite page.

139 **Tentatives d'évangélisation en Côte d'Ivoire à l'époque moderne
1637-1844.** (Attempts at evangelization in Côte d'Ivoire in the modern
period from 1637 to 1844.)
S. P. M'bra Ekanza. *Annales de l'Université d'Abidjan, Série I,
Histoire,* vol. 15 (1987), p. 143-54.
This account of several Christian missionary attempts – in 1637, 1687-1703 and 1844 –
tries to explain the reasons for their failure. There is a brief summary in English.

140 **Aniaba. Un Assinien à la cour de Louis XIV.** (Aniaba. An Assinian
at the court of Louis XIV.)
Henriette Diabaté. Paris: ABC; Abidjan: Nouvelles Editions
Africaines, 1975. 92p. map. (Grandes Figures Africaines).
The story of a young man from Assinie who was sent to the French court, baptised and
educated, and who served in the French army. When he returned to the Côte d'Ivoire,
he claimed to be a son of the King of Assinie, but his claims were denied, and he died
unknown.

141 **Assinie et le royaume de Krinjabo. Histoire et coutumes.**
(Assinie and the kingdom of Krinjabo. History and customs.)
Henri Mouezy. Paris: Larose, 1953. 281p. map. bibliog.
A history of Assinie and the Sanwi kingdom of Krinjabo, founded between 1705 and
1740. The book begins with the first settlements and contacts with European traders in
the seventeenth century, but most material concerns the exploration and colonization
of the area by the French in the nineteenth century, the work of missionaries, and the
decline of the Sanwi kingdom in the early twentieth century.

142   **Une histoire du royaume abron du Gyaman: des origines à la**
      conquête coloniale. (A history of the Abron kingdom of Gyaman:
      from its origins to its colonial conquest.)
      Emmanuel Terray.   Paris: Karthala, 1995. 1056p. maps. bibliog.
      (Hommes et Sociétés).

The kingdom of Gyaman, founded in 1690, was situated in what is now the north-east
corner of the Côte d'Ivoire and neighbouring Ghana. It included Senufo, Mande, Agni
and Abron, but it was the Abron who formed a warrior aristocracy and wielded
political power. The Ashanti conquered the kingdom in 1740, and maintained
domination until they in turn were overcome by Europeans. This study was first
published as a thesis for the University of Paris I in 1984.

143   **'From the best authorities': the Mountains of Kong in the**
      cartography of West Africa.
      Thomas J. Bassett, Philip W. Porter.   *Journal of African History*,
      vol. 32, no. 3 (1991), p. 367-413. maps. bibliog.

An extraordinary account of how a geographical mistake was perpetuated in maps for
several centuries. The Mountains of Kong first appeared in two maps drawn by James
Rennell in 1798, and subsequently appear on all nineteenth-century maps until Binger
proved by his expedition that they did not exist, and removed them from the map
accompanying the account of his explorations in 1889. The authors show how these
legendary mountains, though not named, appeared in works from the sixteenth century
onwards, although they disappeared from eighteenth-century accounts before re-
appearing on Rennell's map.

144   **Les Anyi-Ndenye et le pouvoir aux 18e et 19e siècles.** (The Anyi-
      Ndenye and power in the 18th and 19th centuries.)
      Claude H. Perrot.   Paris: Publications de la Sorbonne; Abidjan:
      CEDA, 1982. 333p. maps. bibliog.

A very detailed, illustrated study of the history of this group, part of the Agni or Anyi
family, who came from the Gold Coast between 1730 and 1850 and settled in an area
just below the centre of the border with what is now Ghana. The illustrations are of
ceremonies, robes and ritual objects which still exist today.

145   **La disparition de la notion de 'caste' à Kong: (XVIIIe-XIXe**
      siècles). (The disappearance of the notion of 'caste' in Kong, 18th-19th
      centuries.)
      Georges Kodjo Niamkey.   In: *Mélanges Pierre Salmon, vol. 2.*
      Edited by G. Thoveron, H. Legros.   Brussels: Institut de Sociologie de
      l'Université Libre de Bruxelles, 1993, p. 133-43. bibliog. (*Civilisation*,
      vol. 41, nos 1-2, 1993).

A short history of changes of social caste among the Dioula or Diula of Kong. Early
categories were freemen, slaves and artisans. The artisans belonged to a caste called
'nyamakala' (those having occult power), and the author considers weavers, forgers
and griots (orators or storytellers). With the development of trade, wealth and merit
determined caste, and all aspired to be rich traders. There is a summary in English.

146 **Note sur l'état baoulé précolonial.** (A note on the precolonial Baule
state.)
J.-N. [Jean-Noël] Loucou. *Annales de l'Université d'Abidjan, Série I,
Histoire,* vol. 13 (1985), p. 25-59. 3 maps.

A history of the Baule state, founded in about 1720, and its constituent ethnic sub-
groups. The author considers the African concept of a state, less centralized than a
traditional European one, and addresses the question of whether it is correct to refer to
the Baule state at all.

147 **La reine Pokou, fondatrice du royaume baoulé.** (Queen Pokou,
foundress of the Baule kingdom.)
Jean-Noël Loucou, Françoise Ligier. Paris: ABC; Abidjan: Nouvelles
Editions Africaines, 1978. 134p. map. (Grandes Figures Africaines).

A re-telling of the epic of Queen Abla Pokou, the niece of Ossei Toutou, an Ashanti
ruler, who, after a civil war among the Ashanti, led her people from Ghana into the
Côte d'Ivoire to form the Baule people. Legend has it that in order to cross the Comoé
she had to sacrifice her child. She died in 1760.

148 **La vie quotidienne au royaume de Krinjabo sous Amon
Ndoufou II.** (Daily life in the kingdom of Krinjabo under Amon
Ndoufou II.)
Koffi Koffi Lazare. *Annales de l'Université d'Abidjan. Série I,
Histoire,* vol. 15 (1987), p. 187-99.

The summary of a thesis presented at the University of Abidjan in 1984. The Sanwi
people left Ghana and founded a kingdom with its capital at Krinjabo between 1705
and 1740. It was assimilated into the French colony in 1893. The reign of Amon
Ndoufou provided a period of stability and prosperity from 1844 to 1886.

Colonial period

149 **Histoire de Kokora Bitty, roi Agni-Amantian de Tiassalé
(Côte d'Ivoire).** (The story of Kokora Bitty, the Agni-Amantian king
of Tiassalé.)
Théodore Kokora Bitty. Abidjan: Imprimerie Nationale, [ca. 1985].
60p. map.

A biography of the last Agni-Amantian king, whose influence extended over the Agni,
Baulé, Abi, Abidji, and other small groups in a region called Apkèliè by the Agni,
now the sub-prefecture of Tiassalé. He was probably born in 1848, and resisted the
French expeditions of Marchand and Manet in 1888, but was defeated. His influence
continued under the colonial regime, and he died in 1944.

150 **Francophone Sub-Saharan Africa 1880-1985.**
Patrick Manning.   Cambridge: Cambridge University Press, 1988.
215p. 13 maps. bibliog.
A study of the effects of colonialism on the political, cultural, religious and social life
of francophone Africa. The last two chapters, on post-war Africa, cover the heritage of
colonialism, in the fields of culture and religion, as well as politics. The index leads to
numerous references to the Côte d'Ivoire.

151 **West Africa partitioned.**
John D. Hargreaves.   London: Macmillan, 1974, 1985. 2 vols. 9 maps.
bibliog.
A history of the 'colonial scramble' for West Africa. Volume one, entitled 'The
loaded pause', covers 1885-89; Volume two, 'The elephants and the grass', studies the
period from 1889 to the mid-1890s in depth, and includes material on the French
colonization of Côte d'Ivoire.

152 **Guinea-Samori.**
Yves Person.   In: *West African resistance. The military response to
colonial occupation.*   Edited Michael Crowder.   London:
Hutchinson, 1971, new ed. 1978, p. 111-43. 3 maps. bibliog.
(Hutchinson University Library for Africa).
An account of Samori who resisted the French from 1881 to 1898. The author has
written fuller accounts in French (see items 153, 154).

153 **Samori. La renaissance de l'empire mandingue.** (Samori. The
renaissance of the Mandingo empire.)
Yves Person.   Paris: ABC; Dakar, Abidjan: Nouvelles Editions
Africaines, 1976. 2 maps. bibliog. (Grandes Figures Africaines).
A biography of the war leader who created two Malinké empires, the first in Senegal
and the second stretching from Central West Africa into the north of the Côte d'Ivoire.
His stronghold, Sikasso, was taken in 1898, and although he won a victory over
Commandant de Lartigue on 20 July 1898 at Owé, his army melted away through lack
of food and he was captured on 29 September 1898 and imprisoned.

154 **Samori. Une révolution Dyula.** (Samori. A Dyula revolution.)
Yves Person.   Dakar: IFAN, 1968-75. (2 vols published 1968, 1 in
1975). 3 vols. bibliog. (Mémoires de l'Institut Fondamental d'Afrique
Noire, no. 80, parts 1, 2, 89).
A full account of Samori, his background and his precursors.

155 **French colonial rule and the Baule peoples: resistance and
collaboration, 1889-1911.**
Timothy C. Weiskel.   Oxford: Clarendon Press, 1980. 7 maps.
bibliog.
A history of Baule relations with the French. At first the Baule cooperated with the
French since they offered trade and prosperity. After the defeat of Samori, however,

the French sought more direct control and reliable comunications with the Niger basin, and the Baule resisted fiercely. Governor Clozel tried a peaceful policy of collaboration from 1903 to 1907, but a final revolt flared up between 1908 and 1911.

156 **La fondation de la colonie française de la Côte d'Ivoire.**
(The foundation of the French colony of the Côte d'Ivoire.)
Fred Bullock. London: The 'Courrier de Londres', 1912. 80p.
bibliog.

An account of the exploration of Marcel Treich-Laplène, an agent of Arthur Verdier, to Bondoukou, and, with Louis-Gustave Binger, to Kong. He signed treaties with local rulers in order to claim territory from the coast to Kong for France.

157 **Marcel Treich-Laplène, précurseur de la Côte d'Ivoire.**
(Marcel Treich-Laplène, harbinger of the Côte d'Ivoire.)
Frédéric Grah Mel. Abidjan: Université Nationale de Côte d'Ivoire, 1991. 207p. bibliog.

A biography of the explorer who arrived in Grand-Bassam to join the Verdier Company in 1883 and became 'Résident de France'. He explored the interior of the country between 1887 and 1888. He died in 1890 on a ship at Grand-Bassam.

158 **La pénétration française dans l'Indénié (1887-1901).** (French penetration into the Indénié, 1887-1901.)
Christian Forlacroix. *Annales de l'Université d'Abidjan, Série F, Ethnosociologie*, vol. 1, fasc. 1 (1969), p. 91-136. bibliog.

The Indénié or N'Dénye was an Agni kingdom in the south-east of the country, stretching from what became the border with the Gold Coast (Ghana) to the Comoé. In 1887 chief Amoakon signed a treaty with Treich-Laplène and in 1889 an Anglo-French treaty recognized the area as falling within French territory. Direct administration was introduced in 1894. Revolt was followed by conquest and in 1896 an administrative region was created with Clozel as its first administrator.

159 **L'Afrique occidentale au temps des Français. Colonisateurs et colonisés, c. 1860-1960.** (West Africa in the time of the French.
Colonizers and colonized, c. 1860-1960.)
Edited by Catherine Coquery-Vidrovitch, aided by Odile Goerg.
Paris: La Découverte, 1992. 460p. maps. bibliog.

The first part of the book covers French colonial policy in West Africa. Pages 289-336 trace the history of colonization in the Côte d'Ivoire, and contain a useful chronology and four maps. One shows the sites of military operations from 1908 to 1915, one indicates hospitals and schools in 1924 and one shows the spread of education by 1983. Politics, trade, population growth and education up to 1960 are covered, and there is a section of the bibliography specific to the Côte d'Ivoire.

160 **La Côte d'Ivoire. Notices historiques et géographiques.** (The Côte
d'Ivoire. Historical and geographical notes.)
Lieutenant [Georges-Auguste] Bonneau.   Paris: Henri Charles-
Lavauzelle, [1899]. 100p.

A history of the colonization of the Côte d'Ivoire up to the time of writing (1899), and
an account of the country at the end of the nineteenth century.

161 **La Côte d'Ivoire par les textes. De l'aube de la colonisation à nos
jours.** (Texts on the Côte d'Ivoire. From the dawn of colonization to
today.)
Guy Cangah, Simon-Pierre Ekanza.   Abidjan: Nouvelles Editions
Africaines, 1978. 237p. 6 maps.

A presentation of historical texts from the National Archives, mostly from colonial
times.

162 **Côte d'Ivoire 1894-1895. La ville de Kong et Samori d'après le
journal inédit du Français Georges Bailly.** (The Côte d'Ivoire
1894-95. The town of Kong and Samori according to the unpublished
diary of the Frenchman Georges Bailly.)
Georges Niamkey Kodjo.   Paris: L'Harmattan, 1991. 147p. 5 maps.
(Racines du Présent).

Georges Bailly spent two years in Kong, a religious and commercial centre controlled
by the French but threatened by Samori. He made notes on politics, trade and prices,
and on his contacts with local merchants and religious leaders. There are interesting
details of daily life and health problems and of the threat posed by Samori.

163 **Changing perspectives on African resistance movements and the
case of the Baule peoples.**
Timothy C. Weiskel.   In: *West African culture dynamics;
archaeological and historical perspectives.*   Edited by B. K. Swartz Jr.,
Raymond E. Dumett.   The Hague: Mouton, 1990, p. 545-61. bibliog.

The author considers, in general, recent studies of resistance to colonialization, and in
particular, the resistance of the Baule (Akan group) from 1893 to 1911. The French
tried to conquer them in 1893, in order to use them as slave porters in an expedition
against Samori, but the Baule successfully resisted. A second attempt at conquest
failed in 1900-2 and trade was opened up. In 1909, ruthless destruction of crops by the
French, followed by famine and epidemics, destroyed Baule resistance and decimated
the population.

164 **Villes de Côte d'Ivoire, 1893-1940.** (Towns of the Côte d'Ivoire,
1893-1940.)
Pierre Kipré.   Abidjan: Nouvelles Editions Africaines, 1985. 2 vols.
maps. bibliog.

Based on a thesis by the author, this is a very full account of the establishment of
towns in the Côte d'Ivoire (vol. 1) and economic and social conditions within the
towns (vol. 2).

165 **Dix ans à la Côte d'Ivoire.** (Ten years in the Côte d'Ivoire.)
François-Joseph Clozel. Paris: Augustin Challamel, 1906.
350p. 14 maps.

The memoirs of Clozel who was administrator of the Indénié or N'Denye region from
1896 to 1897, where he founded Assikasso, near the border with the Gold Coast, in
January 1897. Moving northwards, he explored the area and occupied Bondoukou, just
vacated by the British, in December 1897. He had to relieve a seige of Assikasso in
1898. He was interim governor of the whole country from 1901, and official governor
from 1903 to 1908. He describes tours made in 1904 and 1905, and includes chapters
on the geography of the town and region of Bondoukou and the region of Kong.
Appendices include an early history of Côte d'Ivoire, descriptions of Bingerville and
the lagoon area, and astronomical observations made by Captain Bouvet from 1901 to
1905.

166 **Bingerville, naissance d'une capitale. 1899-1909.** (Bingerville, birth
of a capital. 1899-1909.)
Christophe Wondji. *Cahiers d'Etudes Africaines,* no. 61-2, vol. 16
(1976), cahier 1-2, p. 83-102. 2 maps.

After yellow fever decimated the European population of Grand-Bassam in 1899, it
was decided to build a new administrative capital for the Côte d'Ivoire in a healthier
position further inland. The local Ebrié populaton opposed construction, leading to an
insurrection in 1903. Traders continued to prefer the economic capital Grand-Bassam,
but the economic importance of Abidjan grew, and in 1933 it was declared the capital,
once more uniting administrative and economic capitals. There is a summary in
English.

167 **La politique coloniale des travaux publics en Côte d'Ivoire
(1900-1940).** (Colonial policy on public works in Côte d'Ivoire,
1900-40.)
Zan Semi-Bi. *Annales de l'Université d'Abidjan, Série I, Histoire,*
vol. 2 (1973-74), 359p. maps. bibliog.

This work takes up the whole of this issue of the *Annales.* It is an account of the
construction of the port of Abidjan, the Vridi Canal and of the railway from Abidjan
to Bobo-Dioulasso. The author considers the economic conditions at the time, the
financing of public projects, the consequent growth of trade, and some of the social
effects of construction.

168 **Etude sur la Côte d'Ivoire.** (Essay on the Côte d'Ivoire.)
Cl. Gaube. Paris: Challamel, 1901. 96p. map.

An interesting account of the country in 1901. Sections cover its geography,
agricultural products and social customs. The author recounts some not entirely
successful attempts to prevent human sacrifices on the occasion of the deaths of
chiefs.

169   **Justice indigène et politique coloniale: l'exemple de la Côte d'Ivoire (1903-1940).** (Local justice and colonial policies, 1903-40.) Micheline Landraud. *Penant. Revue de Droit des Pays d'Afrique.* 87th year, no. 759 (Jan.-Feb. 1978), p. 5-41; no. 760 (April-June 1978), p. 205-49.

This two-part article is a history of colonial legislation and the conflicts which ensued between the imposed French-style laws and local customs and beliefs. One example of conflict and difficulty was caused by belief in the power of sorcery.

170   **Notre colonie de la Côte d'Ivoire.** (Our colony of the Côte d'Ivoire.) Roger Villamur, Léon Richaud.   Paris: Augustin Challamel, 1903. 399p. 4 maps.

A fascinating account of the country in its early colonial days. The south-west quarter of the country is marked on the map as unexplored, and the north is dominated by the States of Kong, and the Niéné kingdom in the north-west. The authors describe the country, the flora and fauna, health problems, including 'colonial anaemia' which they say is really pure laziness, mining operations, and the laws and customs of the people.

171   **Souvenirs de brousse. Dahomey–Côte d'Ivoire. 1905-1918.** (Memories of the bush. Dahomey–Côte d'Ivoire. 1905-18.) Marc Simon.   Paris: Nouvelles Editions Latines, 1965. 183p.

The memoirs of a colonial administrator who worked in Tiassalé, Toumodi, Touba and Abidjan between 1907 and 1914.

172   **La pacification de la Côte d'Ivoire 1908-1915.** (The pacification of the Côte d'Ivoire 1908-15.) G. Angoulvant.   Paris: Larose, 1916. 395p.

Gabriel Angoulvant was the sixth governor of the Ivory Coast, from 1908 to 1916. He defends his strong-armed, military methods of occupying the southern part of the country, which were criticized at the time. He derides previous peaceful methods of conquest and describes his military campaigns and methods. Senegalese troops were led by French officers in the brutal suppression of the Baule.

173   **Colonial West Africa. Collected essays.** Michael Crowder.   London; Totowa, New Jersey: Frank Cass, 1978. 341p.

Articles in roughly chronological order on aspects of colonial rule, including the recruitment of African troops for the First World War, and methods of administration using local rulers.

174 **L'appel à l'Afrique. Contributions et réactions à l'effort de guerre
en A. O. F. (1914-1919).** (The call to Africa. Contributions and
reactions to the war effort in French West Africa, 1914-19.)
Marc Michel. Paris: Publications de la Sorbonne, 1982. 533p.
5 maps. bibliog. (Publications de la Sorbonne, Série Afrique, no. 6).
A study of the waves of troop recruitment, the resistance and desertions, and the
increase in exports during the war years. The section on the behaviour of African
troops in Europe concerns the Senegalese, who seems to have become better known,
but more troops were recruited from the Côte d'Ivoire than from Senegal.

175 **La Côte d'Ivoire. Le pays – les habitants.** (The Côte d'Ivoire. The
country – the inhabitants.)
Gaston Joseph. Paris: Emile Larose, 1917. 223p. 3 maps.
An interesting picture of the country in 1917, illustrated with photographs. The first
part deals with the geography of the country. The middle section covers the people,
including some contemporary history, up to 1917. The last part is entitled 'Urban
geography' and describes Bingerville, Grand-Bassam and Bondoukou, with their
recent history.

176 **La crise économique dans les centres urbains en Côte d'Ivoire,
1930-1935.** (The economic crisis in urban centres in Côte d'Ivoire,
1930-35.)
Pierre Kipré. *Cahiers d'Etudes Africaines*, no. 61-2, vol. 16 (1976),
cahier 1-2, p. 119-46.
World recession reached the Côte d'Ivoire in 1931. Many small firms went bankrupt,
urban growth slowed and unemployment rose. The first planters suffered from a fall in
the prices for exported goods. The rehabilitation programme of governor Reste, from
1933 to 1935, was partly successful. A summary in English is included.

177 **La Côte-d'Ivoire. Economie et société à la veille de l'indépendance
(1940-1960).** (The Côte d'Ivoire. Economy and society on the eve of
independence, 1940-60.)
Laurent Gbagbo. Paris: L'Harmattan, 1982. 212p. bibliog.
An account of the country's economic problems during the Second World War and the
emergence of political parties and trade unions dedicated to the pursuit of
independence. Later chapters cover post-war trade; the political position of the Côte
d'Ivoire under the constitution of the French Fifth Republic; and political events up to
independence.

178 **Reform and repression under the Free French: economic and
political transformation in the Côte d'Ivoire, 1942-45.**
Nancy Lawler. *Africa. Journal of the International African Institute*,
vol. 60, no. 1 (1990), p. 88-110. bibliog.
French West Africa continued to support Pétain and Vichy after 1942. In 1943 the
Gaullist André Latrille was appointed, and worked to win support for De Gaulle and
to spur on the war effort. Sympathetic to Africans, he was resented by the Europeans.

Demands for agricultural products for France were sometimes made from areas which could not produce them, latex being the most difficult. Forced labour, low prices, poor conditions and hunger caused discontent and led to a demand for independence. In 1949 the new governor Orseli established a good relationship with Houphouët-Boigny.

179 **Côte-d'Ivoire. Le P. D. C. I. et la vie politique de 1944 à 1985.**
(The Côte d'Ivoire. The PDCI and political life from 1944 to 1985.)
Marcel Amondji. Paris: L'Harmattan, 1986. 207p. bibliog.
In his history of the Parti Démocratique de la Côte-d'Ivoire (PDCI), which was founded on 9 April 1946, the author devotes more space to its early days. In the late 1940s it enjoyed great popular support for its idealism, but corruption grew with power and it was established as a single party in the 1960s. The third part of the book covers the party in recent times, its organization and relation to government.

180 **L'Afrique Occidentale Française de la Conférence de Brazzaville (1944) à l'Indépendance (1960).** (French West Africa from the Brazzaville conference (1944) to independence (1960).)
Joseph-Roger de Benoist. Dakar: Nouvelles Editions Africaines, 1983. 617p. map. bibliog.
A detailed history of official administration, local institutions, politics, social and economic life, and the evolution of nationalism leading to independence.

181 **Journal d'un colonialiste.** (Journal of a colonialist.)
Raymond Gauthereau. Paris: Seuil, 1986. 284p.
Reminiscences of an administrator who took up his post in 1944 in charge of the subdivision of Oumé in south-central Côte d'Ivoire. A lively account from a writer who has also produced five novels.

182 **Decolonization in West African states, with French colonial legacy. Comparison and contrast. Development in Guinea, the Ivory Coast and Senegal (1945-1980).**
Aguibou Y. Yansané. Cambridge, Massachusetts: Schenkman, 1984. 540p. 5 maps. bibliog.
The author begins with a view of French colonial policy and the development of national political structures just before and after independence. Chapter four deals with the economic development of the Côte d'Ivoire under the heading 'private enterprise and state control'. The last part of the book covers relations between West Africa and Europe and trade organizations within West Africa itself. Plentiful statistics are provided, and there are 45 pages of bibliography, in addition to bibliographical footnotes to the chapter on the Côte d'Ivoire.

183 **French West Africa.**
Virginia Thompson, Richard Adloff. London: George Allen &
Unwin, 1958. 626p. map. bibliog.
A history of colonial French West Africa which concentrates on the period from 1945
to 1958. The colony's administration, economy, industry, labour, education, health
and religions are covered, and a short section is devoted specifically to the Côte
d'Ivoire.

184 **Combat pour l'Afrique. 1946-1958. Lutte du R. D. A. pour une
Afrique nouvelle.** (The struggle for Africa. 1946-58. The fight of the
RDA for a new Africa.)
Texts by D. Ouezzin Coulibaly, presented by Claude Gérard.
Abidjan: Nouvelles Editions Africaines, 1988. 531p.
Daniel Ouezzin Coulibaly (1909-58) was a member of the Rassemblement
Démocratique Africain (RDA), the umbrella organization of emerging nationalist
parties in francophone West Africa, from its founding in 1946. He was a senator of the
Côte d'Ivoire from 1953, and a deputy in the French Assemblée Nationale. This is his
account of his activities, his statements and his contributions to the debates of the
Assemblée Nationale on behalf of the nationalist aspirations of the Côte d'Ivoire just
prior to independence.

185 **La marche des femmes sur Grand-Bassam.** (The women's march on
Grand-Bassam.)
Henriette Diabaté. Abidjan: Nouvelles Editions Africaines, 1975.
63p. bibliog.
An account of the march by women of the PDCI–RDA in 1949 from Abidjan to
Grand-Bassam to demand the freedom of imprisoned party members. Some women
ended up in prison, but eventually some political prisoners were freed and conditions
improved for others.

186 **Félix Houphouët et la Côte d'Ivoire. L'envers d'une légende.**
(Félix Houphouët and the Côte d'Ivoire. The other side of the legend.)
Marcel Amondji. Paris: Karthala, 1984. 333p. bibliog.
A survey of the forces which made Houphouët-Boigny so prominent, and the role of
both the ordinary people of the country and of liberal Europeans in the struggle for
independence. The author draws parallels between the anti-colonial movements of the
1940s and resistance to colonialism at the beginning of the century.

187 **West African agent. A British coaster's Anglo-French log.**
T. Rex Young. London: Heath Cranton, 1942. 168p. 2 maps.
The recollections of an Englishman who worked along the coast of Côte d'Ivoire. He
describes his arrival in Grand-Bassam, and the social life of Abidjan, Dabou, Grand
Lahou and Sassandra. Young writes in a lively and popular style.

Independence

188   The apotheosis of Côte d'Ivoire's Nana Houphouët-Boigny.
Jeanne Maddox Toungara.   *Journal of Modern African Studies*,
vol. 28, no. 1 (March 1990), p. 23-54.

A biography of the President. The author examines the role of Houphouët-Boigny as
father of the nation, his retention and exercise of power, his internal policies, and his
relations with France and other African countries.

189   Hommage à Houphouët-Boigny, homme de la terre. (Hommage to
Houphouët-Boigny, a man of the earth.)
Société Africaine de Culture.   Paris: ACCT, Présence Africaine,
1982. 269p.

A book of tributes to the President from French and African contributors.

**190   Houphouët dans mon objectif. 20 ans avec le 'Bélier' de
Yamoussoukro, 1965-1985.** (Houphouët in my viewfinder. 20 years
with the 'ram' of Yamoussoukro.)
Jacob Adjobi.   Abidjan: Fraternité Matin, 1985. 290p.

A pictorial survey of the President's life.

191   Houphouët-Boigny, ou la sagesse africaine. (Houphouët-Boigny, or
African wisdom.)
Paul-Henri Siriex.   Abidjan: Nouvelles Editions Africaines; Paris:
Nathan, 1986. 422p. bibliog.

A biography of the President, praising his achievements. Siriex describes his role in
the independence struggle and the passing of the law which bore his name abolishing
forced labour. He also examines Houphouët-Boigny's part in the growth of the
economy of the Côte d'Ivoire and his role in African and international politics.

192   West African wager.
Jan Woronoff.   Metuchen, New Jersey: Scarecrow Press, 1972.
357p. 2 maps. bibliog.

The wager in the title was the one made between Kwame Nkrumah of Ghana and
Houphouët-Boigny of the Côte d'Ivoire as to which country would be the most
successful after independence. The author compares the two leaders, and the political
struggles, social problems and foreign policy of their two countries.

193   Côte d'Ivoire 1960-1980. 25 ans de liberté, de paix et de progrès.
(Côte d'Ivoire 1960-80. 25 years of liberty, peace and progress.)
Edited by Pierre Cheynier, Charles Koffi.   Abidjan: Fraternité Hebdo,
1986. 198p.

The survey, with photographs and statistics, of the country's achievements in every
field since independence, was produced by an editorial team from the newspaper of

the Parti Démocratique de Côte d'Ivoire. A similar publication appeared in 1980 from the same publisher, marking twenty years' achievements and entitled *Cote d'Ivoire. Vingt ans.*

194   **Le développement du capitalisme en Côte d'Ivoire.**
(The development of capitalism in the Côte d'Ivoire.)
Samir Amin.   Paris: Editions du Minuit, 1967. 330p. bibliog.

A history of the economic development of the Côte d'Ivoire in the 1950s and 1960s, including the commercialization of agriculture and questions of transport, industry, and public and private finances.

West Africa.
See item no. 26.

Kong et sa région. (Kong and its region.)
See item no. 28.

Une vie d'explorateur. (An explorer's life.)
See item no. 77.

Akan weights and the gold trade.
See item no. 707.

Architecture coloniale en Côte d'Ivoire. (Colonial architecture in Côte d'Ivoire.)
See item no. 727.

Afrique Contemporaine. (Contemporary Africa.)
See item no. 774.

Population

195 **Actes du Colloque de démographie d'Abidjan (22-26 janvier 1979).**
(Proceedings of the Colloquium on Demography at Abidjan, 22-26
January 1979.)
Abidjan: Institut de Formation et de Recherche Démographiques, 1980.
4 vols. maps.

This conference on the demography of tropical Africa includes papers on the growth of
Abidjan, its birth and death rates, and on the estimation of the rate of urban migration.

196 **Cheminements migratoires. Maliens, voltaïques et nigériens en
Côte d'Ivoire.** (Migratory paths. People from Mali, Upper Volta
[now Burkina Faso] and Niger in the Côte d'Ivoire.)
Ph. Haeringer. *Cahiers ORSTOM, Série Sciences Humaines,* vol. 10,
nos. 2-3 (1973), p. 195-201. 2 maps.

A considerable number of immigrants travel from the poorer countries north of the
Côte d'Ivoire to the more developed southern part of the country, particularly to the
capital, Abidjan. The author provides some statistics.

197 **Colonisation agricole spontanée et émergence de nouveaux milieux
sociaux dans le sud-ouest ivoirien: l'exemple du canton Bakwé de
la sous-préfecture de Soubré.** (Spontaneous agricultural colonization
and the emergence of new social milieus in south-west Côte d'Ivoire:
the case of Bakwe district in Soubre sub-prefecture.)
Alfred Schwartz. *Cahiers ORSTOM, Série Sciences Humaines,*
vol. 16, nos. 1-2 (1979), p. 83-101. 2 maps.

A study of immigration into this area, mainly of Baule, but also of foreigners, to
create new agricultural land. Colette Vallat writes on the same subject,
'L'immigration baoulé en pays Bakwé: étude d'un front pionnier' (Baule immigration
into Bakwe country: a study of a pioneeer front), in the same issue, pages 103-10.

198 **Demographic aspects of migration in West Africa.**
K. C. Zachariah (et al.). Washington, DC: World Bank, 1980. 2 vols.
maps. bibliog. (World Bank Staff Working Paper, no. 414).

An extemely detailed statistical survey of population movement. Pages 1-166 of
Volume 2, by K. C. Zachariah, cover the Côte d'Ivoire, much of whose rapid
population growth is due to immigration. In 1975 one in five of the population was a
foreign national and in the same year 13 per cent of the population of Burkina Faso
(then called Upper Volta) was resident in the Côte d'Ivoire. Mali was the next largest
source of immigrants, while others came from Guinea, Nigeria, Ghana and Benin.
Thirty-five per cent of immigrants settle in the Abidjan region.

199 **Des ethnies et des villes. Analyse des migrations vers les villes de
Côte d'Ivoire.** (Ethnic groups and towns. Analysis of migrations
towards the towns of the Côte d'Ivoire.)
Yves Marguerat. Abidjan: Centre ORSTOM de Petit-Bassam, 1979.
73p. maps.

A study of migration towards Abidjan and the towns of the Côte d'Ivoire, with
analysis of the ethnic origin of the migrants. The work is illustrated by numerous
maps.

200 **Dynamique de population et stratégies de développement en Côte
d'Ivoire.** (Population dynamics and development strategies in Côte
d'Ivoire.)
Moriba Touré, Souleymane Ouattara, Elizabeth Annan-Yao. In:
Migrations et urbanisation au sud du Sahara. Edited by Moriba
Touré, T. O. Fadayomi. Dakar: CODESRIA; distributed Paris:
Karthala, 1993, p. 1-47. 5 maps.

A history of population growth and movement, including both immigration and
internal migration. The authors look at education and employment in relation to
population growth. They describe the structure of the educational systems and provide
some statistics. They foresee continuing growth, with inevitable demands on
education and public services, and point out the need for local planning, a population
policy, and economic and social development.

201 **Enquête démographique à passages répétés. Agglomération
d'Abidjan.** (Demographic survey with repeated presentations. Abidjan
area.)
Philippe Antoine, Claude Herry. Abidjan: Direction de la Statistique,
1982. 419p. maps. bibliog.

This thorough, but readable survey of the population of the capital is accompanied by
many statistical tables.

202 **Enquête ivoirienne sur la fécondité 1980-81. Rapport principal.**
(Ivoirian survey of fecundity 1980-81. Main report.)
Côte d'Ivoire. Ministère de l'Economie et des Finances, Direction de la
Statistique. Abidjan: Direction de la Statistique, 1984. 2 vols.
2 maps.

A government survey of every aspect of the birth rate, comparing birth rates of
different ethnic groups, educational levels, age groups and areas of residence. It also
included a question on the desire for more children. The second volume consists only
of statistical tables.

203 **Enquête permanente auprès des ménages. Résultats provisoires
1985.** (Standing survey of households. Provisional results 1985.)
République de Côte d'Ivoire. Ministère de l'Economie et des Finances,
Direction de la Statistique. Abidjan: Direction de la Statistique, 1985.
76 leaves.

A summary of the initial findings of a survey of 902 households made between
February and September 1985, a sample which the authors admit is too small to give a
reliable picture. The work consists of charts and tables giving information on the age
structure of the population, birth rates, migration, health, education, employment and
agricultural production.

204 **Le métissage en Côte-d'Ivoire: 1893-1960.** (People of mixed race in
the Côte d'Ivoire: 1893-1960.)
Alain Tirefort. In: *Les jeunes en Afrique. Evolution et rôle (XIXe-XXe
siècles).* Edited by Hélène d'Almeida-Topor (et al.). Paris:
L'Harmattan, 1992, vol. 1, p. 83-102. maps. bibliog.

An interesting survey, with statistics, of children of mixed race, most of whom were
born in the coastal area. If abandoned, they were taken into special ophanages.

205 **Migration in West Africa. Demographic aspects.**
K. C. Zachariah, Julien Condé. New York, Oxford: Published for the
World Bank by the Oxford University Press, 1981. 130p. maps bibliog.

A more general survey of large-scale movements of population than the work cited
above (item no. 198), although using the same statistical evidence. Half the work
concerns international migration, and the other half internal migration and the
migration to the towns. There are several maps showing population density and
internal migration in the Côte d'Ivoire, the main direction being to the Abidjan area.

206 **Les migrations en Côte d'Ivoire d'après le recensement de 1975.**
(Migrations in Côte d'Ivoire, according to the census of 1975.)
Philippe Fargues. *Cahiers Ivoiriens de Recherche Economique et
Sociale,* nos. 31-32 (Dec. 1981-March 1982). 205p. maps. bibliog.

The whole of this double issue is devoted to a study of internal and external
migrations, a study which is supported by statistics from the census.

207 **La nuptialité en Côte d'Ivoire.** (Marriage in the Côte d'Ivoire.)
Monique Barrère. Abidjan: Direction de la Statistique, 1984. 107p.
bibliog.

An analysis of statistics on marriage, including chapters on marriage among immigrants and polygamy, more common among the Mande and Kru and among older people. On the whole, marriage takes place early, particularly for women (in rural areas nearly half were married at 14, and 18 was the overall average age of marriage). There were few divorces or separations, few single people, and a considerable number of elderly widows.

208 **Le peuplement de la Côte d'Ivoire. Problèmes et perspectives de recherche.** (The peopling of the Côte d'Ivoire. Problems and perspectives of research.)
Jean-Noël Loucou. *Annales de l'Université d'Abidjan, Série I, Histoire*, vol. 14 (1986), p. 27-57. bibliog.

A survey of the sources for the history of population movement and of current attitudes towards ethnic history and a feeling of national identity. The author also traces a brief history of the population from prehistoric times.

209 **Population de la Côte d'Ivoire. Analyse des données démographiques disponibles.** (The population of Côte d'Ivoire. Analysis of available demographic data.)
Etienne Ahonzo, Bernard Barrère, Pierre Kopylov. Abidjan: Direction de la Statistique, 1984. 324p. 13 maps.

A very detailed analysis of demographic data, including a section on migration. The population was estimated at 9,300,000 in 1983 – with 2 million of them in Abidjan – with one of the highest rates of growth in Africa, due to a high birth rate and early age of motherhood. The population density, however, is only in the middle range for Africa: 10-20 persons per square kilometre.

210 **Population growth and socioeconomic change in West Africa.**
Edited by John C. Caldwell. New York: Columbia University Press, 1975. 763p. maps.

This work includes articles on fertility levels and control, mortality, migration, and population growth in West Africa generally. There is also a chapter by Louis Roussel on population distribution, trends and migration in the Côte d'Ivoire, in which he includes maps.

211 **Sous-peuplement et développement dans le sud-ouest de la Côte d'Ivoire. Cinq siècles d'histoire économique et sociale.** (Underpopulation and development in the south-west of the Côte d'Ivoire. Five centuries of economic and social history.)
Alfred Schwartz. Paris: ORSTOM, 1993. 490p. 10 maps. bibliog.
(Collection Etudes et Thèses).

After independence, the government launched Operation San Pedro, to develop the hitherto neglected south-west of the country, by creating a port, a town and the development of the hinterland. This study looks at previous attempts to exploit this forest region, and the history of its population, the reasons for its underpopulation, immigration into the area under the plan, and the failure of the plan.

Africa. Endurance and change south of the Sahara.
See item no. 119.

L'émigration baoulé actuelle. (Current Baule emigration.)
See item no. 239.

La part baulé. Effectif de population et domination ethnique: une perspective historique. (The Baule share. The effect of population and ethnic domination: an historical perspective.)
See item no. 247.

Les migrations lobi en Côte d'Ivoire. (Lobi migrations in Côte d'Ivoire.)
See item no. 293.

Effets d'un investissement massif sur les déplacements de populations en Côte d'Ivoire. (The effects of massive investment on population movements in Côte d'Ivoire.)
See item no. 545.

Croissance démographique et prévisions des effectifs scolaires de la population active en Côte d'Ivoire. (Demographic growth and forecasts of educational facilities and of the active population of the Côte d'Ivoire.)
See item no. 640.

Ethnic Groups

General

212 **Africa, its peoples and their culture history.**
George Peter Murdock. New York: McGraw-Hill, 1959. 456p. maps. bibliog.
This standard reference work includes information and a bibliography on the ethnic groups of the Côte d'Ivoire in the chapters on the Nuclear Mande and the Voltaic peoples.

213 **Les coutumes indigènes de la Côte d'Ivoire.** (Native customs of the Côte d'Ivoire.)
F.-J. Clozel, Roger Villamur. Paris: Augustin Challamel, 1902. 539p. map. bibliog.
A codification of the local laws and customs of the various ethnic groups of the country, with an introduction giving brief histories of some of the groups. A fascinating historical picture of traditional social structures.

214 **Le noir de Bondoukou. Koulangos – Dyoulas – Abrons – etc.**
(The negro of Bondoukou. Koulangos – Diulas – Abrons – etc.)
L. Tauxier. Paris: Ernest Leroux, 1921. 770p. (Etudes Soudanaises).
A detailed survey of the ethnic groups of the Bondoukou region in the north-east of the country. The work begins with a description of the geographical features of the region, and its history, including a section on the history of the kingdom of Bouna. The main part of the work is devoted to the way of life and beliefs of the Kulango, the Diula and the Abron, with a section on the smaller groups. The last third of the book consists of appendices, many of which provide vocabulary lists of the languages of the area: Kulango, Diula, Abron, Agni, Doma, Nanfana, Huéla, Noumou, Degha, Tégué, Sya and Siti.

215 **Le saga des peuples d'Afrique.** (The saga of the peoples of Africa.)
     Ibrahima Baba Kake.   Paris: Africa Media International, 1903. 137p.
     (Collection Peuples et Civilisations d'Afrique).

A work on some of the main peoples of Africa, written in a popular style. Of the
peoples from the Côte d'Ivoire there can be found chapters on the Malinké or
Mandingo group, the Akan, the Baule and the Lobi.

Historical dictionary of the Ivory Coast.
See item no. 132.

**Essai de nomenclature des populations, langues et dialectes de Côte
d'Ivoire.** (An attempt to classify the populations, languages and dialects of
the Côte d'Ivoire.)
See item no. 307.

Arts de la Côte d'Ivoire dans les collections du Musée Barbier-Mueller.
(Arts of the Côte d'Ivoire in the collections of the Barbier-Mueller Museum.)
See item no. 698.

Akan group (including Lagoon)

216 **La division du temps et le calendrier rituel des peuples lagunaires
     de Côte d'Ivoire.** (Division of time and the ritual calendar among the
     Lagoon people of the Côte d'Ivoire.)
     Georges Niangoran-Bouah.   Paris: Institut d'Ethnologie, 1964. 164p.
     bibliog. (Université de Paris. Travaux et Mémoires de l'Institut
     d'Ethnologie, no. 68).

An ethnologist compares the calendars of various ethnic groups who form the larger
Lagoon group, in which he includes the Abbé, Abure, Adioukrou, Alladian, M'batto,
Attié, Abidji and Ebrié. The second part of the work covers rituals and ceremonies
throughout the year. It is a matter of debate as to whether the Lagoon group are part of
the Akan cluster or not. The Abbé, for example, are called Lagoon by some authorities
and Akan by others.

217 **Introduction au problème des migrations Akan.** (Introduction to the
     problems of Akan migration.)
     Elizabeth Yao Annan.   *Kasa Bya Kasa. Revue Ivoirienne
     d'Anthropologie et de Sociologie*, no. 6 (April-June 1985), p. 53-73.

A survey of the latest research on Akan migrations over the centuries. The author
accepts that members of the Akan group migrated from Ghana, but it is now thought
that part of the Akan group may have originated in the Côte d'Ivoire, before moving
to Ghana and back again, and that others originating in the Côte d'Ivoire may have
migrated to the coast or the forests, to be joined later by groups from Ghana. Many
authorities now include the Lagoon group as part of the Akan cluster.

218   **Symboles institutionnels chez les Akan.** (Institutional symbols
       among the Akan.)
       Georges Niangoran-Bouah. *L'Homme*, vol. 13, no. 1-2 (Jan.-June
       1973), p. 207-32.
An illustrated description of figurative weights whose forms have historical or
mythical significance. The author describes ceremonies featuring the dja (sacred
bundles containing the figures) and analyses the types and what they signify. A short
summary in English is provided.

The Akan doctrine of God.
See item no. 369.

Sorciers noirs et diables blancs. (Black sorcerers and white devils.)
See item no. 380.

West African traditional religion.
See item no. 381.

Théorie des pouvoirs et idéologie. (A theory of powers and ideology.)
See item no. 427.

Akan weights and the gold trade.
See item no. 707.

Abidji

219   **Religion, magie, sorcellerie des Abidji en Côte d'Ivoire.** (Religion,
       magic and sorcery among the Abidji of the Côte d'Ivoire.)
       Fernand Lafargue.   Paris: Nouvelles Editions Latines, 1976. 302p.
       2 maps. bibliog.
The Abidji are a small group in the Lagoon cluster, who live to the north-east of
Abidjan. The author has studied their clan structure, their social relationships,
including marriage (polygamy), their cults and ceremonies, magic and charms. One
chapter describes the Dipri festival, which celebrates the sacrifice by the primordial
clan chief of his son Bidjo in order to gain food for his tribe. Another chapter
describes the effects of imported religions.

Abron

220   **Gli Abron della Costa d'Avorio. Una cultura teocratica che
       sopravive e si rinnova.** (The Abron of the Côte d'Ivoire. A theocratic
       society which survives and renews itself.)
       Marco Lunghi.   Milan, Italy: Vita e Pensiero,1984. 158p. bibliog.
       4 maps. (Scienze Storiche, no. 35).
The author researches and dates the oral traditions of the Gyaman kingdom of the
Abron, who migrated into the north-east of the Côte d'Ivoire from the Gold Coast, and

founded a powerful kingdom at the end of the seventeenth and beginning of the eighteenth centuries. They were defeated and made vassals by the Ashanti (Asante). The author describes their social and political structures and includes photographs of the current king, of chiefs and of ordinary people and their houses.

221 **Un mouvement de réforme religieuse dans le royaume abron précolonial: le culte de Sakrobundi.** (A movement of religious reform in the Abron kingdom: the cult of Sakrobundi.) Emmanuel Terray. *Cahiers d'Etudes Africaines,* no. 73-6, vol. 19 (1979), cahiers 1-4, p. 143-76. map. bibliog.
A study of a cult which arose in the Abron kingdom in the north-east of the Côte d'Ivoire, and the north-west of Ghana during the last twenty or thirty years of the nineteenth century. The author considers the cult in its historical context. The volume, which replaces all four volumes for the year, is a tribute to Denise Paulme.

222 **When the spider danced. Notes from an African village.** Alexander Alland, Jr. Garden City, New York: Anchor Press, 1975. xii, 227p.
An account of the Abron. The ethnologist author lived among them in 1960, 1961-62 and 1973. This book was published in French as *La danse de l'araignée. Un ethnologue américain chez les Abron (Côte d'Ivoire),* in a translation by Didier Pemerle (Paris: Plon, 1984. 338p. 3 maps) in the series Terre Humaine, with additional notes on medicine, sorcery, and the conflict between traditional and Western ways.

Une histoire du royaume abron du Gyaman. (A history of the Abron kingdom of Gyaman.) *See* item no. 142.

Le noir de Bondoukou. (The negro of Bondoukou.) *See* item no. 214.

L'Abron: langue sans consonnes nasales. (Abron: a language without nasal consonants.) *See* item no. 316.

Abure (Abouré)

223 **Les Abouré. Une société lagunaire de Côte d'Ivoire.** (The Abure. A lagoon society of Côte d'Ivoire.) Georges Niangoran-Bouah. *Annales de l'Université d'Abidjan, Lettres et Sciences Humaines,* vol. 1 (1965), p. 37-171. 2 maps. bibliog.
The author classifies the Abure as being both Lagoon and Akan. His detailed study takes up most of this issue, and covers the history of the Abure and their social structures, in particular their system of marriage, and ceremonies associated with puberty, marriage and childbirth.

Adioukrou

224 **Le système politique de Lodjoukrou. Une société lignagère à classes d'âge. Côte d'Ivoire.** (The political system of the Lodjoukrou. A lineal society with age classes.)
Harris Memel-Fotê.   Paris: Présence Africaine; Abidjan: Nouvelles Editions Africaines, 1980. 479p. 4 maps. bibliog.

The name of this small ethnic group has been transcribed in many ways, and within the text the author has used non-Roman phonetic script to convey the sound of their name, but the *Grand dictionnaire encyclopédique de la Côte d'Ivoire* enters them under the form Adioukrou and places them in the Lagoon group, which it considers part of the Akan cluster. This is a detailed study of the origin and social organization of the Adioukrou, who are situated to the north of the Ebrié lagoon. The original people migrated from the west, but were joined by an Akan group who dominated them culturally, and they changed from patrilinear to matrilinear succession. They were originally settled in the forest near Gagnoa, but pressure from the Bété drove them across the Bandama to their present position.

Agni

225 **Les Agni devant la mort (Côte d'Ivoire).** (The Agni in the face of death.)
Jean-Paul Eschlimann.   Paris: Karthala, 1985. 277p. map. bibliog.

Funerals are central to the Agni: an occasion for which all return to the village. This is a profound study of attitudes and ceremonies. A good death is that of an old person with plentiful progeny. The author considers the death of the great, and the problem of 'bad' deaths, such as suicides.

226 **Les Agni (Païpi-Bri).**
Maurice Delafosse.   *L'Anthropologie,* vol. 4 (1893), p. 402-43. map.

An early account of the Agni, in particular a group called the Païpi-Bri, who were slightly paler than other groups. The author describes their appearance, way of life, beliefs, language and arts. He includes some photographs and four short chants.

227 **Les coutumes Agni, rédigées et codifiées d'après les documents officiels les plus récents.** (Agni customs, edited and codified according to the most recent official documents.)
Roger Villamur, Maurice Delafosse.   Paris: Augustin Challamel, 1904. 174p.

A handbook of local customs and laws, designed to serve as a code for local tribunals and administrators. There are sections on marriage, inheritance, property, crime and judicial procedures.

228 **Croyances religieuses et coutumes juridiques des Agni de la Côte d'Ivoire.** (Religious beliefs and judicial customs of the Agni in the Côte d'Ivoire.)
F. J. Amon D'Aby. Paris: Larose, 1960. 184p. map.
A study of religious beliefs, with sections on festivals, the gods, dreams, healing, and the special properties of pearls. The second half of the book covers the rituals of birth and death, and those engendered by the succession of chiefs, and the traditional laws concerning marriage, divorce and inheritance. There are photographs of some ceremonies.

229 **Fear thy neighbour as thyself. Psychoanalysis and society among the Anyi of West Africa.**
Paul Parin, Fritz Morgenthaler, Goldy Parin-Matthèy. Chicago, Illinois; London: University of Chicago Press, 1980. 408p. bibliog.
A psychoanalytical study which begins with some more general information on the Agni or Anyi, their history and family organization. The authors, Swiss psycho-analysts, originally published their study in German in 1971, under the title 'Fürchte deinen Nächsten wie dich selbst: Psychoanalyse und Gesellschaft am Modell der Agni in Westafrika'.

230 **Naître sur la terre africaine.** (To be born on African earth.)
Jean-Paul Eschlimann. Abidjan: INADES, 1982. 149p. map. bibliog.
A study of rituals concerning children among the Agni-Bona, a branch of the Agni. The author explains the position of children in society, and considers problems associated with childbirth, such as abortion and still births.

231 **Sagesse ancienne.** (Ancient wisdom.)
Barthélemy Comoé Krou. *Annales de l'Université d'Abidjan, Série F, Ethnosociologie*, vol. 5 (1973), p. 5-67.
The re-telling and analysis of an Agni tale about a young girl's marriage, revealing social customs and beliefs. The third section of this article is a short play illustrating the same theme.

Assinie et le royaume de Krinjabo. (Assinie and the kingdom of Krinjabo.)
See item no. 141.

Les Anyi-Ndenye et le pouvoir aux 18e et 19e siècles. (The Anyi-Ndenye and power in the 18th and 19th centuries.)
See item no. 144.

La vie quotidienne au royaume de Krinjabo sous Amon Ndoufou II. (Daily life in the kingdom of Krinjabo under Amon Ndoufou II.)
See item no. 148.

Essai de manuel de la langue Agni. (Sketch for an Agni language manual.)
See item no. 318.

Assongu: a terracotta tradition of southeastern Ivory Coast.
See item no. 370.

Notes sur les Agni de l'Indénié. (Notes on the Agni of Indénié.)
See item no. 375.

Riches paysans de Côte d'Ivoire. (Rich peasants of Côte d'Ivoire.)
See item no. 583.

Ahizi *(see* Kru group, items 256, 257)

Ahouan

Yam cultivation and socio-ecological ideas in Aouan society, Ivory Coast.
See item no. 588.

Alladian

232 **Sites littoraux du pays Alladian (Côte d'Ivoire): premières enquêtes et premiers sondages.** (Coastal sites of the Alladian region: first enquiries and surveys.)
Josette Rivallain. *Annales de l'Université d'Abidjan, Série I, Histoire,* vol. 11 (1983), p. 27-60.
An archaeological survey to establish the early history of the Alladian, together with an account of more recent traditional activities, some of which are still carried out today, including pottery and salt production, fishing and basketry.

Voyage au Dahomey et à Côte d'Ivoire. (Voyage to Dahomey and Côte d'Ivoire.)
See item no. 78.

Ano

233 **Une société paysanne de Côte d'Ivoire: les Ano.** (A peasant society from the Côte d'Ivoire: The Ano.)
Raymond Deniel. Abidjan: INADES, 1976. 225p. 2 maps. bibliog.
A survey for the general reader of an small ethnic group, part of the Akan cluster, who live in the Prikro region, in the east-central, Baule part of the country. The author looks at their social structures, their daily life, their beliefs and their schools,

Attié (Akyé, Atié)

234 **Mission en pays atié, Côte d'Ivoire.** (Mission in Atié territory in the
Côte d'Ivoire.)
Denise Paulme. *L'Homme,* vol. 5, no. 1 (Jan.-March 1965), p. 105-9.
The author studied the Atié and the M'batto, small groups in the south-east numbering
80,000 and 20,000 respectively, considered by Delafosse to be from the Lagoon
group, and by Murdock and the *Grand dictionnaire encyclopédique de la Côte
d'Ivoire* to be from the Akan. The author is inclined towards the former theory. A
complex social system groups people into three age classes. Each man always
remained in the same class, e.g. A, his son in B, his grandson in C, and his great-
grandson in A, etc.

235 **Le pays akyé (Côte d'Ivoire). Etude de l'économie agricole.**
(The Akyé region. A study of the agricultural economy.)
Dian Boni. *Annales de l'Université d'Abidjan, Série G, Géographie,*
vol. 2, fasc. 1 (1970), p. 7-206. 12 maps. bibliog.
This study forms the entire contents of this fascicule. Despite its title, it is a complete
study of the Akyé, called the Attié or Atié by Europeans and the Agni. Topics covered
are the physical geography of the area, the origin and social structure of the group, and
their agricultural practices.

236 **Première approche des Atié.** (First approach to the Atié.)
Denise Paulme. *Cahiers d'Etudes Africaines,* no. 21, vol. 6 (1966),
cahier 1, p. 86-120. map.
The Atié, or Akyé, are a small group living in the south-east corner of the Côte
d'Ivoire, near, but not on the coast. The author lived in the Alépé region, and
describes the social structures and lines of descent of the group.

Six mois dans l'Attié. (Six months in the Attié.)
See item no. 76.

Avikam

237 **Légende et histoire du peuple Avikam ou Brignan.** (Legend and
history of the Avikam or Brignan people.)
Lohou Abby Ahikpa. Abidjan: Imprimerie Nationale, 1985. xi, 87p.
2 maps. bibliog.
The Avikam or Brignan are a small ethnic group, driven by wars from Ghana, who are
settled on the Grand Lahou lagoon and the lower Bandama river. They are situated
west of the Alladian and south of the Dida peoples. The author has collected their oral
history from named narrators, and some written sources, and also gives a brief sketch
of their present way of life.

Baule

238 **Dans le pays baoulé. Monographie de la commune de Tomidi.**
Origine et histoire. (In Baule country. A study of Tomidi commune.
Origin and history.)
Gabriel Kouadio Tiacoh. Abidjan: Imprimerie Nationale, 1983. 109p.
map.

In this history of Tomidi and its surroundings, the author tells the story of the Baule,
since many of its leaders came from this town. The author recounts the legends of the
initial migrations and settlement of the Baule, and traces their history through colonial
times to the present day.

239 **L'émigration baoulé actuelle.** (Current Baule emigration.)
P. Etienne, M. Etienne. *Cahiers d'Outre-Mer*, vol. 21, no. 82
(April-June 1968), p. 155-95. 7 maps.

A description of the migration of the Baule to the towns or plantations, and of the
social conditions of the migrants.

240 **Le goli. Contribution à l'étude des masques baoulé.** (The goli.
A contribution to the study of Baule masks.)
Fernand Lafargue. *Annales de l'Université d'Abidjan, Série F,
Ethnosociologie*, vol. 5 (1973), p. 69-98.

This study of the goli ritual, its masks and dances, is part of a wider study of the Baule
traditional religion being undertaken by the author. A short vocabulary of religious
terms is included at the end of the article.

241 **L'histoire socio-économique des peuples baule: problèmes et**
perspectives de recherche. (The socio-economic history of the Baule:
problems and perspectives of research.)
Timothy C. Weiskel. *Cahiers d'Etudes Africaines*, no. 61-2, vol. 16
(1975), cahier 1-2, p. 357-95. 4 maps. bibliog.

A look at attempts to reconstruct the precolonial history of the Baule. Until recently,
historians have relied on oral traditions published by Maurice Delafosse in 1900, but
recent anthropological and linguistic research has questioned the stories of mass
migration and military conquest. An outline chronology is presented, with suggestions
for future research. There is a summary in English.

242 **Life with the Baoulé.**
Vincent Guerry, translated Nora Hodges. Washington, DC: Three
Continents Press, 1975. 172p.

An account of the social life and beliefs of the Baule, written by a priest who has lived
with them, without trying to convert them. Originally published in French as *La vie
quotidienne dans un village Baoulé* (Abidjan: INADES, 1972), it was re-issued in
French by INADES in 1980 with a 24-page bibliography by Jean-Pierre Chauveau.

243 **Maternité sociale, rapports d'adoption et pouvoir des femmes chez les Baoulé (Côte d'Ivoire).** (Social maternity, adoption relations and the power of women among the Baule.)
Mona Etienne. *L'Homme*, vol. 19, no. 3-4 (July-Dec. 1979), p. 63-107. bibliog.

An investigation into the practice of adoption which sheds light on the social structure of the Baule and on the relationships between men and women. Adoption can give a woman autonomy and a more equal relationship with men, an advantage that is becoming lost to urban women where a money economy favours men. There is a summary in English.

244 **Naissance de l'intelligence chez l'enfant baoulé de Côte d'Ivoire.** (The birth of intelligence in the Baule child of Côte d'Ivoire.)
P. R. Dasen, B. Inhelder, M. Lavallée, J. Retschitzki. Berne: Hans Huber, 1978. 321p. 2 maps. bibliog.

Chapter two of this study of child development describes the Baule environment and way of life, with particular emphasis on customs associated with birth and children. The rest of the work is a detailed study of the Baule child's interaction with his or her mother, his or her learning of motor skills and psychological development and the influence of nutrition on this development. One of the conclusions was that the child benefited from being carried around by his or her mother, being stimulated by contact and observation of daily activities.

245 **Notes sur les échanges dans le Baulé précolonial.** (Notes on exchanges among precolonial Baule.)
Jean-Pierre Chauveau. *Cahiers d'Etudes Africaines,* no. 63-4, vol. 16 (1976), cahier 3-4, p. 567-602. 8 maps.

After a brief introduction on the settlement and social organization of the Baule, the author looks at the system of trading by personal exchange, since traditions excluded the formation of a merchant class.

246 **Notes sur l'histoire économique et sociale de la région de Kokumbo (Baoulé-sud, Côte d'Ivoire).** (Notes on the economic and social history of the Kokumbo region, South-Baule, Côte d'Ivoire.)
Paris: ORSTOM, 1979. 227p. 24 maps. (Travaux et Documents d'ORSTOM).

A collection of essays on the early history of the Baule, their settlement in the Kokumbo region and their social and economic organization, including a study of marriage relationships.

247 **La part baulé. Effectif de population et domination ethnique: une perspective historique.** (The Baule share. The effect of population and ethnic domination: an historical perspective.)
Jean-Pierre Chauveau. *Cahiers d'Etudes Africaines,* no. 105-6, vol. 27 (1987), cahier 1-2, p. 123-65. bibliog.

The author considers whether the demographic importance of the Baule explains its domination of the Côte d'Ivoire today. He looks back at a century of high population growth, with some fluctuations. He also considers the readiness of young Baule women to migrate and intermarry, while retaining Baule identity for their offspring because of their matrilineal traditions.

248 **Quand les dieux dansent les dieux créent.** (When the gods dance the gods create.)
Bernard Courteau. Montreal: Leméac, 1974. 278p. (Collection Francophonie Vivante).

The author, a Canadian, spent several years as a guest lecturer at the Ecole Normale at Bouaké. He has collected reminiscences and stories about the customs and traditions of the Baule and some of their folk-tales, which he studied further on his return to Québec.

249 **Sur les traces probables de civilisation égyptienne et d'hommes de race blanche à la Côte d'Ivoire.** (On the probable track of Egyptian civilization and white-skinned men in the Côte d'Ivoire.)
Maurice Delafosse. *L'Anthropologie*, vol. 11 (1900), p. 431-51, 543-68, 677-90.

The author proposes the theory that Egyptian civilization was transmitted across the Sahara via the Tuareg and Songhai to the Baule of the Côte d'Ivoire. He describes the customs, religion and art of the Baule and claims similarities with Egyptian art and religion. When one studies the examples and illustrations, however, one can see no greater affinity than there would be between any two different religions or artistic objects. The articles do not develop the idea of a white race. At the time of writing many Europeans believed that any sign of 'civilization' must have been transmitted from Egyptian, 'nearly-white' sources.

250 **Terminologie de la parenté et de l'alliance chez les Baoulé.**
(The vocabulary of kinship and alliance among the Baule.)
Pierre Etienne, Mona Etienne. *L'Homme,* vol. 7, no. 4 (Oct.-Dec. 1967), p. 50-76. 2 maps. bibliog.

A study, with explanatory diagrams, of the terminology which specifies the complex relationships of kinship and descent.

Note sur l'état baoulé précolonial. (A note on the precolonial Baule state.)
See item no. 146.

La reine Pokou, fondatrice du royaume baoulé. (Queen Pokou, foundress of the Baule kingdom.)
See item no. 147.

French colonial rule and the Baule peoples: resistance and collaboration, 1889-1911.
See item no. 155.

Changing perspectives on African resistance movements and the case of the Baule peoples.
See item no. 163.

La pacification de la Côte d'Ivoire 1908-1915. (The pacification of the Côte d'Ivoire 1908-15.)
See item no. 172.

Colonisation agricole spontanée et émergence de nouveaux milieux sociaux dans le sud-ouest ivoirien. (Spontaneous agricultural colonization and the emergence of new social milieux in south-west Côte d'Ivoire.)
See item no. 197.

Phénomènes religieux et facteurs socio-économiques dans un village de la région de Bouaké. (Religious phenomena and socio-economic factors in a village in the Bouaké region.)
See item no. 376.

Espace vécu et milieu de contact forêt–savane chez les paysans Baoulé et leurs enfants dans le sud du 'V Baoulé' (Côte d'Ivoire). (Baule life-space in a forest/savannah contact zone: research on Baule farmers and their children in the south of the 'Baule V', Côte d'Ivoire.)
See item no. 413.

Ebrié

251 **Les Ebrié et leur organisation politique traditionnelle.** (The Ebrié and their traditional political organization.)
Georges Niangoran-Bouah. *Annales de l'Université d'Abidjan, Série F, Ethnosociologie,* vol. 1, fasc. 1 (1969), p. 51-89. map.
An article on the social structures of the various sub-groups of the Ebrié, who are found around the Ebrié lagoon on the coast of the Côte d'Ivoire.

252 **Histoire et coutumes de la Côte d'Ivoire. Cercles des lagunes. Les Ebriés.** (History and customs of the Côte d'Ivoire. Lagoon region. The Ebrié.)
Direction des Archives Nationales. Abidjan: Imprimerie Nationale, [ca. 1985]. 98p.
The administration of the National Archives intends to publish documents from the DD series concerning the administration of the country. They will be studies of the history and customs of a region or ethnic group, based on historical documents recording customs before they were Westernized. This first volume concerns the Ebrié from the lagoon region around the capital, who in this publication are considered to be descended from the Ashanti and part of the Akan group. Their relationships and customary law concerning inheritance and contracts are described. The second half of this short work concerns a survey of customary law from the beginning of this century and instructions on the administration of customary versus French law written in the 1930s.

M'batto

253 **Le langage des amulettes en pays M'Batto.** (The language of amulets in the M'Batto area.)
J.-M. Kihm, G. Tape. *Annales de l'Université d'Abidjan, Série D, Lettres*, vol. 10 (1977), p. 123-52. bibliog.

A survey, with photographs, carried out in the village of Akouré, thirty kilometres east of Abidjan, of amulets worn by children. Some are intended as protection from disease, and others reflect relationships with parents or deceased adults. The M'Batto are a small group of about 5,000 people in the Lagoon group.

Kru group

254 **The economic anthropology of the Kru (West Africa).**
Andreas Massing. Wiesbaden, Germany: Franz Steiner, 1980. 281p. bibliog. (Studien zur Kulturkunde, no. 55).

The Kru group are located in the coastal regions of Liberia and the Western Côte d'Ivoire. The book begins with the geography of the region and the history of the Kru group. The author then describes their social organization and agricultural practices. An appendix lists ethnic groups and their populations, and indicates their territories on a detailed map.

255 **Etude sociolinguistique de l'aire kru de Côte d'Ivoire.**
(Sociolinguistic study of the Kru region of Côte d'Ivoire.)
Suzanne Lafage. Abidjan: Université d'Abidjan, Institut de Linguistique Appliquée, 1982- . 8 maps. bibliog. (Etudes, no. 83).

A study of the Kru group in the south-west of the Côte d'Ivoire, which the author points out is not the same as the smaller Krou group in the extreme south-west corner of the country. Only the first volume, 'Analyse des données ethnodémographiques et socioculturelles' has appeared at the time of writing. It analyses statistics of ethnic groups and sub-groups in the area by administrative district, together with figures on language use and education.

Ahizi

256 **Appartenance et dépendance. L'exemple du système de classes d'âge des Aïzi (basse Côte d'Ivoire).** (Belonging to / depending on: the age-set system of the Ahizi, lower Côte d'Ivoire.)
François Verdeaux. *Cahiers d'Etudes Africaines*, no. 68, vol. 17 (1977), cahier 4, p. 435-61. bibliog.

A study of the age-set and lineage systems and of their combination in a matrilineal society. The system institutionalizes men as social seniors or juniors, or exchangers/exchangees, with children as the ultimate object of exchange.

257 **Tiagba. Notes sur un village aïzi.** (Tiagba. Notes on an Ahizi village.)
C. Bonnefoy. *Etudes Eburnéennes,* vol. 3 (1954), p. 7-129. 2 maps.
bibliog.

The Ahizi or Aizi are a small ethnic group classed by Lavergne de Tressan as part of
the Kru group, but by others as also having Akan descent, living in the Jacqueville
sub-prefecture. The Tiagba form a sub-group of the Ahizi and the village of Tiagba is
considered the 'mother-village' of the Ahizi. This description of their way of life, their
demographic structure, housing, agriculture and fishing is illustrated with
photographs.

Bété

258 **Economie marchande et structures sociales: le cas des Bété de Côte
d'Ivoire.** (Market economy and social structures: the Bété of Côte
d'Ivoire.)
Jean-Pierre Dozon. *Cahiers d'Etudes Africaines*, no. 68, vol. 17
(1977), cahier 4, p. 463-83.

Some notes on male–female relationships and division of labour among the Béte of
Gagnoa. Agriculture used to be the province of women, but since colonization men
and women both take part in the plantation economy.

259 **L'image du monde bété.** (The image of the Bété world.)
B. [Bohumil] Holas. Paris: Presses Universitaires de France, 1968.
401p. bibliog.

The author limits himself to an exploration of the spiritual world of the Bété, and does
not extend to social aspects or practical matters.

260 **Une société de Côte d'Ivoire. Les Bété.** (A society in the Côte
d'Ivoire. The Bété.)
Denise Paulme. Paris: Mouton, 1962. 200p. 3 maps. bibliog.
(Le Monde d'Outre-Mer Passé et Présent. Ecole Pratique des Hautes
Etudes. Documents, vol. 8).

A comprehensive survey of this people, frequently cited by later researchers. The
author covers their origin and social structures, their management of agriculture, and
their beliefs and rituals. Paulme provides her own photographs.

261 **La société bété. Histoires d'une 'ethnie' de Côte d'Ivoire.**
(Bété society. Stories of an 'ethnic group' of the Côte d'Ivoire.)
Jean-Pierre Dozon. Bondy, France: ORSTOM; Paris: Karthala, 1985.
367p. 3 maps. bibliog. (Hommes et Société).

A comprehensive study of the Bété, their history and social organization and their
material conditions.

262 **Vers une définition de l'art bété: le mythe de Srele.** (Towards a definition of Bété art: the myth of Srele.)
Zadi Grékou, Séri Dédy. *Annales de l'Université d'Abidjan, Série F, Ethnosociologie*, vol. 7 (1978), p. 49-76. bibliog.
A study of a mythical figure and what it reveals about the Bété conception of the artist and, in particular, the musician.

Bheteh-nini. Contes bété. (Bété tales.)
See item no. 685.

Godié

263 **Organisation familiale des Godié de Côte d'Ivoire.** (Family structure of the Godié of the Côte d'Ivoire.)
Raymond Degri de Djagnan. *Cahiers d'Etudes Africaines*, no. 27, vol. 7 (1967), cahier 3, p. 399-433.
An analysis of the complex family structure and marriage customs of the Godié. They form a small group on the coast east of the Sassandra, probably of Kru origin with some Akan descent.

Kru or Krou

264 **Images de la femme kru à travers une cérémonie de funérailles (Côte d'Ivoire).** (Images of the Kru woman through a funeral ceremony.)
Alfred Schwartz. *Cahiers d'Etudes Africaines,* no. 73-6, vol. 19 (1979), cahiers 1-4, p. 323-7.
A short contribution, in this volume of *Cahiers* which replaces all four parts for the year and is dedicated to Denise Paulme. The author gives an interesting report of a Kru funeral ceremony. The translated songs of the women show their rejection of traditional male domination borne out by the fact that 23 per cent of marriageable Kru women were not married at the time of the study. The Kru or Krou proper inhabit the south-west corner of the Côte d'Ivoire and the adjoining part of Liberia, and form part of the larger Kru cluster.

265 **Krou popular traditions in the Ivory Coast.**
Bohumil Holas. In: *The realm of the extra-human, ideas and actions.* Edited by Agehananda Bharati. The Hague: Mouton, 1976, p. 365-77. (9th International Congress of Anthropological and Ethnological Sciences, Chicago, 1973).
A brief contribution on the need to create myths in order to explain natural phenomena, including material on the animals and characters of Kru myths.

266 **Traditions krou.** (Kru traditions.)
Bohumil Holas. Paris: Nathan, 1980. 573p. maps. bibliog.
An extended survey of Kru social life and customs, illustrated by photographs.

Sous-peuplement et développement dans le sud-ouest de la Côte d'Ivoire.
(Underpopulation and development in the south-west of the Côte d'Ivoire.)
See item no. 211.

Neyo

Essai de manuel de la langue néoulé. (An outline manual of Néoulé.)
See item no. 329.

Wè

267 **Dynamique de la société Ouobé. Loi des masques et coutume.**
(Dynamic of Wobé society. The law of masks and costume.)
J. Girard. Dakar: IFAN, 1967. 352p. map bibliog. (Mémoires de
l'Institut Fondamental d'Afrique Noire, no. 78).
A study of the customs and social structures of the Wobé, now considered with the
Guéré to form one group, the Wè. The masks and their use are covered in the first part,
while later chapters deal with sorcery, the initiation of young people, marriage and
agricultural practices. The appendix includes traditional tales.

268 **The Guéré excision festival.**
Elizabeth Tucker. In: *Time out of time. Essays on the festival.*
Edited by Alessandro Falassi. Albuquerque, New Mexico: University
of New Mexico Press, 1987, p. 276-85.
After a brief introduction on the Guéré, who have largely resisted conversion to
Christianity or Islam, the author describes excision festivals performed in 1972 and
1974, when they were already limited by the government. Now they are even further
limited. The operation and the following ceremonies are described.

269 **Masque en pays Guéré.** (Masks among the Guéré.)
H.-B. Tiabas. *Annales de l'Université d'Abidjan, Série F,
Ethnosociologie*, vol. 7 (1978), p. 85-90.
The origin and role of the mask in Wè society.

270 **La mise en place des populations Guéré et Wobé. Essai d'interprétation historique des données de la tradition orale.** (The settlement of the Guéré and Wobé populations. An attempted historical interpretation of oral tradition.)
Alfred Schwartz. *Cahiers ORSTOM, Série Sciences Humaines*, vol. 5, no. 4 (1968), p. 2-38; vol. 6, no. 1 (1969), p. 2-56. 13 maps.
A study of this ethnic group, the Wè, perceived by colonial studies as being two groups. Schwartz describes their clans, their social structures and the traditions of their origins.

271 **Le nom africain, ou langage des traditions.** (African names, or the language of traditions.)
Alphonse Tiérou. Paris: G.-P. Maisonneuve et Larose, 1977. 158p.
The author is from the Guéré group, which he calls Ouehi, and which is now considered part of the Wè. He writes about the history and significance of names, different categories of names and what they reveal about Guéré society, beliefs and ceremonies. A person has different names which reflect his relationship to both sides of his family and his role in ceremonies and in religion. There is a glossary.

272 **Tradition et changements dans la société guéré.** (Tradition and changes in Guéré society.)
Alfred Schwartz. Paris: ORSTOM, 1971. 259p. maps. bibliog.
(Mémoire ORSTOM, no. 52).
A study of the social structures and agriculture of the Guéré and Wobé, now recognized as one group, the Wè, who live in the western border of the country between latitudes 5°50 and 7°43 in the forest zone. The author notes the effects of colonization by the French on their way of life.

273 **La vérité première du second visage africain.** (The first truth about the second African face.)
Alphonse Tiérou. Paris: G.-P. Maisonneuve et Larose, 1975. 135p.
A young French-educated Guéré pursues a journalistic type of enquiry into the masks of his people, their form and symbolism, their use in ceremonies and dances, and their religious significance. He describes some of the ceremonies and talks to people taking part in them. The masks cover most of the body since they have a long grass skirt attached to them, as shown in the illustrations.

Women and masks among the Western Wè of Ivory Coast.
See item no. 716.

Mande group

Northern or Nuclear Mande

274 **Manding. Focus on an African civilisation.**
Edited by Guy Atkins. London: Centre for African Studies, School of
Oriental and African Studies, 1972. 33p. 2 maps.

An introductory booklet on the Manding, published in connection with a programme
of research on the group. The term Manding is the equivalent of Nuclear Mande, or, in
relation to the Côte d'Ivoire, Northern Mande. It includes Bambara and Diula as well
as Malinké. This booklet gives a brief history of the Manding empire of Mali, and
information on social structures, arts and crafts, music and literature. The research
programme included a Manding conference held in 1972 at the School of Oriental and
African Studies (SOAS), London. A short report on the conference was also published
by SOAS in 1972, entitled *Manding Conference 1972.*

275 **Papers on the Manding.**
Edited by Carleton T. Hodge. Bloomington, Indiana: Indiana
University Press; The Hague: Mouton, 1971. 307p. bibliogs. (Indiana
University Publications, African Series, vol. 3).

A collection of studies on the Manding or Northern Mande group which includes
general contributions on the Mande, and articles on the Malinké and Diula.

Manding art and civilisation.
See item no. 710.

Bambara

276 **Les Bambara.**
Viviana Paques. Paris: Presses Universitaires de France, 1954. 123p.
map. bibliog. (Monographies Ethnologiques Africaines).

The Bambara are widely distributed in West Africa, with only a small proportion
living in the north-west of the Côte d'Ivoire. This work examines the migrations and
sub-groups of the Bambara, their history and social organization and aspects of their
culture and language.

277 **Histoire des Bambara.** (History of the Bambara.)
Louis Tauxier. Paris: Paul Geuthner, 1942. 226p. map.

The Bambara are a Mande group who are found in Upper Guinea, Senegal,
Mauritania, Mali, Burkina Faso and the north-west of the Côte d'Ivoire. This history
of the group deals mainly with the Bambara of Mali and Upper Guinea, all part of the
French Sudan at the time.

Essai sur la langue bambara. (A sketch of the Bambara language.)
See item no. 338.

La religion bambara. (Bambara religion.)
See item no. 377.

Diula

278   **Traders without trade. Responses to change in two Dyula communities.**
Robert Launay.   Cambridge: Cambridge University Press, 1982.
188p. 2 maps. bibliog. (Cambridge Studies in Social Anthropology, no. 42).

A history of the Diula, their trade and social organization. The second part of the book examines the life of the Diula in the twentieth century, their Muslim faith today, and patterns of migration and kinship.

Table ronde sur les origines de Kong. (Round table on the origins of Kong.)
See item no. 138.

La disparition de la notion de 'caste' à Kong: (XVIIIe-XIXe siècles). (The disappearance of the notion of 'caste' in Kong, 18th-19th centuries.)
See item no. 145.

Beyond the stream.
See item no. 394.

Toura

279   **Les Toura. Esquisse d'une civilisation montagnarde de Côte d'Ivoire.** (The Toura. Sketch of a mountain civilization of the Côte d'Ivoire.)
Bohumil Holas.   Paris: Presses Universitaires de France, 1962. 234p. bibliog.

More than a sketch, this is a considerable study of the Toura, also known as the Weingmé, a very small but distinctive group of mountain people who live in the Man mountains, the highest part of the Côte d'Ivoire on the western border of the country.

Southern or Peripheral Mande

280 **Nègres gouro et gagou.** (Guro and Gagou negroes.)
L. Tauxier. Paris: Paul Geuthner, 1924. 369p. bibliog. (Etudes
Soudanaises).

The Guro is the larger of these two Southern Mande groups who, after much
migration, are to be found in an area around the towns of Zuenoula and Bouaflé just
west of the centre of the country. The Gagou, who call themselves Gban, are a much
smaller group of ancient origin, who are also diminutive in stature. This work begins
with the geography and fauna of the region. Successive chapters give details of
anthropometric measurements, and cover elements of their languages, history, ethnic
sub-divisions, their customs, beliefs, and finally folklore.

281 **Variations ivoiriennes sur un thème omaha.** (Variations on an
Omaha theme.)
Ariane Deluz. *L'Homme*, vol. 13, no. 3 (July-Dec. 1973), p. 31-44.
bibliog.

A comparative analysis of kinship terminology between the Dan and the Guro, in
which the author draws parallels with the Omaha. A table compares conventions of
kinship, marriage and female behaviour between the Dan and the Guro.

Beng

282 **Cousin marriage, birth order and gender-alliance models among
the Beng of the Ivory Coast.**
Alma Gottlieb. *Man. The Journal of the Royal Anthropological
Society,* new series, vol. 21, no. 4 (Dec. 1986), p. 697-722. bibliog.

The Beng constitute a small group within the Peripheral or Southern Mande group in
the east-central Côte d'Ivoire. Although technically illegal under recent law, marriages
are still arranged among the Beng. Varieties of cousin marriage are common, but
restricted by rules forbidding marriage between certain relations and people already
linked by marriage. Birth order is significant in candidacy for such arrangements, as is
the consideration as to whether the cousin is on the mother's or father's side, and
these relationships determine the amount of authority a husband has over his wife.
Among these complexities there is some interesting information on relations between
the sexes: women's hearts are considered 'harder' than men's, quicker to anger and
more bitter afterwards.

283 **Parallel worlds. An anthropologist and a writer encounter Africa.**
Alma Gottlieb, Philip Graham. New York: Crown Publishers, 1993.
324p. 2 maps.

A diary of travels in 1979-81 and 1985 in the Beng region in the east-centre of the
country. This husband-and-wife team give a lively account of their stay with the
people among whom they felt both welcome and unwelcome as outsiders.

284 **Sex, fertility and menstruation among the Beng of the Ivory Coast: a symbolic analysis.**
Alma Gottlieb.   *Africa: Journal of the International African Institute*, vol. 52, no. 3 (1982), p. 34-47. bibliog.
The author introduces briefly the Beng, a small group of about 7,000 in the Southern Mande group, who have a cult of the earth. Menstruating women may not work in the forest or the fields (which are in the forest), nor touch a corpse, nor cook for their husbands. [Perhaps these restrictions were invented by a woman!] The earth is polluted by menstrual blood or by sexual intercourse in the forest.

285 **Under the kapok tree. Identity and difference in Beng thought.**
Alma Gottlieb.   Bloomington and Indianapolis, Indiana: Indiana University Press, 1992. 184p. 3 maps. bibliog.
A study of the world of ideas among the Beng, their social structures and beliefs.

Dan (*see also* Southern Mande)

Classification stylistique du masque dan et guéré. (Stylistic classification of Dan and Guéré masks.)
See item no. 712.

The arts of the Dan in West Africa.
See item no. 713.

Musique dan. La musique dans la pensée et vie sociale d'une société africaine. (Dan music. Music in the thought and social life of an African society.)
See item no. 736.

Gagou

286 **Le Gagou. Son portrait culturel.** (The Gagou. A cultural portrait.)
B. Holas.   Paris: Presses Universitaires de France, 1975. 233p. bibliog.
The Gagou, who call themselves the Gban, are a small group of hunter-gatherers in the south-centre of the country, and are among the oldest inhabitants of the country. They are included in the Southern Mande group. The author describes their appearance and habits and discusses their origin, language, agriculture, rituals and beliefs.

Guéré (*see* Wè: items 267-73)

Guro

287   **Anthropologie économique des Gouro de Côte d'Ivoire. De
l'économie de subsistance à l'agriculture commerciale.** (Economic
anthropology of the Guro of the Côte d'Ivoire. From a subsistence
economy to commercial agriculture.)
Claude Meillassoux.   Paris; The Hague: Mouton, 1964.
382p. 17 maps. bibliog.
A very full survey of the history of the Guro, their lands and their social organization.
Their agriculture has gone through three phases: subsistence farming; forced labour;
commercial agriculture. A critique of this work is offered by Ariane Deluz and
Maurice Godelier in *L'Homme*, vol. 7, no. 3 (July-Sept. 1967), p. 78-91. The author
responds on p. 91-7 of the same issue.

288   **Anthroponymie et recherche historique.** (Anthroponymy [the study
of family names] and historical research.)
Ariane Deluz.   *L'Homme*, vol. 7, no. 1 (Jan.-March 1967), p. 32-49.
bibliog.
A study of the usage, transmission and meanings of personal names among the Guro.

289   **Les masques et leur fonction sociale chez les Gouro.** (Masks and
their social function among the Guro.)
Venance Kacou.   *Annales de l'Université d'Abidjan, Série F,
Ethnosociologie*, vol. 7 (1978), p. 77-84.
A short article on the origins and uses of masks.

290   **Organisation sociale et tradition orale. Les Guro de Côte d'Ivoire.**
(Social organization and oral tradition. The Guro of Côte d'Ivoire.)
Ariane Deluz.   Paris; The Hague: Mouton, 1970. 196p. map. bibliog.
(Cahiers de l'Homme. Nouvelle Série, no. 19).
A survey conducted in 1958-59 of the social structures of the Guro. It includes a
detailed classification of tribes by region.

291   **Villages et lignages chez les Guro de Côte d'Ivoire.** (Villages and
lineages among the Guro of Côte d'Ivoire.)
Ariane Deluz-Chiva.   *Cahiers d'Etudes Africaines*, no. 19, vol. 5
(1965), cahier 3, p. 388-52. map.
The Guro occupy an area west of the centre of the Côte d'Ivoire, around Bouaflé. The
author has studied the organization of Guro villages and their genealogical structures
in great detail.

Die Kunst der Guro, Elfenbeinküste. (The art of the Guro, Côte d'Ivoire).
See item no. 714.

Voltaic group

Kulango

Le noir de Bondoukou. (The negro of Bondoukou.)
See item no. 214.

Phonologie de Koulango de la région de Bondoukou. (Phonology of
Kulango from the Bondoukou region.)
See item no. 358.

Lobi

292 **Les Lobi.**
Léon Charles. *Revue d'Ethnologie et de Sociologie* (Institut
Ethnographique International de Paris), vol. 2 (1911), p. 202-20.
5 plates.
A short description of the appearance of the Lobi, their social organization and their
customs, written by a European who seems to have disapproved of them strongly and
talks of their 'inherent vices'. The five plates are photographs of musical instruments,
statuettes and ornaments.

293 **Les migrations lobi en Côte d'Ivoire; archaïsme ou création
sociale.** (Lobi migrations in the Ivory Coast; archaism or social
creation.)
Michèle Fiéloux. In: *Les migrations africaines.* Edited by Jean-Loup
Amselle. Paris: Maspero, 1976, p. 43-61. map. (Dossiers Africains).
A history of the migration of the Lobi into Burkina Faso in the nineteenth century, and
from there to the north-eastern corner of the Côte d'Ivoire at the end of the nineteenth
and in the early twentieth centuries. At the time of writing, up to 100,000 lived in
Burkina Faso and 65,000 in the Côte d'Ivoire. The author examines the causes of
migrations and provides a map with dates indicating the settlement of various areas.

294 **Organisation sociale des Lobi. Une société bilinéaire du Burkina
Faso et de Côte d'Ivoire.** (The social organization of the Lobi.
A bilinear society from Burkina Faso and Côte d'Ivoire.)
Cécile de Rouville. Paris: L'Harmattan, 1987. 259p. map. bibliog.
(Connaissance des Hommes).
The Lobi are divided between Burkina Faso and the extreme north-east of Côte
d'Ivoire. The author challenges the view that theirs is a matrilinear society, and finds
that individuals have a double affiliation, to both their mother's and father's clans. In a
society without chiefs, social order is maintained by adhesion to collective cults, since
the Lobi have resisted both Islam and Christianity.

295 **Les tribus du rameau Lobi.** (The tribes of the Lobi branch.)
Henri Labouret.   Paris: Institut d'Ethnologie, 1931. 510p. 31 plates.
(Travaux et Mémoires de l'Institut d'Ethnologie, Université de Paris,
no. 15).

An ethnographic study of the Lobi group and the history of their territory, with
photographs of their artefacts and some photographs of the people themselves and
their ceremonies. Their agriculture, trade, crafts, and artistic activities are surveyed,
together with their social organization, customs and religion.

Kunst und Religion der Lobi. (Art and religion of the Lobi.)
See item no. 726.

Senufo

296 **Divination bei den Kafibele-Senufo. Zur Aushandlung und
Bewältigung von Alltagskonflikten.** (Divination among the Kafibele-
Senufo. The treatment and resolution of daily conflicts.)
Till Förster.   Berlin: Dietrich Reimer, 1985. 360p. map. bibliog.

The Kafibele are a Senufo sub-group, living along the River Bou, in the region of
Sirasso in the north-centre of the country. This is a detailed study of their beliefs and
ceremonies.

297 **J'ai changé de nom. . . Pourquoi?** (I changed my name. Why?)
Charles-Valy Tuho.   Abidjan: Nouvelles Editions Africaines, 1984.
103p. bibliog.

A former Rector of Abidjan University and ambassador to the European Communities
writes of his background as a Senufo. He explains the Senufo way of life, its social
structures, names, ceremonies and beliefs. He also writes of the history of the Senufo
and of their cultural identity. The last chapter is a testimony to the Christian faith
which has led him to change his name.

298 **Kunst und Religion bei den Gbato-Senufo, Elfenbeinküste.** (Art and
religion among the Gbato-Senufo, Côte d'Ivoire.)
Karl Heinz Krieg, Wulf Lohse.   Hamburg, Germany: Hamburgisches
Museum für Völkerkunde, 1981. 144p. 2 maps. bibliog. (Wegweiser
zur Völkerkunde, no. 26).

A well-illustrated study of the art and religion of the Gbato, a Senufo sub-group
settled around Boundiali, in the north-west of the Côte d'Ivoire.

299 **Le paysan Senoufo.** (The Senufo peasant.)
Sinali Coulibaly.   Abidjan: Nouvelles Editions Africaines, 1978.
245p. 11 maps. bibliog.

A study of the traditional way of life among the Senufo of the Korhogo department,
which Coulibaly wished to record before it was swept away by the 'new' society. The
author describes the geography and vegetation of the area, and then moves on to the

history of the Senufo, their traditional huts, their religious beliefs, and political and family structures. The last part of the book deals with traditional agricultural methods.

300 **Les Sénoufo (y compris les Minianka).** The Senufo (including the Minianka.)
B. [Bohumil] Holas. Paris: Presses Universitaires de France, 1966. 2nd ed. 183p. 4 maps. bibliog. (Monographies Ethnologiques Africaines).
The author remarks that even since his first edition in 1957 some Senufo had moved away from their roots and migrated to the cities. He analyses the location and population density of the Senufo, who reside in the central-north of the country, and across the northern border in Mali and part of Burkina Faso. A map indicates the location of thirty dialects. The author then covers the history of the Senufo, their way of life, their customs and traditional laws, and their religion.

301 **Les Senoufo face au cosmos.** (The Senufo in the face of the cosmos.)
Jean Marie Keletigui. Abidjan: Nouvelles Editions Africaines, 1978. 102p. (La Voix de . . .).
The beliefs of the Senufo concerning the origin of the cosmos and man, and about God and death.

302 **Le sens initiatique du secret dans le poro senoufo. L'exemple du Noncara chez les Fodonnon.** (The meaning of the secret initiation into the Senufo poro. The example of the Noncara of the Fodonnon.)
Bêh Ouattara. *Kasa Bya Kasa*, no. 3 (Feb.-April 1983), p. 63-77.
The Noncara is is a specialized 'poro' or secret society, whose members, after initiation, devote themselves to healing among the Fodonnon sub-group of the Senufo.

303 **Woman power and art in a Senufo village.**
Anita J. Glaze. *African Arts*, vol. 8, no. 3 (Spring 1975), p. 24-9, 64-8, 90-1. bibliog.
An account of research conducted in a cluster of villages to the south-west of Korhogo in the Kufuru area. It is inhabited by a mixture of dialect and occupational groups, although the Fodonnon group is dominant. The role of women in rituals, particularly in poro activities, is examined, with explanations of beliefs and myths.

Les jeunes Djimini. Essai sur la dynamique des groupes de jeunes. (Young Djimini. An essay on young people's group dynamics.)
See item no. 419.

Art and death in a Senufo village.
See item no. 717.

L'art sacré sénoufo. Ses différentes expressions dans la vie sociale. (Sacred Senufo art. Its different expressions in social life.)
See item no. 718.

Bestiaire et génies. Dessins sur tissus des Sénoufo. (Bestiaries and spirits. Senufo drawings on cloth.)
See item no. 719.

Le double monstrueux. Les masques-hyène des Sénoufo. (The double monster. Hyena-masks of the Senufo.)
See item no. 721.

Glänzend wie Gold: Gelbguss bei den Senufo, Elfenbeinküste. (Glitters like gold: brass casting among the Senufo of the Côte d'Ivoire.)
See item no. 722.

Kreenbele Senufo potters.
See item no. 723.

Senufo ornament and decorative arts.
See item no. 724.

Musique et excision chez les Djimini (Côte d'Ivoire). (Music and excision of the Djimini.)
See item no. 737.

Languages

General

304 Alphabets de langues africaines. (Alphabets of African language.)
Edited by Rhonda L. Hartell.   Dakar: UNESCO – Bureau Régional de
Dakar, Société International de Linguistique, 1993. 311p. bibliog.
The section on the Côte d'Ivoire begins with a history of efforts to transcribe the
country's oral languages into written symbols. The phonemes and written symbols are
given for nineteen languages, together with a word to illustrate each sound and its
translation into French. The bibliography suggests at least one item under each
language, but many of them are on a specialized aspect, or locally produced and may
be difficult to obtain elsewhere, demonstrating the lack of basic texts for the outsider
on most of the languages of the Côte d'Ivoire.

305 Annales de l'Université d'Abidjan. Série H. Linguistique. (Annals
of the University of Abidjan. Series H. Linguistics.)
Abidjan: University of Abidjan, 1966- . annual.
Studies in West African languages and linguistics, in English and French.

**306 Esquisse générale des langues de l'Afrique et plus particulièrement
de l'Afrique Française.** (A general outline of the languages of Africa,
and more particularly of French Africa.)
Maurice Delafosse.   Paris: Masson, 1914. 42p. map. (Part of Enquête
sur la Famille, la Propriété, la Justice chez les Indigènes des Colonies
Françaises d'Afrique, published by the Société Antiesclavagiste de
France).
An introduction to the broader groups of languages, followed by a listing of languages
and their dialects, and indicating the ethnic group name and location of the speakers.
It forms part of a survey of the family, property and justice among the native peoples

75

of French African colonies, that survey being published by the Anti-slavery Society of France.

307 **Essai de nomenclature des populations, langues et dialectes de Côte d'Ivoire.** (An attempt to classify the populations, languages and dialects of the Côte d'Ivoire.)
Pierette Ceccaldi. Paris: Centre d'Etudes Africaines, CARDAN, 1974. 2 parts.

Two large folders of sheets give the names of dialects or languages and the corresponding ethnic groups in alphabetical order, with notes on the origin and meaning of the name, and variations; for example, what the people call themselves, and what they are called by neighbours and administrators. Citations are given for the first official use of the name and for reference works providing information on the language or group. The location of the group or language is described, along with its relationship to larger language groups. As this work is published by the major centre for French studies in Paris, it does not solve the problem of translation or transcription into English. It was reviewed in the *Journal des Africanistes,* vol. 50, fasc. 1 (1980), p. 154-7.

308 **Inventaire préliminaire des langues et dialectes en Côte d'Ivoire.** (Preliminary inventory of languages and dialects of the Côte d'Ivoire.)
Esther Frick, Margrit Bolli. *Annales de l'Université de l'Abidjan, Série H, Linguistique,* vol. 1 (1971), p. 395-416. bibliog.

A contribution to the Eighth International Congress of African Linguistics, this is a listing of languages and dialects giving their locations.

309 **The languages of West Africa.**
Diedrich Westermann, M. A. Bryan. Folkestone, England; London: Dawsons, for the International African Institute, 1970. 2nd ed. 277p. map. bibliog.

This standard scholarly work lists the languages of West Africa in their groups, indicating the area where each language is spoken and by which ethnic group. It gives alternative and local names for both the languages and the groups, and estimates the number of speakers. There are linguistic notes, an extensive bibliography, a detailed map, and an index giving references from variant forms of name. The classification of so many oral languages with variant names is complex and debatable, and speakers from different groups may inhabit the same areas.

310 **La numération cardinale dans quelques langues de Côte d'Ivoire.** (Cardinal numbers in some languages of the Côte d'Ivoire.)
E. Grandet. *Annales de l'Université d'Abidjan, Série H, Linguistique,* vol. 6, fasc. 1 (1973), p. 47-102. bibliog.

The enquiry, conducted by questionnaire, was originally intended to cover cardinal and ordinal numbers as well as fractions, in about thirty languages representing the various linguistic groups of the Côte d'Ivoire. Since the information received was unequal, the enquirers had to limit themselves to cardinal numbers.

311 **La politique linguistique en Afrique francophone. Une étude**
comparative de la Côte d'Ivoire et de Madagascar. (Linguistic
policy in francophone Africa. A comparative study of the Côte d'Ivoire
and Madagascar.)
Denis Turcotte.   Quebec: Les Presses de l'Université Laval, 1981.
(Travaux du Centre International de Recherche sur le Bilinguisme,
A-17).
The Côte d'Ivoire is a mosaic of over sixty ethnic groups, none of which make up
more than a quarter of the population. The first article of the constitution lays down
French as the official language and this is still government policy. French is used in
education and administration, but some Ivoirian languages are used in the media.
Although Diula is widely known, the south and Christian communities would resent
its imposition as an official language. This is a survey of language use and policy, and
includes a chapter on linguistic research.

312 **Polyglotta Africana; or a comparative vocabulary of nearly three**
hundred words and phrases in more than one hundred distinct
African languages.
S. W. Koelle.   London: Church Missionary Society, 1854. 188p.
This large-format book sets out in columns translations of some basic words into
many languages. In their turn, the languages are placed in related groups. This is a
source book for many later studies, and is useful for noting related languages.

313 **The spread of Dyula and popular French in Côte d'Ivoire:**
implications for language policy.
Paulin G. Djité.   *Language Problems and Language Planning*,
vol. 12, no. 3 (Fall 1988), p. 213-25. bibliog.
Standard French is not used by the mass of the people, who prefer popular French or
Diula as a lingua franca, especially since migration and high drop-out rate from school
hinder the teaching of standard French. Dyula lacks a writing system, apart from
phonetic transcriptions, and popular French would not be much easier to write than
Standard French for the illiterate. There was no majority support for a change to the
current policy of Standard French as the national official language.

314 **Vocabulaires comparatifs de plus de 60 langues et dialectes parlés**
à la Côte d'Ivoire et dans les régions limitrophes. (Comparative
vocabularies from more than 60 languages and dialects spoken in the
Côte d'Ivoire and neighbouring regions.)
Maurice Delafosse.   Paris: Ernest Leroux, 1904. 284p. map. bibliog.
A comparative study of basic common words and phrases, with introductory material
on the language groups and a map. Many of the languages and dialects are still little
known, and subsequent classifications are based on this book.

Le noir de Bondoukou. (The negro of Bondoukou.)
See item no. 214.

Akan group

315 **Atlas linguistique de Côte d'Ivoire. Les langues de la région lagunaire.** (Linguistic atlas of Côte d'Ivoire. The languages of the Lagoon region.)
G. Dumestre. Abidjan: Université d'Abidjan, Institut de Linguistique Appliquée, 1970. 323p. maps. bibliog.
The Lagoon group of languages differ from other language groups in Côte d'Ivoire in that they do not resemble each other closely. This study compares 400 words in Ebrié, Attié, Abbey, Krobou, Abure, Adioukrou, Alladian, Aïzi, Etiolé, Avikum, Abidji and M'batto, with a translation of each word into French.

Abron

316 **L'Abron: langue sans consonnes nasales.** (Abron: a language without nasal consonants.)
Lawrence Tufuor. *Annales de l'Université d'Abidjan, Série H, Linguistique,* vol. 13, fasc. 2 (1984), p. 159-96. map.
This article begins with general information about the Abron, part of the Akan group, who number about 40,000 in Côte d'Ivoire and about 766,500 in Ghana. This phonological study concludes that there are nasal vowels but not nasal consonants in Abron.

Adioukrou

317 **Eléments d'enquête lexicale en Adioukrou.** (Some questions of vocabulary in Adioukrou.)
G. Hérault. *Annales de l'Université d'Abidjan, Série H, Linguistique,* vol. 3, fasc. 1 (1970), p. 71-96.
A short vocabulary of agricultural and domestic terms, with explanatory notes. The author has also written *Eléments de grammaire Adioukrou*, published by the Institut de Linguistique Appliquée of the Université d'Abidjan in 1978 (477p.).

Agni

318 **Essai de manuel de la langue Agni.** (Sketch for an Agni language manual.)
Maurice Delafosse. Paris: J. André, 1900. 226p. map. bibliog.
A manual of vocabulary and some material on the grammar and pronunciation of the language. There is an anthology of Agni stories and traditions, with translations into French, and information on the history and grouping of tribes.

Attié (or Akyé)

Six mois dans l'Attié. (Six months in the Attié.)
See item no. 76.

Baule

319 **Notes on Baule phonology.**
J. M. Stewart. *Bulletin of the School of Oriental and African Studies*,
vol. 18, no. 2 (1956), p. 353-65.
A provisional phonological analysis of Baule, a member of the Anyi-Baule dialect
cluster of the Akan language group, which does not attempt to examine tones.

320 **Les tons du Baoulé (Parler de la région de Toumodi).** (Baule tones.
Toumodi dialect.)
Denis Creissels, N'Guessan Kouadio. Abidjan: Université d'Abidjan,
1979. 123p. (Linguistique Africaine, no. 75).
Exercises in the Baule tonal system, with introductory explanations.

321 **Les tons du Baoulé: comparaison de deux dialectes.** (Baule tones: a
comparison of two dialects.)
Judith Timyan. *Annales de l'Université d'Abidjan, Série H,
Linguistique,* vol. 8, fasc. 1 (1975), p. 261-81. bibliog.
A study of tones in two dialects, Kodé from Totokro village in the Béoumi region, and
Fali from Bamoro, in the Bouaké region. Baule uses both level and rising or falling
tones. The differences between dialects is above all a difference in tones.

Ebrié

322 **Esquisse d'une phonologie de l'Ebrié.** (Outline of Ebrié phonology.)
P. Vogler. *Annales de l'Université d'Abidjan, Série H, Linguistique*,
vol. 1 (1968), p. 60-5.
An article on the Ebrié sound system. Ebrié is a Lagoon language in the eastern sub-
group, spoken in the sub-prefecture of Bingerville and in Abidjan. G. Dumestre
supplements this article by a short 'Contribution à l'étude de l'Ebrié' in the same
periodical, vol. 3, fasc. 1 (1970), p. 19-30.

323 **The tones of the Ebrié associative construction.**
Constance Kutsch Lojenga. *Journal of African Languages and
Linguistics*, vol. 7, no. 1 (April 1985), p. 1-22. bibliog.
An article on the Ebrié tone system, with some general information on Ebrié. The
researcher found substiantial variation in the tones between older and younger
speakers.

Kru group

324 **Atlas linguistique kru.** (A linguistic atlas: the Kru languages.)
Lynell Marchese. Paris: ACCT; Abidjan: Université d'Abidjan,
Institut de Linguistique Appliquée, 1984. 3rd ed. 424p. 16 maps. bibliog.

A survey of Kru languages, their relationships and common features. General
grammatical constructions are described and compared in different languages. There
are two word-lists at the end of the volume, one comparing 306 common words in 12
Ivoirian dialects, and another comparing 66 words in 21 Ivoirian and Liberian dialects.

325 **The Kru languages: a progress report.**
Wm. E. Welmers. In: *Language and linguistic problems in Africa.*
Proceedings of the VIIth conference on African Linguistics. Edited
by Paul F. A. Kotey, Haig Der-Houssikian. Columbia, South
Carolina: Hornbeam Press, 1977, p. 353-62. map. bibliog.

A critical survey of recent research into the Kru languages, their position in the Niger-
Congo group, and the relationships among themselves. A map indicates the location of
various languages and dialects, in an area along the coast in Liberia and the Côte
d'Ivoire.

326 **On assertive focus and the inherent focus nature of negatives and
imperatives: evidence from Kru.**
Lynell Marchese. *Journal of African Linguistics,* vol. 5, no. 2
(Oct. 1983), p. 115-29. bibliog.

A study of the form and distribution of assertive markers in several Kru languages.

327 **Tense/aspect and the development of auxiliaries in Kru languages.**
Lynell Marchese. Dallas and Arlington, Texas: Summer Institute of
Linguistics and University of Texas at Arlington, 1986. 301p. 9 maps.
bibliog. (Publications in Linguistics of the Summer Institute in
Linguistics, no. 78).

A detailed study for the specialist philologist of syntactic changes in fourteen Kru
languages, focusing on tense, aspect, negation, modality and word order.

Godié

328 **Morphotonologie du Godié.** (Morphotonology of Godié.)
C. Gratrix. *Annales de l'Université d'Abidjan, Série H, Linguistique,*
vol. 8, fasc. 1 (1975), p. 99-114. bibliog.

Godié or Godyé is a language in the Bété sub-group of the Kru group, spoken by
about 20,000 people in the south-west of the Côte d'Ivoire. This study is based on the
Kojiwali dialect, and describes the tonal system of Godié. In the same issue, on pages
215-39, is an article by L. Marchese entitled 'Morphonologie du verbe godié'
(Morphonology of the Godié verb), based on the same dialect.

Néoulé

329 **Essai de manuel de la langue néoulé parlée dans la partie occidentale de la Côte d'Ivoire.** (An outline manual of Néoulé (or Neyo) spoken in the western part of the Côte d'Ivoire.)
Georges Thomann. Paris: Ernest Leroux, 1905. 198p. map. bibliog.

A dialect of the Bété sub-group of the Kru main group, spoken on the coast between Niéga and Dagbégo, in the Néyo and Kébé cantons of the Sassandra sub-prefecture. Because the Neyo were widely employed as seafarers their language was widely understood along the coast. This manual provides notes on the grammar and vocabulary lists, and concludes with notes on the Bété and Bakwé sub-groups of the Kru and a comparison of some words in Néyo with translations into other Bété and Bakwé dialects.

Nyabwa

330 **Le Niaboua, langue sans consonnes nasales?** (Nyabwa, a language without nasal consonants?)
J. Bentinck. *Annales de l'Université d'Abidjan, Série H, Linguistique,* vol. 8, fasc. 1 (1975), p. 5-14. map.

A study of nasalization in Niaboua or Nyabwa, a language in the Guéré sub-group of the Kru group, spoken by about 15,000 people between the Sassandra in the west, the Lobo in the east, Pelézi in the north and Gninikabo in the south. The research was done in Guéssabo.

Wobé

331 **Le comportement tonal des constructions associatives en wobé.** (The tonal behaviour of associative constructions in Wobé.)
Carole Paradis. *Journal of African Languages and Linguistics,* vol. 6, no. 2 (Oct. 1984), p. 147-71. bibliog.

Wobé is a member of the Wè sub-group of the Kru group of languages, spoken by nearly 180,000 people. The study includes some explanation of the tonal system and consonants of Wobé.

332 **Précis de grammaire wobé.** (An outline of Wobé grammar.)
Inge Egner. *Annales de l'Université d'Abidjan, Série H, Linguistique,* vol. 15 (1989), p. 1-238. 2 maps. bibliog.

This complete grammar comprises the whole contents of this issue. It is prefaced by a chapter on the sounds and the alphabet of Wobé.

333 **Système vocalique et sandhi vocalique en Wobé.** (Vowel system and vocalic sandhi in Wobé.)
V. Hofer, T. Bearth. *Annales de l'Université d'Abidjan, Série H, Linguistique,* vol. 8, fasc. 1 (1975), p. 135-58.
A study of the vowel system and of vocal conjunctions in Wobé.

Mande group

Northern Mande

334 **Etude comparée des parlers manding ivoiriens.** (A comparative study of Manding dialects.)
Marie-Jo Derive. Paris: ACCT; Abidjan: Université d'Abidjan, Institut de Linguistique Appliquée, 1983. 327, 194 leaves. maps. bibliog.
A very detailed survey of Manding dialects, spoken in the north-west of the country, with maps to indicate their ranges and a series of maps to indicate the variations in particular sounds. The author prefers the term Manding which she uses to include the group of languages also known as Northern Mande which include Malinké in the north-west and Diula or Dioula in the north-east. A lengthy review by David J. Dwyer appears in the *Journal of African Languages and Linguistics,* vol. 14, no. 1 (Nov. 1993), p. 61-9.

335 **Etude dialectologique de l'aire manding de Côte d'Ivoire.** (A study of the dialects of the Manding area of Côte d'Ivoire.)
Marie-Jo Derive. Paris: Peeters, 1990. 2 fasc. (270p. and 137p.). 94 maps. (Langues et Cultures Africaines, nos 11, 12).
Grammatical and phonetic comparisons are made between the dialects in order to group and map them.

336 **Etudes sur le mandingue de Côte d'Ivoire.** (Studies on the Manding language of the Côte d'Ivoire.)
Cassian Braconnier, John Maire, Kalilou Tera. Paris: ACCT; Abidjan: Université d'Abidjan, Institut de Linguistique Appliquée, 1983. 199 leaves.
Three studies on the phonology and syntax of Diula (also spelled as Dioula or Jula) and the search for a 'standard' Diula, and one article on the extent to which speakers of different Manding dialects understand each other. The dialect of Diula which has been christened 'Côte d'Ivoire Diula' (or Diula véhiculaire) was the most widely understood and was recommended for a programme of literacy and literature which would reach most Manding-speaking people.

337   **La langue mandingue et ses dialectes (Malinké, Bambara, Dioula).**
(The Manding language and its dialects: Malinké, Bambara and Diula.)
Maurice Delafosse.   Paris: Paul Geuthner, 1929, 1955. 2 vols.
(Bibliothèque de l'Ecole Nationale des Langues Orientales Vivantes,
vols 10, 15).

Manding, or Mandingo or Mande, is one of the major languages of the Côte d'Ivoire,
spreading across the north of the country. Volume one of this work consists of a guide
to the grammar of the language in fairly formal terms and a guide to some vocabulary
and forms of address, together with a French–Manding dictionary. The second
volume, issued some time later, is a Manding–French dictionary with copious
explanations of terms. Many of the words are common to all the dialects.

Bambara

338   **Essai sur la langue bambara.** (A sketch of the Bambara language.)
G. Binger.   Paris: Maisonneuve, 1886. 132p. map.

Gustave Binger wrote this outline of Bambara after his work in Senegal but before he
explored the Côte d'Ivoire and became its first governor. He gathered his information
in the Kaarta area, now in Mali, and he gives an outline of the grammar and
pronunciation, some phrases and a little dictionary. As with many African language
groups, it is a matter of terminology whether one calls Bambara a language in the
Mande or Manding group, or a dialect of the Manding language.

339   **Grammaire et méthode Bambara.** (Bambara grammar and method.)
Capitaine Delaforge.   Paris: Charles Lavauzelle, 1947. 4th ed. 202p.

A brief grammar and vocabulary list.

340   **Manuel de la langue bambara.** (Manual of the Bambara language.)
[Un missionnaire de Ségou].   Algiers: Maison-Carré, 1905. 154p.

Bambara is a dialect of Manding, closely related to Diula. This grammar was
compiled by a missionary in Ségou in Mali. The Bambara are distributed in Senegal,
Mauretania, Mali and Burkina Faso, as well as in a small area of the north-east of the
Côte d'Ivoire.

Les Bambara.
See item no. 276.

Diula

341   **Dioula d'Odienné (parler de Samatiguila): matériel lexical.**
(Odiénné Diula [Samatiguila dialect]: lexical material.)
C. Braconnier, S. Diaby.   Abidjan: Institut de Linguistique Appliquée;
Paris: ACCT, 1982. 130p.

Diula is a dialect which has evolved from Manding, and is close to Bambara. There are three main forms of Diula: the Diulas of Kong and Odienné, and 'véhiculaire' or tàgbusikan Diula, spoken by non-Diula all over the country. This vocabulary list, with the Diula words noted in phonetic transcription since there is no formal written Diula language, was compiled from the usage of speakers from Samatiguila village, 39 kilometres north of Odienné, in the north-west of the country.

342   **Eléments de grammaire dioula.** (Elements of Diula grammar.)
G. Dumestre.   Abidjan: Université d'Abidjan, Institut de Linguistique
Appliquée, 1970. 97 leaves. (Documents Linguistiques).

Notes from a course on Diula grammar held at the University of Abidjan.

343   **Essai de manuel pratique de la langue mandé ou mandingue.**
(A practical manual of the Mande or Manding language.)
Maurice Delafosse.   Paris: Ernest Leroux, 1901. 304p. map. bibliog.
(Publications de L'Ecole des Langues Orientales Vivantes, 3rd series,
vol. 14).

Delafosse refers to the Mande or Manding language, and calls Diula, Malinké and Bambara dialects, where other writers speak of a Mande group of languages and Diula, Malinké and Bambara as languages. Delafosse found the three dialects fairly similar. He devotes most of this work to Diula, partly because he spent some time in a Diula area, and partly because, at the time, Malinké was more widely spoken, and he felt that less had been published about Diula. The first part of the book is a grammatical study of Diula, the second part a French–Diula vocabulary list, and the third part a history of Samori in Diula as a study text. The last part is brief comparison of Mande dialects and includes information on other dialects from smaller groups. The bibliography, obviously enough, lists nineteenth-century works on Mande dialects,

344   **Petit dictionnaire dioula. Dioula–français. Français–dioula.**
(Little Diula dictionary. Diula–French. French–Diula.)
C. Braconnier, M. J. Derive.   Abidjan: Université d'Abidjan, Institut
de Linguistique Appliquée, 1978. 141p.

A small collection of words and phrases, with illustrative examples, to aid the beginner. Most of the terms are common to all the forms of Diula.

345   **Phonologie du Dioula d'Odienné.** (Phonology of Odienné Diula.)
Cassian Braconnier.   Paris: ACCT; Abidjan: Université d'Abidjan,
Institut de Linguistique Appliquée, 1983. 131p.

A guide to the sound-system of Diula.

346 **Propositions pour la création d'un vocabulaire scientifique en Jula.**
(Suggestions for the creation of a scientific vocabulary in Diula.)
Kalilou Tera, Siaka Touré. Paris: ACCT; Abidjan: Université
d'Abidjan, Institut de Linguistique Appliquée, 1983. 87p. (Promotion
des Langues Manding et Peul).

As a practical step towards the use of national languages instead of French in
education, the authors propose scientific neologisms in Diula (or Dioula or Jula) and
provide a small dictionary.

347 **Quelques remarques sur le Dioula véhiculaire en Côte d'Ivoire.**
(Some remarks on common Diula in Côte d'Ivoire.)
Gayle Partman. *Annales de l'Université d'Abidjan, Série H,
Linguistique*, vol. 8, fasc. 1 (1975), p. 241-59. bibliog.

Diula or Dioula is not only the language of the people of that name, but became the
language of trade, and is now commonly understood all over the Côte d'Ivoire and
spoken by those who do not use French. Research was done on its use in the town of
Bouaflé, which has good road links to other parts of the country, including the capital.
The author looks at pidginization of the language by native and non-native speakers,
and variations of usage in speakers of different ethnic origins.

348 **The role of accent in the tonal system of Odyene Dyula.**
Moussa Bamba. *Current Approaches to African Linguistics*, vol. 7
(1990), p. 1-14.

A paper read at the 19th Annual Conference on African Linguistics, which took place
at Boston University in 1988. It gives a metrical analysis of Odyene (Odiénné) Dyula
(or Diula).

349 **Le système tonal du Dioula d'Odienné.** (The tonal system of
Odienné Diula.)
Cassian Braconnier. Paris: ACCT; Abidjan: Université d'Abidjan,
Institut de Linguistique Appliquée, 1983. 2nd ed. 2 vols. map. bibliog.

A linguistic study of the tonal system of Odienné Diula, based on information from a
speaker from Samatiguila.

350 **Les tons d'Odienné: guide pratique.** (Odienné tones: a practical
guide.)
Cassian Braconnier, Sanoussi Diaby. Paris: ACCT; Abidjan:
Université d'Abidjan, Institut de Linguistique Appliquée, 1983. 26p.

A brief text-book with exercises.

Malinké

351 **Dictionnaire français–malinké et malinké–français. Précédé d'un abrégé de grammaire malinké.** (French–Malinké and Malinké–French dictionary. Preceded by a summary of Malinké grammar.)
Père Abiven. Conakry: Mission des PP. du Saint-Esprit, 1906. xliv, 176p.
A short outline of the structure of the language prefaces this dictionary.

352 **Essai de dictionnaire pratique français–malinké.** (An outline practical French–Malinké dictionary.)
[Un père de la congrégation du Saint-Esprit et du Saint-Coeur de Marie: Père Abiven]. Saint-Louis, Senegal: [n.p.], 1896. 429p.
A dictionary with explanatory notes.

Southern Mande

353 **Atlas des langues Mandé-sud de Côte d'Ivoire.** (Atlas of Southern Mande languages of the Côte d'Ivoire.)
Nazam Halaoui, Kalilou Tera, Monique Trabi. Paris: ACCT; Abidjan: Université d'Abidjan, 1983. 227p. map. bibliog.
Not an atlas, although a map indicating the areas covered by the languages is provided, but a comparative study of the Southern Mande languages, the most important of which are Dan and Guro. Chapters cover phonology, syntax and vocabulary, the last chapter providing a lexical list of 200 French words translated into nine Mande languages.

Nègres gouro et gagou. (Guro and Gagou negroes.)
See item no. 280.

Gagou or Gban

354 **Etude descriptive du Gban (Côte d'Ivoire); phonétique et phonologie.** (A descriptive study of Gban, Côte d'Ivoire; phonetics and phonology.)
Joseph Le Saout. Paris: Société d'Etudes Linguistiques et Anthropologiques de France (SELAF), 1976. 447p. 2 maps. bibliog. (Langues et Civilisations à Tradition Orale, no. 21).
The Gban are among the oldest inhabitants of the Côte d'Ivoire. This phonological description was originally a thesis and is a fairly technical analysis designed to shed light on wider questions of phonology in African languages. The fourth annexe is a Gban–French vocabulary of 1029 entries.

Le Gagou. Son portrait culturel. (The Gagou. A cultural portrait.)
See item no. 286.

Voltaic or Gur group

355 **Atlas de langues gur de Côte d'Ivoire.** (Atlas of Gur languages in the
Côte d'Ivoire.)
E. N. A. Mensah, Z. Tchagbale. Paris: ACCT; Abidjan: Institut de
Linguistique Appliquée, Université d'Abidjan, 1983. 316p. 2 maps.
bibliog.

The Gur languages, also known as Voltaic, are spoken in a large zone of West Africa,
of which the Côte d'Ivoire forms the south-west corner, although this area is actually
the north-eastern part of the Côte d'Ivoire. The first chapter explains how the group
consists of sub-groups: Senufo, Lobi, Kulango, Kirma-Tyurama, Gurunsi and Oti
Volta, a sub-group which includes Kamara, Sofalaba and Birifor. The bulk of the book
is taken up by word-lists. For a hundred French words, each of which is given at the
top of the page, the authors give a translation, in the singular and the plural, into
twenty-three Gur languages.

Kulango

356 **Description sommaire du Kulango (Dialecte de Bouna, Côte
d'Ivoire).** (A summary description of Kulango, Bouna dialect, Côte
d'Ivoire.)
André Prost. *Annales de l'Université d'Abidjan, Série H,
Linguistique*, vol. 7, fasc. 1 (1974), p. 21-74.

A brief description, with some vocabulary, of the Kulango language.

357 **Petit lexique koulango–français.** (Little Kulango–French dictionary.)
Lawrence Tufuor. *Cahiers Ivoiriens de Recherches Linguistiques*,
vol. 15 (1984), p. 83-161.

A Kulango–French vocabulary list to aid students.

358 **Phonologie de Koulango de la région de Bondoukou.** (Phonology of
Kulango from the Bondoukou region.)
A. Bianco. *Annales de l'Université d'Abidjan, Série H, Linguistique,*
vol. 12, fasc. 2 (1979), p. 5-123. 2 maps. bibliog.

A general introduction to the language, its dialects and speakers, prefaces a detailed
enquiry into its sound-system.

Loron

359 **Esquisse phonologique du Loron.** (Phonological description of
Loron.)
I. Leenhouts, I. Person. *Annales de l'Université D'Abidjan, Série H,
Linguistique,* vol. 10, fasc. 1 (1977), p. 53-82.
Loron is a dialect of Kulango spoken, at the time, by about 3,000 to 5,000 people in
the extreme north-east of the Côte d'Ivoire. This is a description of its sound-system.

Senufo

360 **Senoufo phonology, discourse to syllable (A prosodic approach).**
Elizabeth Mills. Dallas, Texas: Summer Institute of Linguistics and
University of Texas at Arlington, 1984. 217p. map. bibliog.
After a general preface on the Senufo languages, the author concentrates on the
official Senufo of the Côte d'Ivoire, spoken around Korhogo, and provides a complex
analysis of problems of phonology which have not been resolved. A detailed review
by Mary Laughren appears in the *Journal of African Languages and Linguistics,*
vol. 8, no. 1 (April 1986), p. 87-94.

French

361 **The acquisition and use of French as a second language in Africa
(Sociolinguistic, historical-comparative and methodological
perspectives).**
Emmanuel N. Kwofie. Grossen-Linden, Germany: Hoffmann-Verlag,
1979. 122p. bibliog. (Giessener Beiträge zur Sprachwissenschaft,
vol. 15).
The first chapter covers the history of the introduction of French into Africa. The
second chapter examines the acquisition of French by African children, based on a
survey of Ivoirian children. In the rest of the book, the author looks at contact
situations between French and African languages, the characterisitcs of pidgins and
creoles, and the linguistic interference of African languages with French.

362 **Contribution à l'étude lexicale du français de Côte d'Ivoire.**
(Contribution to the lexical study of Côte d'Ivoire French.)
L. Duponchel. Abidjan: Université d'Abidjan, Institut de
Linguistique Appliquée, 1972. 168p. bibliog. (Enseignement du
Français, vol. 35).
A survey of the influence of African vocabulary on the French spoken in the Côte
d'Ivoire, with a lexicon of terms used.

363 **Le français: langue africaine.** (French: an African language.)
Pierre Dumont. Paris: L'Harmattan, 1990. 173p. bibliog.

The author examines the use of French in Africa: its role in countries of language conflicts, its use by uneducated peole, the teaching of vocabulary and the production of dictionaries. The author also studies the usage by people in Cameroon, Senegal, Benin and the Côte d'Ivoire.

364 **Le français populaire d'Abidjan: un cas de pidginisation.** (Popular French of Abidjan: a case of pidginization.)
Jean-Louis Hattiger. Abidjan: Université d'Abidjan, Institut de Linguistique Appliquée, 1983. 348p. bibliog. (Publication, no. 87).

A study of French-language usage based on recordings made in Abidjan and its suburbs in 1977.

365 **Francophonie et pratique linguistique en Côte d'Ivoire.** (The use of French and other languages in the Côte d'Ivoire.)
J. Derive, M.-J. Derive. *Politique Africaine,* no. 23 (Sept. 1986), p. 42-56. bibliog.

A majority of urban dwellers in the Côte d'Ivoire speak French, but fewer of the rural population do so, particularly in the north. Because of the linguistic diversity of the country, French still continues in use as the one common language. The authors consider the options of whether to teach and promote the use of French universally or whether to teach the country's major languages.

366 **The grammar of spoken French in the Ivory Coast; a study in second language acquisition.**
Emmanual N. Kwofie. Grossen-Linden, Germany: Hoffmann, 1976. 47p. (Giessener Beiträge sur Sprachwissenschaft, vol. 5).

The author conducted a number of interviews with African speakers of French in 1968, and categorizes aspects of grammar and usage. These are mostly deviations from the absolutely correct forms.

367 **Le nouchi abidjanais, naissance d'un argot ou mode linguistique passagère?** (Abidjan nouchi, the birth of a slang or a passing linguistic fashion?)
Jérémie Kouadio N'Gessan. In: *Des langues et des villes. Actes du colloque international . . . à Dakar, du 15 au 17 décembre, 1990.* Paris: ACCT (Diffusion Didier), [ca. 1993], p. 373-83.

A description, with examples of vocabulary, of a slang derived from French and spoken by young people in Abidjan.

Religion

General

368 **Religions dans la ville. Croyances et changements sociaux à Abidjan.** (Religions in the city. Beliefs and social changes in Abidjan.) Raymond Deniel. Abidjan: INADES, 1975. 208p. 2 maps.

A survey of attitudes to religion among adults and young people in Abidjan. The 700 interviewees, who were drawn from all religious traditions and ethnic groups, were questioned on attitudes to tradition, the family, success, money and the development of the country.

Traditional

369 **The Akan doctrine of God. A fragment of Gold Coast ethics and religion.**
J. B. Danquah. London: Frank Cass, 1968. 2nd ed. 206p. (Africana Modern Library, no. 2).

The Akan group extends from Ghana into the eastern coastal region of the Côte d'Ivoire. A Ghanian lawyer expounds traditional Akan religion for Westerners. He compares its beliefs and moral values with those of Christianity and the philosophies of Ancient Greece, and with nineteenth-centry Germany. Most people would not agree with his thesis that the Akan are monotheistic and that fetish worship is a late 'foreign acquisition'. The work was first published in 1944.

370 **Assongu: a terracotta tradition of southeastern Ivory Coast.**
Robert T. Soppelsa. *Africa. Journal of the International African Institute*, vol. 57, no. 1, p. 57-73. bibliog.

Assongu are small terracotta figures representing a spirit force said to emanate from an island in the Aby lagoon in the south-east of the country. The author researched the origin of the spirit, which first appeared in the late seventeenth century among the Eotilé, and he describes and illustrates types of figure, their functions and their symbolism.

371 **Essai sur la religion bambara.** (An essay on Bambara religion.)
Germaine Dieterlen. Paris: Presses Universitaires de France, 1951.
240p. bibliog. (Bibliothèque de Sociologie Contemporaine).

The Bambara, part of the Mande group, are situated on the north-western border of the Côte d'Ivoire in the Goulia sub-prefecture, and extend into Mali. This work reflects research done in the late 1940s on traditional beliefs, although the people are nominally Muslim. The author explores myths, cults and beliefs, sacrifices, rites, divination and crafts. The supreme deity is known as Faro.

372 **La magie à l'école.** (Magic at school.)
Jean-Marie Gibbal. *Cahiers d'Etudes Africaines*, no. 56, vol. 14 (1974), cahier 4, p. 627-50.

Some school-children were interviewed to give their opinions on magic and sorcery, and how they can affect success at school if, for example, children from another ethnic group wished them to fail.

373 **La mort africaine. Idéologie funéraire en Afrique noire.** (African death. Funeral ideology in Black Africa.)
Louis-Vincent Thomas. Paris: Payot, 1982. 272p. bibliog.
(Bibliothèque Scientifique).

A study of myths and rituals associated with death and African attitudes to death and ancestors, with many references to the people of the Côte d'Ivoire.

374 **Notes sur certains rites magico-religieux de la haute Côte d'Ivoire. Les gbons.** (Notes on certain magico-religious rites of the upper Côte d'Ivoire. The gbons.)
M. Prouteaux. *L'Anthropologie*, vol. 29, no. 1-2 (1918-19), p. 37-52.

Six issues for these two years were published as one volume very much in arrears, the volume and page number being sufficient for identification. Gbons are large, hideous masks and the author describes their use in rituals among several different ethnic groups. Some photographs are included.

375 **Notes sur les Agni de l'Indénié.** (Notes on the Agni of Indénié.)
M. P. Chéruy. *Revue d'Ethnographie et de Sociologie*, vol. 5, no. 5-6 (May-June 1914), p. 155-67.

Notes on the beliefs, cults, legends and superstitions of the Agni, and the spirits they honour. The author intended to continue his article, but war brought an end to the journal.

376 **Phénomènes religieux et facteurs socio-économiques dans un village de la région de Bouaké.** (Religious phenomena and socio-economic factors in a village in the Bouaké region.)
Pierre Etienne. *Cahiers d'Etudes Africaines,* no. 23, vol. 6 (1966), cahier 3, p. 367-401. bibliog.

An enquiry into two cults, Tete-Kpa and Tigali [these are rough transliterations] among the Baule of the Bouaké region in the centre of the country. The author explains the beliefs and organization of the cults and the costs of membership.

377 **La religion bambara.** (Bambara religon.)
L. [Louis] Tauxier. Paris: Paul Geuthner, 1927. 472p.

A very detailed survey of Bambara religious ideas, myths and practices, based on notes made in 1913. The author interviewed the son of a priest of the Komo religious society and other religious practitioners, and supplemented his information with help from a missionary.

378 **Sacrifices dans la ville. Le citadin chez le devin en Côte d'Ivoire.** (Sacrifices in the town. The citizen visits the diviner in the Côte d'Ivoire.)
Abdou Touré, Yacouba Konaté. Abidjan: Douga, 1990. 257p. map. bibliog.

This study of animal sacrifices is based on 1160 questionnaires returned to the authors from a cross-section of Côte d'Ivoire society, including Muslim, Christian and traditional believers. There is a chapter on the use of the cola bean.

379 **Savoir voir et savoir vivre: les croyances à la sorcellerie en Côte d'Ivoire.** (The skill of seeing and knowing: beliefs in sorcery in the Côte d'Ivoire.)
Marc Augé. *Africa. Journal of the International African Institute,* vol. 46, no. 2 (1976), p. 128-45.

The author conducted his research in the late 1960s among the Alladian, Avikam and Ebrié, and consulted prophets from the Harrist tradition. The powers of sorcerers and counter-sorcerers can directly affect only someone from the same lineage, but wider influence can be cast through the cooperation of other sorcerers.

380 **Sorciers noirs et diables blancs. La notion de personne, les croyances à la sorcellerie et leur évolution dans les sociétés lagunaires de basse Côte d'Ivoire (Alladian et Ebrié).** (Black sorcerers and white devils. The idea of the person, beliefs in sorcery and their evolution among the Lagoon societies of lower Côte d'Ivoire, Alladian and Ebrié.)
Marc Augé. In: *La notion de personne en Afrique noire. Colloques Internationaux du CNRS, no.* 544. Paris: CNRS, 1973. Reprinted Paris: L'Harmattan, 1993, p. 519-27.

A short essay on beliefs in sorcery.

381 **West African traditional religion.**
Kofi Asare Opoku. Accra; London: FEP International Private Ltd,
1978. 182p. map. bibliog.

Although this book is based on the peoples of Ghana, the author gives a clear and interesting outline of West African concepts of God. The main features of traditional religion are a belief in God, in lesser deities, in ancestral spirits and in the spirits involved in sorcery, a form of totemism, and the use of charms and amulets. The Akan, who inhabit both Ghana and the south-east Côte d'Ivoire are studied in more detail.

382 **Witches, kings and the sacrifice of identity, or the power of paradox and the paradox of power among the Beng of the Ivory Coast.**
Alma Gottlieb. In: *Creativity of power. Cosmology and action in African societies.* Edited by W. Arens, Ivan Karp. Washington, DC;
London: Smithsonian Institution Press, 1989, p. 245-72. bibliog.

The information for this article was gathered from a witch who 'sold' her menstrual cycle to buy her powers as a witch. The author explores the idea of sacrificing an aspect of one's identity to gain such powers. She describes the system of two kings for the two political regions of the Beng area, their powers of withchcraft and their obligations to sacrifice their uterine kin. A witch's talents may be inherited or bought.

Christianity

383 **Deima. Prophètes paysans de l'environnement noir.** (Deima.
Peasant prophets in the Black environment.)
Jean Girard. Grenoble, France: Presses Universitaires de Grenoble,
1974. 2 vols. 3 maps. bibliog. (Collection Actualité Recherche).

A study of the prophetic Deima movement, its beliefs and cosmology, its clergy and ritual. Derived from Christianity, it holds a basic belief in the sin of humanity against the earth-mother and nature. The writings of Bagué Aonoyo or Honoyo, a prophetess, are published in Volume 2. The church has 400,000 members, mostly forest-dwellers who are caught up in conflicts caused by urbanization and deforestation.

384 **The message as the medium. The Harrist churches of the Ivory Coast and Ghana.**
Sheila S. Walker. In: *African Christianity. Patterns of religious continuity.* Edited by George Bond, Walton Johnson, Sheila S.
Walker. New York: Academic Press, 1979, p. 9-64. bibliog.

A summary of Harris's mission and church, and of other Ivoirian prophets who founded churches in his tradition, including Jonas Zaka, Bébéh Gra, Papa Nouveau, Crastchotche and Boto Adai who all founded cults in the 1930s and 1940s. These cults, however, died out with the death of their leaders. Another movement which survived was the Deima church founded by Marie Lalou which gives an important role to women.

385 **Nkipiti; la rancune et le prophète.** (Nkipiti; spite and the prophet.)
Marc Augé, Jean-Pierre Colleyn. Paris: Editions de l'Ecole des Hautes Etudes en Sciences Sociales, 1990. 85p. (Anthropologie Visuelle, no. 2).

Published in conjunction with a video of the same name produced by Radio-T.V. de la Communauté Française de Belgique. The subject of both is Sebim Odjo, a prophet and healer in the tradition of Harris. Augé has transcribed his biographical details and describes the making of the film in 1981, at Vieux-Badiem in the Lagoon region. More interviews were held in 1983.

386 **The prophet Harris. A study of an African prophet and his mass-movement in the Ivory Coast and Gold Coast, 1913-1915.**
Gordon Mackay Haliburton. London: Longman, 1971. 250p. 2 maps. bibliog.

A full biography of the prophet William Wade Harris, who founded his own Christian movement, with background history on the church and the country at the time. A Kru from Liberia, he saw a vision of the Angel Gabriel while in prison in Liberia. He preached in the coastal regions of the Côte d'Ivoire and the Gold Coast from 1913 to 1914 and retired to his village in Liberia in 1915 where he lived a holy life until 1929. With great success, he urged the banishment of paganism and adherence to the Bible. The Methodist missionary W. J. Platt succeeded in converting many Harris followers to Methodism, and wrote a book which is rather short on precise facts: *An African prophet. The Ivory Coast and what came of it* (London: SCM Press, 1934).

387 **Le prophète Harris et le harrisme.** (The prophet Harris and Harrism.)
René Bureau. *Annales de l'Université d'Abidjan, Série F, Ethnosociologie*, vol. 3 (1971), p. 29-196. bibliog.

A study in three parts. The first covers the life of William Wade Harris. The second part concerns the movement as it now functions in the south of the Côte d'Ivoire, and the work of the healer Albert Atcho. The third part looks at the sermons of Albert Atcho.

388 **Le prophète Harris, Le Christ noir des lagunes.** (The prophet Harris. The black Christ of the lagoons.)
Christophe Wondji. Paris: ABC; Dakar, Abidjan: Nouvelles Editions Africaines, 1977. 96p. (Grandes Figures Africaines).

A biography of the prophet William Harris, who founded his Christian movement 1913-14. There is a map of his progress along the coast.

389 **Une religion syncrétique en Côte d'Ivoire: le culte deima.**
(A syncretic religion in Côte d'Ivoire: the Deima cult.)
Denise Paulme. *Cahiers d'Etudes Africaines,* no. 9, vol. 3 (1962),
cahier 1, p. 5-90. map. bibliog.

The Deima cult was founded by a woman, Marie Lalou Dawono in about 1942. She
was inspired by the prophet Harris. The author met her successor in Treichville,
Abidjan, and followers in Daloa, among the Bété. She tells the history of Lalou and
the cult, transcribes a biography of Blé Nahi (Lalou's successor), and recounts some
of the sacred legends of the cult.

390 **The religious revolution in the Ivory Coast. The prophet Harris
and the Harrist church.**
Sheila S. Walker. Chapel Hill, North Carolina: University of North
Carolina Press, 1983. 206p. bibliog. (Studies in Religion).

A study of the origins, development and recent state of the Harrist church, based on
research conducted during the 1970s in Lagoon villages around Abidjan. The book
begins with a biography of William Wade Harris and his mission of 1913. He
preached a Christianity more adapted to Africans than the doctrines of the Western
missionaries, and at the same time, his form of Christianity helped his believers adapt
more easily to life under their colonial masters than their traditional beliefs did.

391 **La vie religieuse en Afrique.** (Religious life in Africa.)
Nil Guillemette, Jean Guerber, Sidbe Sempore. Abidjan: INADES,
1983. 3rd ed. 112p.

Religious life here means the Roman Catholic religion, and three Catholic priests
write of the priesthood and missionary work in Africa, and its basis in the Bible.

392 **Witchcraft and healing in an African Christian church.**
Sheila S. Walker. *Journal of Religion in Africa*, vol. 10 (1979),
fasc. 2, p. 127-38.

The author describes the work of the Harrist healer Atcho in the village of Bregbo
near Abidjan.

393 **Young men, old men, and devils in aeroplanes. The Harrist church,
the witchcraft complex and social change in the Ivory Coast.**
Sheila S. Walker. *Journal of Religion in Africa,* vol. 11, fasc. 2
(1980), p. 106-23.

New (European) values, and the wealth and power available to some young people
have upset traditional respect for the old, and those who cling to old beliefs seek
explanations in theories of witchcraft.

Islam

394 **Beyond the stream. Islam and society in a West African town.**
Robert Launay. Berkeley, California: University of California Press,
1992. 258p. bibliog.

The author spent a year studying the Diula in the Koko district of Korhogo, and here
he records his observations of a Muslim community.

395 **Etudes sur l'Islam en Côte d'Ivoire.** (Studies on Islam in Côte
d'Ivoire.)
Paul Marty. Paris: Ernest Leroux, 1922. 457p. 2 maps. bibliog.
(Collection de la Revue du Monde Musulman).

Despite the title, this is a comprehensive study of Islam in 1922. One in sixteen of the
population were Muslim at the time. The coastal and forest regions of the country are
dismissed in the first 76 pages, since Islam has not made much impact there. Animism
is described briefly, and condemned, and the growth of Christianity noted. Most of the
book is devoted to the northern savannah region, in which one in six of the population
is Muslim. The strength of Islam in each region is assessed, and the author analyses
religious practices and the influence of Islam on education, law, social life and
economic conditions. He also looks at the survival of traditional rituals.

396 **The history of Islam in West Africa.**
J. Spencer Trimingham. London; Oxford: Oxford University Press,
1970. 262p. 6 maps.

A history of the Islamic states of West Africa, with a few references to the Côte
d'Ivoire.

397 **Islam in West Africa.**
J. Spencer Trimingham. Oxford: Clarendon Press, 1959. 262p. map.

A study of Islam and its relationship with pagan religions, its theology, practices,
institutions and sociology. The pattern of Islam in the Côte d'Ivoire was of isolated
settlements in an animist community.

398 **Les musulmans d'Abidjan.** (The Muslims of Abidjan.)
Raymond Delval. Paris: Fondation Nationale des Sciences Politiques,
Centre de Hautes Études sur l'Afrique et l'Asie Modernes, 1980.
106 leaves. 3 maps. bibliog. (Cahiers du C. H. E. A. M., no. 10).

Over a third of the population of Abidjan are Muslim. The author provides statistics
which indicate the ethnic origins of Muslims, and the percentages in each quarter of
the city. He also gives a history of the growth of their communities. Abidjan is the
spiritual centre of Islam in Côte d'Ivoire, since the main associations and reformist
movements are led from there. The last part of the book describes the activities of the
main Muslim organizations and reformist movements, while the appendix lists the
statutes of the main organizations.

399 **Samori and Islam.**
Yves Person. In: *Studies in West African Islamic history*, vol. 1. *The cultivators of Islam.* Edited by John Ralph Willis. London: Frank Cass, 1979, p. 259-77. bibliog.
An account of Islam among the Mande people. Samori, the war leader who resisted the French until 1898, was a Muslim, but not an ardent one, and he used animist troops against other Muslims to further his own ambitions. But he allied himself mainly with Muslims, extended Islamic law and practice in his territory, and suppressed animism around Sikasso, his stronghold.

Les Agni devant la mort. (The Agni in the face of death.)
See item no. 225.

Croyances religieuses et coutumes juridiques des Agni de la Côte d'Ivoire. (Religious beliefs and judicial customs among the Agni of the Côte d'Ivoire.)
See item no. 228.

Divination bei den Kafibele-Senufo. (Divination among the Kafibele-Senufo.)
See item no. 296.

Kunst und Religion bei den Gbato-Senufo. (Art and religion among the Gbato-Senufo.)
See item no. 298.

Les Senufo face au cosmos. (The Senufo in the face of the cosmos.)
See item no. 301.

Prophétisme et thérapeutique. Albert Atcho et la communauté de Bregbo. (Prophecy and healing. Albert Atcho and the community of Bregbo.)
See item no. 630.

L'art sacré sénoufo. (Sacred Senufo art.)
See item no. 718.

Kunst und Religion der Lobi. (Art and religion of the Lobi.)
See item no. 726.

Social Life

400 **Abidjan au coin de la rue. Eléments de la vie citadine dans la métropole ivoirienne.** (Abidjan on the corner of the street. Elements of city life in the capital of the Côte d'Ivoire.)
Edited by Philippe Haeringer. Paris: ORSTOM, 1983. (*Cahiers ORSTOM. Série Sciences Humaines*, vol. 19, no. 4 (1983), p. 363-592. map).
A collection of articles on the struggle for daily existence in the capital. The page numbering is continuous throughout the year.

401 **Abidjan 'côté cours'. Pour comprendre la question de l'habitat.**
(Abidjan, the 'courtyard side'. To understand the housing question.)
Philippe Antoine, Alain Dubresson, Annie Manou-Savina. Paris: ORSTOM, Karthala, 1987. 274p. map. bibliog.
A history of population structure and growth in the capital, and of housing and town planning.

402 **Abidjan: quand les 'petits' deviennent des pauvres.** (Abidjan: when the 'small people' become the poor.)
Claudine Vidal. *Politique Africaine*, no. 39 (Sept. 1990), p. 166-70.
A short survey of the growth of poverty and unemployment in the capital.

403 **Abobo-Sagbé 1986.**
Institut Africain pour le Développement Economique et Social, Action Social en Milieu Urbain. Abidjan: INADES, [1986]. 114p. 3 maps.
A survey of Sagbé, a heavily populated area of Abobo, one of the ten communes of Abidjan. The questionnaires sought information on the social welfare of the inhabitants, their housing, their links within the community and with relatives in the country, and their employment and the ways young people can improve their prospects.

404 **L'autre Abidjan. Histoire d'un quartier oublié.** (The other Abidjan. The story of a forgotten district.)
Alain Bonnassieux.   Abidjan: INADES; Paris: Karthala, 1987. 220p. bibliog.

A history and survey of the Vridi Canal area of Abidjan, a poor, peripheral area which has grown up in the last forty years as host to immigrants from Burkina Faso and other West African countries, together with a growing number of Ivoirians. The author recounts the personal stories and miseries of those who scrape a living on the streets from their crafts or trading.

405 **Citadins et paysans dans la ville africaine. L'exemple d'Abidjan.** (Citizens and peasants in the African town. The example of Abidjan.)
Jean-Marie Gibbal.   Grenoble, France: Presses Universitaires de Grenoble; Paris: Maspero, 1974. 398p. 2 maps. (Bibliothèque d'Anthropologie).

A study of the social stratification of Abidjan, in particular the insertion at the bottom of the scale of new arrivals from the countryside. The author focuses on two different quarters: Marcory, a prosperous area, and Nouveau Koumassy, a poor one. The immigrants from the countryside take poorly paid jobs and struggle to help their extended families in the village, while not taking a full part in city life. The author looks at their relationship with their village and their visits home.

406 **La civilisation quotidienne en Côte-d'Ivoire. Procès d'occidentalisation.** (Everyday life in the Côte d'Ivoire. A process of Westernization.)
Abdou Touré.   Paris: Karthala, 1981. 279p. bibliog.

An ironic study of the heritage of French colonialism. The wealthier, urbanized sections of the community seek to create an reflection of France, and in particular of Paris, in the Côte d'Ivoire. The media extol the French way of life, and the government imposes European values in the fields of marriage and education. Even such an apparently laudable aim as universal literacy and the spread of education entails the imposition of French language and culture.

407 **Côte d'Ivoire, la société au quotidien.** (Daily life in the Côte d'Ivoire.)
[Various authors].   *Politique Africaine,* no. 24 (Dec. 1986), 163p. bibliogs.

Most of this issue is devoted to the Côte d'Ivoire, and includes articles on funeral customs, agriculture and agricultural salaries, political conflicts in Abidjan, trade unions, and television education programmes.

408 **Les danseuses d'Impé-Eya. Jeunes filles à Abidjan.** (The dancers of Impé-Eya. Young girls in Abidjan.)
Simone Kaya.   Abidjan: INADES, 1976. 127p.

The author's reminiscences of a girlhood in Abidjan in the 1950s. The title comes from a dance-game. As her family moved from the north of the country, she has some memories of village life.

409 **The demand for urban housing in the Ivory Coast.**
Christian Grootaert, Jean-Luc Dubois.   Washington, DC: World Bank,
1986. viii, 70p. bibliog. (LSMS Working Paper, no. 25).
Recent years have shown a rapid growth of the urban population of the Ivory Coast,
leading to a steep rise in the price of accommodation and a fall in its quality. This
statistical survey examines the income and structure of households. Eighty per cent of
housing in Abidjan is rented, with some of it sub-let. In other towns slightly more than
half is rented. *Comportement économique des ménages urbains de Côte d'Ivoire en
matière d'habitat,* by the same authors, was also published by the World Bank in 1986
and provides a French version of the same material.

410 **Des conséquences de la sous-représentation statistique des femmes
sur le développement national.** (The consequences of statistical
under-representation of women on national development.)
Aminata Traoré.   *Kasa Bya Kasa,* no. 6 (April-June 1985), p. 3-34.
An argument for more attention to be given to women's role in national development,
since their attitudes to health and family planning are vital for the future of the
country.

411 **Le développement urbain en Côte d'Ivoire.** (Urban development in
Côte d'Ivoire.)
Thierry Paulas.   Paris: Karthala, 1995. 184p. bibliog.
An examination of World Bank projects to promote urban developement from 1970 to
the early 1990s. The World Bank has played an important role in the rapid
urbanization of Côte d'Ivoire, both by its loans and by its studies on urbanization in
developing countries.

412 **Du mariage en Afrique occidentale.** (Marriage in West Africa.)
[Various authors].   *Cahiers ORSTOM, Série Sciences Humaines,*
vol. 8, no. 2 (1971), 231p. bibliogs.
This issue is devoted to marriage customs and the status of women, and most of the
articles concern the Côte d'Ivoire. There are articles on the Alladian, the Baule, the
Guéré, and the town-dwellers of Abidjan. Another study of attitudes towards marriage
and the economic activities of women is included in 'Economic activity and marriage
among Ivoirian urban women' by Barbara Lewis in *Sexual stratification: a cross-
cultural view* by L. Schlegel (New York: Columbia University Press, 1977, p. 161-91).

413 **Espace vécu et milieu de contact forêt–savane chez les paysans
Baoulé et leurs enfants dans le sud du 'V Baoulé' (Côte d'Ivoire).**
(Baule life-space in a forest/savannah contact zone: research on Baule
farmers and their children in the south of the 'Baule V', Côte d'Ivoire.)
Chantal Blanc-Pamard.   *Cahiers ORSTOM, Série Sciences Humaines,*
vol. 15, no. 2 (1978), p. 145-72. map. bibliog.
An enquiry into the life of the Baule and of their relationship to the environment, their
agricultural work and their hunting activities. Children's perceptions of their lives are
also recorded.

414 **Gender aspects of household expenditures and resource allocation in the Côte d'Ivoire.**
Lawrence Haddad, John Hoddinott. Oxford: University of Oxford Institute of Economics and Statistics, 1991. 59p. bibliog. (Applied Economics Discussion Paper Series, no. 112).
This paper uses a household survey from the Côte d'Ivoire to examine patterns of household expenditure. Doubling women's share of the household cash income led to an increase in money spent on food and a one per cent improvement in child height-for-age (but greater for boys than for girls). There was less money spent on cigarettes and alcohol. Another study of household consumption and standards of living is found in *The distribution of welfare in the Republic of Côte d'Ivoire in 1985* by Paul Glewwe (Washington, DC: World Bank,. 1987. 80p. bibliog.).

415 **Guerre des sexes à Abidjan. Masculin, féminin, CFA.** (War of the sexes in Abidjan. Masculine, feminine, and cash.)
Claudine Vidal. *Cahiers d'Etudes Africaines*, no. 65, vol. 27 (1977), cahier 1, p. 121-53.
A lively sketch of life in Abidjan and the war between the sexes. Illustrating his article with many case-histories, the author describes the struggles of women to scrape a living, and their exploitation inside marriage – where they are neglected in favour of mistresses – or on the streets. Lack of formal education and qualifications limits their earning power and independence.

416 **Un impossible amour. Une ivoirienne raconte.** (An impossible love. An Ivoirian woman tells her story.)
Akissi Kouadio. Abidjan: INADES, 1983. 102p.
Autobiography from tape-recordings of a Baule Catholic, who became involved in Catholic organizations, and whose marriage broke down because of conflicts between her religion and her Western-orientated way of life – which included visits to France – and the traditional way of village life of her husband and family.

417 **In the shadow of the sacred grove.**
Carol Spindel. New York: Vintage Books, 1989. 318p.
The author spent a year in a Senufo village – to which she gives a fictitious name – and this is a lively account of her experiences and of the lives of the women of the village.

418 **Inox, l'enfant inoxydable d'Abidjan.** (Inox, the rustproof child of Abidjan.)
Christine Denot. *Politique Africaine*, no. 53 (March 1994), p. 108-16.
A sketch of the life of a child nicknamed Inox. The child of Burkinabe immigrants, he has been forced to leave school in order to scratch a living on the streets of the capital, but has aspirations to a better life.

419 **Les jeunes Djimini. Essai sur la dynamique des groupes de jeunes.**
(Young Djimini. An essay on young people's group dynamics.)
Jean-Claude Thoret. Paris: Ecole Pratique des Hautes Etudes;
Abidjan: Institut d'Ethno-Sociologie, Université d'Abidjan, 1973.
340 leaves. (duplicated). maps. bibliog.

A thesis on young Djimini and Djamala (part of the Senufo group) in the north-east of
the country, based on residence in the region from 1969 to 1972, in the village of
Nassoulo, in Dabakala and in Bouaké. There is a good deal of general information on
the general social life of the region, as well as material on young people, their
education, employment, initiation rituals, marriage, and their clubs.

420 **Libéralisme et vécus sexuels à Abidjan.** (Liberalism and sexual
experience in Abidjan.)
Marc Le Pape, Claudine Vidal. *Cahiers Internationaux de
Sociologie*, vol. 76 (Jan.-June 1984), p. 111-18.

The researchers interviewed women and homosexuals about their lives and attitudes.
The conflict of traditional and Western values brings frustration to women, while the
number of single mothers is high.

421 **Parenté, échange matrimonial et réciprocité. Essai d'interprétation
à partir de la société dan et de quelques autres sociétés de Côte
d'Ivoire.** (Kinship, matrimonial exchange and reciprocity. An attempt
at interpretation from Dan and some other societies in the Côte
d'Ivoire.)
Alain Marie. *L'Homme,* vol. 12, no. 4 (Oct.-Dec. 1972), p. 5-36.
bibliog.

A study conducted among the Baule, the Alladian and the Dan, of a matrimonial
system based on reciprocal exchanges and the rights that men thereby acquire over
women and children.

422 **Les petits métiers à Abidjan. L'imagination au secours de la
conjoncture.** (Small trades in Abidjan. Imagination in the face of
circumstances.)
Abdou Touré. Paris: Karthala, 1985. 290p. 2 maps.

A lively series of interviews with people who scratch a living on the streets of Abidjan
as small traders, hairdressers, money-lenders, car-washers, pumpers of car tyres, and
even a circumciser.

423 **Poverty and the social dimensions of structural adjustment in Côte
d'Ivoire.**
Ravi Kanbur. Washington, DC: World Bank, 1990. 51p. bibliog.
(Social Dimensions of Adjustment in Sub-Saharan Africa. Policy
Analysis).

A study of living standards and poverty in fairly technical terms. The Social
Dimensions of Adjustment Project was launched in 1987 as a joint venture by the
UNDP Regional Programme for Africa, the African Development Bank and the World

Bank, to integrate social dimensions into development plans. This study analyses the evolution of poverty under the programme of structural adjustment which has been supported by World Bank funds in the 1980s.

424 **La prostitution en Afrique. Un cas: Abidjan.** (Prostitution in Africa. An example: Abidjan.)
Golj Kouassi. Abidjan: Nouvelles Editions Africaines, 1986. 325p.

A study in depth of the history, causes, types and social organization of prostitution. The author also looks at attempts at suppression and the links between alcohol and the trade.

425 **Sapore di terra.** (A smell of earth.)
Piero Boselli. Naples, Italy: Società Editrice Napoletana, 1980. 115p.

The diary of a journey which is 'not quite anthropological research, but aims to be more than a tourist diary'. The author visits Bondoukou and some villages of the region and ends his trip in Abidjan.

426 **Social welfare in Africa.**
Edited by John Dixon. London; New York; Sydney: Croom Helm, 1987. 358p. bibliog.

The chapter on the Côte d'Ivoire (p. 69-99) is by Adama Bakayoko and Sylvestre Ehouman. They begin with the ideological environment of the welfare system, its history and the problems it faces. They describe the structure of the welfare services, the official organizations, and the benefits and pensions which are available. Then they give details of the organizations which provide welfare services, including those for abandoned children, the blind and the disabled, and conclude by considering some shortcomings of the system.

427 **Théorie des pouvoirs et idéologie. Etude de cas en Côte d'Ivoire.**
(A theory of powers and ideology. A study of some examples in the Côte d'Ivoire.)
Marc Augé. Paris: Hermann, 1975. 439p. map. bibliog.

The author explores the social structures, customs and beliefs of three ethnic groups living in the coastal region of the Côte d'Ivoire. These are the Alladian, the Avikam and the Ebrié, all part of the Akan group. They are described in detail, with many case-studies. Traditional values come into conflict with modern, Westernized attitudes, especially in a part of the country so close to the capital.

428 **Tradition et modernisme en pays lagunaires de basse Côte d'Ivoire.** (Traditions and modernism in the lagoon region of the lower Côte d'Ivoire.)
Henri Berron. Gap, France: Ophrys, 1980. 386p. maps. bibliog.

A well-documented study of life in the coastal region of the Côte d'Ivoire around Abidjan. The author considers the lagoons both as source of food and as a means of communication. Agriculture, fishing, trade, transport and services in the villages and in the urban area are studied, and the encroachment of the city upon the surrounding villages is examined.

429 **Univers économique traditionnel et évolution du système de production guéré.** (The traditional economic world and the evolution of the Guéré system of production.)
Alfred Schwartz. *Cahiers ORSTOM, Série Sciences Humaines*, vol. 8, no. 3 (1971), p. 255-70.

A study of agricultural and craft production, and changes wrought by the introduction of a money economy. In this issue are other articles on the introduction of a cash economy: 'Les Baoulé face aux rapports de salariat' (Baule facing a system of salaries), by Pierre Etienne, p. 235-42, and 'Les effets de la disparition du commerce précolonial sur le système de production koulango' (The effects of the disappearance of precolonial commerce on the Kulango system of production), by J.-L. Boutillier, p. 243-54.

430 **Urban policy and political conflict in Africa. A study of the Ivory Coast.**
Michael A. Cohen. Chicago, Illinois: University of Chicago Press, 1974. 261p. bibliog.

The control of the central authorities over public resources and the solution of urban problems leads to political conflicts. Other topics examined are social mobility and stratification in the city, the emergence of political groups and the political process of decision-making.

Naître sur la terre africaine. (To be born on African earth.)
See item no. 230.

Tradition et changements dans la société Guéré. (Tradition and changes in Guéré society.)
See item no. 272.

Beyond the stream. Islam and society in a West African town.
See item no. 394.

Les investissements publics dans les villes africaines 1930-1985. (Public investment in African towns, 1930-1985.)
See item no. 608.

Politics

431 **Côte d'Ivoire. Agir pour les libertés.** (The Côte d'Ivoire. Acting for freedom.)
Laurent Gbagbo. Paris: L'Harmattan, 1991. 206p.

A record of interviews given from 1980 by Laurent Gbagbo, the secretary general of the Front Populaire Ivoirien (FPI), and unsuccessful opposition candidate in the 1990 presidential elections. There are also propostions put forward by the FPI in the face of the political and economic problems of the country.

432 **Côte d'Ivoire, après la faillite, l'espoir?** (Côte d'Ivoire, after failure, hope?)
Antoine Séry. Paris: L'Harmattan, 1990. 200p.

The author presents a grim picture of a weak economy, high prices and high unemployment, dirty ill-equipped hospitals and inadequate schools. He attacks the policies of President Houphouët-Boigny for too much dependence on France, allowing French firms to profit from the country, and for relying on State enterprises which line the pockets of administrators. He places hope in the emergence of opposition parties and in the leadership of Laurent Gbagbo.

433 **Côte d'Ivoire: la dépendance et l'épreuve des faits.** (Côte d'Ivoire: subjection and the test of achievements.)
Marcel Amondji. Paris: L'Harmattan, 1988. 188p. bibliog.

A chronicle of political events from 1980 to 1985, from hopes of democratization in 1980 to a regression into autocracy in 1985. President Houphouët-Boigny resolved some of the tensions in society without making major changes or upheavals, and without losing his grip on power.

434 **Côte-d'Ivoire. Histoire d'un retour.** (Côte d'Ivoire. The story of a return.)
Laurent Gbagbo. Paris: L'Harmattan, 1989. 75p.

Transcriptions of interviews with Laurent Gbagbo, the opposition leader, in which he explains the reasons for his exile in 1982 after government action against the teachers' strike, and the reasons for his return to the Côte d'Ivoire in 1988. He discusses the aims of the Front Populaire Ivoirien and the arrest of Innocent Anaky, a prominent member of the party.

435 **Côte-d'Ivoire: pour une alternative démocratique.** (Côte d'Ivoire: in favour of a democratic alternative.)
Laurent Gbagbo. Paris: L'Harmattan, 1983. 177p.

The opposition leader traces the history of the single party of the Côte d'Ivoire, the Parti Démocratique de Côte d'Ivoire, from 1951 to 1965. He gives instances of plots against it and their repression, including the story of Kraghé Gnagbé who created a Parti Nationaliste in 1967, was confined to a lunatic asylum, but who later called a strike in Gagnoa sub-prefecture, his home area, and was killed, along with 3,000 to 4,000 other people when the army moved in to repress the ensuing disorders in October 1970. Gbagbo criticizes the running of the state-controlled enterprises, riddled with nepotism and corruption, in which the managers become rich at the expense of the peasants, who fail to get their fair profits. He also criticizes the lack of provision of health and social services and the declining economic conditions.

436 **La démocratie par le haut en Côte d'Ivoire.** (Democracy from the top in the Côte d'Ivoire.)
Tessy D. Bakary Akin. Paris: L'Harmattan, 1992. 318p.

A professor of political sciences from Laval University, Québec, studies political changes in the Côte d'Ivoire since 1990, and considers the problem of transition from autocracy to democracy. He studies the role of the Parti Démocratique de la Côte d'Ivoire, until recently the only permitted party, and the problem of whether democracy can extend beyond the élite.

437 **L'économie politique d'une démocratisation. Élements d'analyse à propos de l'expérience récente de la Côte d'Ivoire.** (The political economy of a process of democratization. Analysis of the recent experience of the Côte d'Ivoire.)
Yves-A. Fauré. *Politique Africaine,* no. 43 (Oct. 1991), p. 31-49.

An account of the elections of 1990 and reasons why the opposition did not perform as well as expected.

438 **Evolution politique et constitutionnelle en cours et en perspective en Côte d'Ivoire.** (Political and constitutional evolution in progress and in perspective in the Côte d'Ivoire.)
René Dégni-Ségui. In: *L'Afrique en transition vers le pluralisme politique. Colloque, Paris, 12-13 décembre 1990.* Edited by Gérard Conac. Paris: Economica, 1993, p. 291-300.

The author describes recent moves towards a multi-party state, the revision of the constitution on 6 November 1990, and challenges to the autocracy of the President. Other papers from the conference cover the general move in Africa towards multi-party states. A recent survey of the emergence of a multi-party system in the Côte d'Ivoire is *Le multipartisme en Côte d'Ivoire* by Jean-Noël Loucou (Abidjan: Editions Neter, 1992. 213p. bibliog.).

439 **Guide des elections.** (Guide to elections.)
Albert Aggrey. Abidjan: Juris Conseils, 1983. 85p.

An explanation of the election system at local and national level with a glossary of terminology and some sample forms. The third part of the text consists of the relevant legal texts.

440 **Jeunes et aînés en Côte d'Ivoire. Le VIIe congrès du P. D. C. I.–R. D. A.** (Young and old in the Côte d'Ivoire. The VIIth congress of the PDCI–RDA).
Jean-François Médard. *Politique Africaine,* vol. 1, no. 1 (Jan. 1981), p. 102-19.

A report of this party conference during which announcements were made on the promotion of younger people to the party hierarchy. The article includes a transcript of the closing speech by Djedje Mady.

441 **Jeunesse et parti unique. Le Mouvement des Etudiants et des Elèves de Côte d'Ivoire.** (Youth and the single party. The Movement of Students and Pupils of the Côte d'Ivoire.)
Tape Dimi Gagbo. Paris: La Pensée Universelle, 1980. 123p. bibliog.

A history of the Mouvement des Etudiants et des Elèves de Côte d'Ivoire, a youth movement affiliated to the Parti Démocratique de Côte d'Ivoire. The second half deals with the movement's aims and weaknesses, and suggests a way forward.

442 **La marche du siècle. Félix Houphouët-Boigny. Que restera-t-il de lui?** (The progress of the century. Félix Houphouët-Boigny. What will remain of him?)
Edited by Gilletie Sarl. *Africa International,* Hors série (special number) no. 3 (Feb. 1994), 48p.

A special number in tribute to President Houphouët-Boigny, the 'last of the fathers of Independence'. It opens with an account of the unsuccessful challenge by Alassane Dialmmane Ouattara, the Premier Ministre, to the assumption of presidential power by Henri Konan Bédié, Houphouët-Boigny's chosen successor. Other articles look back on Houphouët-Boigny's career, his creation of the Rassemblement Démocratique Africain, his role in African politics, and his encouragement of literature and the arts.

443 **Nouvelle donnée en Côte d'Ivoire: le VIIIe congrès du PDCI–RDA (9-12 Oct. 1985).** (New deal in the Côte d'Ivoire: the VIIIth congress of the PDCI–RDA, 9-12 Oct. 1985.)
Yves-André Fauré. *Politique Africaine,* no. 20 (Dec. 1985), p. 96-109.

This report of the 1985 conference of the Parti Démocratique de Côte d'Ivoire – the only permitted party at the time – gives a useful account of economic and political difficulties in the previous five years, of economic improvements at the end of those five years, and a discussion of methods of electing a successor to the President.

444 **Le PDCI a 40 ans.** (The PDCI is 40.)
Edited by the editorial team of Fraternité Hebdo. Abidjan: Fraternité Hebdo, 1986. 239p.

A look back at the beginnings of the Parti Démocratique de Côte d'Ivoire (PDCI) by the editors of the official government and party newspaper. The PDCI was founded on 9 April 1946 by Houphouët-Boigny, who later that year founded the Rassemblement Démocratique Africain (RDA), a West African movement, of which the PDCI became a local organ. The party was referred to as the PDCI–RDA, and the Côte d'Ivoire dominated the RDA. Houphouët-Boigny steered both away from their Communist affiliation.

445 **La politique intérieure d'Houphouët-Boigny.** (The internal policy of Houphouët-Boigny.)
Jacques Baulin. Paris: Eurafor Press, 1982. 255p. bibliog.

A rather critical history of the political career of the President. It includes a chapter on his monopoly of power and one on plots against him. Included in the appendices is an account of the death of one of his political opponents, Ernest Boka, issued by the Ivoirian Revolutionary Party.

446 **Propositions pour gouverner la Côte d'Ivoire.** (Propositions for governing the Côte d'Ivoire.)
Front Populaire Ivoirien, introduction by Laurent Gbagbo. Paris: L'Harmattan, 1987- .

Although the first volume (204p.) was published in 1987, no more volumes had appeared by the time of compilation of this bibliography in 1995. The Front Populaire Ivoirien was created in the early 1980s to bring together scattered clandestine left-wing militants opposed to the government. Here they put forward their proposals for the government and the economy of the country, for foreign relations, health and education. The preface is written by the unsuccessful challenger in the presidential elections of 1990.

447 **State, society and political institutions in Côte d'Ivoire and Ghana.**
Richard Crook. *IDS [Institute of Development Studies] Bulletin,*
vol. 21, no. 4 (Oct. 1990), p. 24-34.

A comparison between the political stability of the Côte d'Ivoire since independence
and Ghana's instability. The author describes the Ivoirian political élite, the role of the
government in controlling society and the economy, and in suppressing or defusing
discontent.

448 **La succession d'Houphouët-Boigny.** (The succession to Houphouët-
Boigny.)
Jacques Baulin. Paris: Eurafor Press, 1989. 160p.

Despite the efforts of President Houphouët-Boigny to prepare the way for his own
choice of presidential successor, Konan Bédié, the succession had not been settled at
the time of the writing of this book. [Konan Bédié is now President.] The career of
Bédié is examined in the context of the country's political and economic problems and
the struggle for greater democracy. This is the third book the author has written about
the President.

449 **Who's who in Africa. Leaders for the 1990s.**
Alan Rake. Metuchen, New Jersey; London: Scarecrow Press, 1992.
448p.

This collection of pen portraits provides more than bare biographical details of
political figures, as the author seeks to explain each subject's role in the affairs of his
country. Thirteen figures are included in the chapter on the Côte d'Ivoire, including
Houphouët-Boigny and his successor Henri Konan Bédié.

The political economy of Ivory Coast.
See item no. 505.

Constitution and Legal System

Constitution

450 **L'article 11 de la constitution de 1960 dans le système politique ivoirien.** (Article 11 of the 1960 constitution in the Ivory Coast political system.)
Zogbélémou Togba. *Penant. Revue de Droit des Pays d'Afrique,* 93rd year, no. 780 (April-July 1983), p. 153-75.

Article 11 of the constitution concerns the designation of a presidential successor, and the author considers revisions made to the text in 1975 and 1980, and the actual legal process of revising the constitution. In 1980 provision was made for the election of a Vice-President at the same time as the President, who would assume power in the event of the death of the President. Comparisons are made with the United States, but in the Côte d'Ivoire there is the additional question of the ethnic background of both candidates; whether they should be the same or different, and whether an ambitious Vice-President could oust the President.

451 **Côte d'Ivoire.**
In: *Constitutions of the countries of the world.* Edited by Albert P. Blaustein, Gisbert H. Flanz. Dobbs Ferry, New York: Oceana Publications, 1971- . Section issued June 1987. vii, 21p.

This is a loose-leaf publication, updated as the need arises. A chronology of the political history of the country is followed by the text of the constitution in English. A supplement was issued in July 1992, to cover changes made as regards the powers and the succession of the President.

452 **Le droit des conventions internationales dans la constitution ivoirienne de 1960.** (The law of international conventions in the Côte d'Ivoire constitution of 1960.)
Zogbélémou Togba. *Penant. Revue de Droit des Pays d'Afrique,* 97th year, no. 793 (Jan.-April 1987), p. 49-86.

The constitution of 1960 accepts the force of international conventions in diplomatic fields, following the example of the French constitution of 1958. The author explains international conventions and their implementation within the legal framework of the Côte d'Ivoire. The relevant parts of the constitution are printed as an annexe.

Law

453 **The civil code of the Ivory Coast.**
Alain A. Levasseur. Charlottesville, Virginia: The Michie Company, 1976. 609p. map.

This work includes the text in English and an analysis of laws passed between 1964 and 1970 on marriage, divorce, inheritance and the care of children, together with an introduction on the creation of these laws. There are chapters on the implementation of the laws, and their effect on the African family in transition between traditional customs and the Westernized urban way of life. An annexe gives the original French text of a number of laws on family life published in 1964 and 1970 in the *Journal Officiel.*

454 **Codes et lois usuelles de Côte d'Ivoire.** (Common codes and laws.)
Edited by A. Aggrey. Abidjan: Juris Conseil, 1984. 6 vols.

A compilation of legislation covering legal institutions, internal security, defence, the economy and trade, foreign relations, and international conventions.

455 **La Cour suprême. Composition, organisation, attributions et fonctionnement.** (The Supreme Court. Composition, organization, attributions and proceedings.)
Albert Aggrey. Abidjan: Editions Juris Conseil, 1982. 85p.

The text of legislation passed in 1978 governing the Supreme Court, together with a supplementary decree passed in 1982. A subject index makes the texts more accessible.

456 **Le droit des successions en Côte d'Ivoire: tradition et modernisme.** (The right of succession in the Côte d'Ivoire: tradition and modernism.)
Jacqueline Oblé. Abidjan: Nouvelles Editions Africaines, 1984. 493p.

The law on inheritance illustrates a conflict in Ivoirian society between traditional custom and modern, Westernized ways. In traditional law, a man's possessions and obligations went to a younger brother or nephew. The law passed in 1964 ordered that the children and spouse should inherit, and the author explores the problems raised by this conflict.

457 **Le droit du mariage en Côte d'Ivoire.** (Law on marriage in Côte d'Ivoire.)
Marc Dumetz. Paris: Librairie Générale de Droit et de Jurisprudence R. Pichon et R. Durand-Auzias, 1975. bibliog. (Bibliothèque Africaine et Malgache, vol. 24).

A detailed study of the law of marriage, and the difficulties posed by the determination of the government to impose Western family values and systems, as well as equality for women, in a country of very different traditional marriage and family customs. Rules on inheritance which are not based on the nuclear family also cause problems.

458 **L'enfant naturel en droit ivoirien.** (The illegitimate child in Ivoirian law.)
Yacinthe Sarassoro. Abidjan: Les Nouvelles Editions Africaines, 1984. 111p. bibliog.

A lecturer in law expounds the legal situation of the growing number of illegitimate children born from free, adulterous or incestuous unions. He examines, among other problems, the child's right or lack of right to seek out his or her father, and problems of recognition and inheritance.

459 **Un jeune homme de bonne famille. Logique de l'accusation et de la confession en Côte d'Ivoire.** (A young man of good family. The logic of accusation and confession in the Côte d'Ivoire.)
Marc Augé. *Cahiers d'Etudes Africaines,* no. 73-6, vol. 19 (1979), cahiers 1-4, p. 177-218.

In this Festschrift volume for Denise Paulme, Marc Augé analyses in detail a confession of causing six deaths by sorcery made by Aka Blaise, an Alladian, at Bregbo in 1966. It raises complex questions of relationships according to lineage, since the sorcerer is effective only on members of his lineage, and the denunciations and witness statements must be interpreted according to these relationships. Causes of death which can be attributed to sorcery are also studied.

460 **Les lois sur le nom, l'état civil et le droit de famille dans la République de Côte d'Ivoire.** (Laws concerning names, the civil state and the family in the Cote d'Ivoire.)
Paul Dacoury. Milan, Italy: A Giuffrè, 1966. 112p. (Università degli Studi di Camerino. Istituto Giuridico. Testi per esercitaziono, sezione 11, no. 2).

A collection of texts relating to nationality and the registration of births and names, and to marriage, paternity, inheritance and adoption. A short introduction comments on the innovations in these constituents of a civil code in comparison with traditional law.

461 **The modernization of law in Africa with particular reference to family law in the Ivory Coast.**
Alain A. Levasseur. In: *Ghana and the Ivory Coast. Perspectives on modernization.* Edited by Philip Foster, Aristide R. Zolberg. Chicago, Illinois; London: University of Chicago Press, 1971, p. 151-66.

In the Ivory Coast civil code of 1964, the Ivoirian national assembly attempted a bold reform of law to reflect the European concept of monogamous marriage and the European family, abolishing the bride-price and demanding the consent of the bride to a marriage. However, there were many concessions in the code to the traditional practice of polygamy and informal marriages, and to the fact that a husband's children by other 'wives' have the same rights as the 'legitimate' ones. The previous chapter in the book, 'Attempts to change the marriage laws in Ghana and the Ivory Coast', by Dorothy Dee Vellenga, p. 125-50, deals very briefly with the abolition of the dowry and the suppression of polygamy, but since a man's children are all treated equally, there is no special protection for the legitimate wife or her children.

462 **Penant (Receuil Penant). Revue de Droit des Pays d'Afrique.**
(Penant. A Review of African Law.)
Le Vésinet: Ediéna, 1891- . 3 issues per year.

Penant was the name of the founder of this serial. Most issues include judgments from the courts of the Côte d'Ivoire, among other countries, as well as articles on points of law.

463 **Précis de droit pénal général.** (A summary of criminal law.)
J.-P. Brill. Abidjan: CEDA, 1985. 85p. (Collection Juridique).

A summary of criminal law, working from the crime to the criminal, the responsibility of the criminal, punishments and rehabilitation.

464 **Revue Ivoirienne de Droit.** (Ivory Coast Review of Law.)
Abidjan, 1969- . quarterly.

A journal for professional lawyers including articles, new laws and cases.

Les coutumes indigènes de la Côte d'Ivoire. (Native customs of the Côte d'Ivoire.)
See item no. 213.

Les coutumes Agni. (Agni customs.)
See item no. 227.

Croyances religieuses et coutumes juridiques des Agni de la Côte d'Ivoire. (Religious beliefs and judicial customs of the Agni in the Côte d'Ivoire.)
See item no. 228.

Organisation politique, administrative et judiciaire de la Côte d'Ivoire. (Political, administrative and judicial organization in Côte d'Ivoire.)
See item no. 470.

Administration and Local Government

Administration

465 **L'administration ivoirienne.** (The Ivoirian administration.)
Hugues Tay. Paris: Berger-Levrault, 1974. 129p. bibliog.
(Encyclopédie Administrative).
A study of the structures and functions of government organizations in the fields of planning, culture, education, media, and health.

466 **Budget général de fonctionnement.** (General administration budget.)
Ministère de l'Economie et des Finances. Direction Générale des Finances, Direction du Budget. Abidjan: Direction du Budget, [1973]- . annual.
An annual summary of government expenditure.

467 **Le droit administratif ivoirien.** (Ivoirian administrative law.)
Alain Serge Mescheriakoff. Paris: Economica, 1982. 247p. bibliog.
The legal framework for the government and administration of the Côte d'Ivoire is analysed in this work. The second section of the book covers the legal powers of administrators, from the top to the bottom of the chain, and the third looks at specific legislation controlling the administration.

468 **Eléments juridiques du diagnostic de l'informatisation de l'administration ivoirienne.** (Legal elements of the diagnosis of the computerization of the administration of the Côte d'Ivoire.)
Mamadi Kourouma. *Penant. Revue de Droit des Pays d'Afrique*, 102nd year, no. 809 (May-Sept. 1992), p. 197-214.
A study of the legal questions raised by the computerization of government records. The Côte d'Ivoire is one of the heaviest users of computers in tropical Africa. The

author looks at the qualifications and inadequate pay of staff implementing the computerization, the need for legal protection of software, and the need for legislation to protect civil liberties.

469   **Un example éphémère de planification du développement: l'AVB en Côte d'Ivoire centrale (1969-1980).** (An ephemeral example of development planning: the AVB in central Côte d'Ivoire, 1969-80.) Véronique Lassailly-Jacob. *Cahiers d'Etudes Africaines*, no. 103, vol. 26 (1986), no. 3, p. 333-48. 3 maps. bibliog.

The history of the Autorité pour l'Aménagement de la Vallée du Bandama (AVB), (Authority for the Management of the Bandama Valley), formed to plan the future of the central part of the country after its geography was radically altered by the building of the Kossou dam and the creation of a large artificial lake. Despite its successes in resettling displaced people, transport links across the lake were not established, and problems arose with new settlers acquiring rights to land. It could not resolve conflicts with other government authorities, and, isolated from the actual area by being in Abidjan, it became increasingly bureaucratized and expensive. It was closed down in 1980.

470   **Organisation politique, administrative et judiciaire de la Côte d'Ivoire. Guide de préparation aux concours administratifs.** (Political, administrative and judicial organization in Côte d'Ivoire. Guide for administration examinations.) Alexandre Tagro. Abidjan: Imprimerie Nationale, 1986. 79p.

A short guide to the law governing the presidency and its powers, the government and National Assembly, the organization of the administration from the central to the local level, and the structure of the legal system. The system and the names used reflect those of France. The last section is on the PDCI (Parti Démocratique de Côte d'Ivoire).

471   **Planification et politique économique en Côte d'Ivoire 1960-1985.** (Planning and political economy in Côte d'Ivoire 1960-85.) Jean-Pierre Foirry, Denis Requier-Desjardins. Abidjan: CEDA, 1986. 272p. bibliog. (Collection Economie et Gestion).

The authors introduce their subject with a general section on development planning, and then move on to economic planning in the Côte d'Ivoire. They examine the five-year plans up to 1985 and the role of agriculture, industry and public services under the plans.

472   **La réforme administrative en Côte d'Ivoire.** (Administrative reform in the Côte d'Ivoire.) Ministère de la Fonction Publique. Secrétariat Général à la Réforme Administrative. Abidjan: Le Secrétariat, 1980. 40 leaves.

An outline of the structure of government in the Côte d'Ivoire, and an official plan for its reform, with the aim of aiding the development of the country and the democratization of its administration.

473 **Régions et régionalisation en Côte d'Ivoire.** (Regions and regionalization in Côte d'Ivoire.)
L. [Laurent] Nguessan-Zoukou. Paris: L'Harmattan, 1990. 179p. 2 maps. bibliog.

The Côte d'Ivoire preserved the colonial administrative divisions and centralized administration after independence, and regional inequalities have grown. Areas which were responsible for the country's economic growth have not seen social rewards, and leading figures have directed investment towards their own regions, or towards development showcases. The author, a 'regionalist', argues for more autonomy and fair resources for each of the eight 'natural' regions of the country. He devotes a chapter to the resources and potential of each of the regions.

474 **Le statut des fonctionnaires parlementaires en Côte-d'Ivoire.** (The status of parliamentary officials in the Côte d'Ivoire.)
M. Kourouma. *Penant. Revue de Droit des Pays d'Afrique*, 99th year, no. 799 (Jan.-April 1989), p. 103-25. bibliog.

The deputies of the Assemblée Nationale are bound to depend for information on its permanent employees and risk being influenced by the the employees' wish to support their own ethnic group or area. The author studies the recruitment of personnel, their salaries, pensions, rights and obligations to neutrality and availability at all times.

475 **Wage differentials and moonlighting by civil servants: evidence from Côte d'Ivoire and Peru.**
Jacques van der Gaag, Morton Stelcner, Wim Vijverberg. *World Bank Economic Review*, vol. 3, no. 1 (Jan. 1989), p. 67-95. bibliog.

Both Peru and the Côte d'Ivoire, in an attempt to reduce government expenditure, have allowed public-sector salaries to erode, encouraging moonlighting among public servants. The authors found that in the Côte d'Ivoire wages in the public sector were indeed well below the private sector, and an increasing number of public servants are likely to seek a second job, but remain in public employ because of the security and the fringe benefits such as paid holidays and pensions. The authors conclude that a reduction in the number employed would be more effective than further reductions in wages.

Local government

476 **Le contentieux electoral municipal en Côte d'Ivoire.** (Municipal election litigation in the Côte d'Ivoire.)
Mamadi Kourouma. *Penant. Revue de Droit des Pays d'Afrique*, 94th year, no. 785 (July-Sept. 1984), p. 290-306.

New legislation on local elections in 1980, and complaints about the elections of November 1980, were brought before the Supreme Court. The author examines legislation controlling the elections and the response of the Supreme Court to the complaints brought after the elections.

477 **Dix ans de contentieux électoral municipal en Côte d'Ivoire (1981-1991).** (Ten years of municipal election litigation, 1981-91.) Mamadi Kourouma. *Penant. Revue de Droit des Pays d'Afrique,* 103rd year, no. 813 (Oct.-Dec. 1993), p. 292-322.

A study of cases brought before the administrative chamber of the Supreme Court under the laws passed on municipal elections of 1980, 1985 and 1990.

478 **L'Etat et les municipalités en Côte d'Ivoire: un jeu de cache-cache?** (The state and the municipal administrations in the Côte d'Ivoire: a game of hide-and-seek?) Alphonse Yapi Diahou. *Politique Africaine,* vol. 40 (Dec. 1990), p. 51-9.

An account of the conflicts between central government and local mayors. Local authorities have little real power even over property and housing.

479 **Les nouvelles municipalités en Côte d'Ivoire.** (New municipal authorities in Côte d'Ivoire.) Fraternité Hebdo, Charles Koffi. Abidjan: Fraternité Hebdo, 1981. 232p.

The official newspaper of the Parti Démocratique de Côte d'Ivoire produced this handbook to municipal authorities. It contains the legislation concerning municipal administration, including local statutes for Abidjan, and lists the elected officials and very brief details of all municipal authorities, although these are hard to find in the mass of advertising.

Foreign Relations

Burkina Faso

480 **Ouaga et Abidjan: divorce à l'africaine?** (Ouagadougou and
Abidjan: an African divorce?)
Yves-André Fauré. *Politique Africaine*, no. 20 (Dec. 1985), p. 78-86.
Despite the number of Burkina immigrants in the Côte d'Ivoire, relations between the
Côte d'Ivoire and Burkina Faso deteriorated after the coup of August 1983 when the
youthful Captain Sankara came to power. In 1987 (that is, after the article was
written), Sankara was overthrown and assassinated. He was succeeded by Blaise
Compaoré, whose wife was a relative of Houphouët-Boigny's, and relations improved
again. There are references in this article to relations between the Côte d'Ivoire and its
other neighbours.

Europe

481 **L'économie ivoirienne et la Communauté Economique**
Européenne. (The economy of the Côte d'Ivoire and the European
Economic Community.)
Charles Valy Tuho. Abidjan: CEDA, 1992. 288p. (Collection
Economie et Gestion).
This work traces the evolution of cooperation between the European Community and
the Côte d'Ivoire from the Yaoundé conventions through to the three Lomé
conventions. In the Côte d'Ivoire, industry has grown, exports have diversified
(though they are still concentrated on a few agricultural products), and imports have
continued to grow. The Côte d'Ivoire depends on European markets, but its products
are insignificant for Europe, particularly since the GATT agreements have reduced the

possibility of preferential treatment for the Côte d'Ivoire. Financial and technical aid from Europe is also documented and Chapter 6 looks in detail at the third Lomé convention, which ran from 1986 to 1990.

France

482 **La France et l'Afrique. Vade-mecum pour un nouveau voyage.**
(France and Africa. Vade-mecum for a new journey.)
Edited by Serge Michailof. Paris: Karthala, 1993. 510p. (Hommes et Sociétés).

A collection of rather pessimistic essays on many aspects of French aid and cooperation with its former African colonies. The economy, industry, agriculture and education are included and in every field affairs seem to be on the edge of crisis.

483 **French African policy: towards change.**
Tony Chafer. *African Affairs. The Journal of the Royal African Society,* vol. 91, no. 362 (Jan. 1992), p. 37-51.

The author considers President Mitterrand an obstacle to a much-needed change in French African policy, which has always put strategic and political considerations before economic ones and French prestige before more practical needs. Jean-Pierre Cot's attempts to distribute aid more widely, to end military intervention and to take a stand on human rights were all thwarted. These changes are still desirable, as is cooperation with other donors of aid. The Franc Zone, with its deficit, is a drain on the French Treasury. France is likely in the future to concentrate on its traditional close allies, namely, Gabon, Senegal and the Côte d'Ivoire.

484 **Pervasive entente. France and Ivory Coast in African affairs.**
Rajen Harshé. New Delhi: Arnold-Heinemann, 1984. 184p. 3 maps. bibliog.

A consideration of the relations between France and the Côte d'Ivoire and the influence this relationship has had on the role of the Côte d'Ivoire in African affairs. The author begins with the colonial relationship, and then devotes considerable space to the early days of independence and the attitude of President Houphouët-Boigny to Pan-Africanism. The President continued a close relationship with France and Europe, and the author analyses the economic aspects of these ties. A recent study of the President's foreign policy is *La politique étrangère de la Côte d'Ivoire (1959-1993). Une diplomatie au service de la paix et du développement* (The foreign policy of the Côte d'Ivoire, 1959-1993. Diplomacy in the service of peace and development) by Marc Aiko Zike (Abidjan: Copreca-edition, 1994. 161p.).

Economy and Finance

Economy

485 **Adjustment and equity in Côte d'Ivoire.**
Hartmut Schneider. Paris: Development Centre of the Organization
for Economic Cooperation and Development, 1992. 168p. (Adjustment
and Equity in Developing Countries).
A study of recent austerity measures and their effects on prices, public services,
employment, and the standard of living.

486 **African economic handbook.**
London: Euromonitor Publications, 1986. 335p. maps.
The first part of the book places Africa in a world economic context, and then passes
to a view of the regions. The section on West Africa gives an outline of politics,
population growth, agriculture, trade and debt, government expenditure and economic
performance, including statistics for the Côte d'Ivoire, while pages 108-13 specifically
cover the Côte d'Ivoire.

487 **L'ajustement structurel en Afrique. (Sénégal, Côte d'Ivoire,
Madagascar).** (Structural adjustment in Africa. Senegal, Côte d'Ivoire,
Madagascar.)
Gilles Duruflé. Paris: Karthala, 1988. 205p.
In the second section of this work, the author examines the economic crisis suffered
by the Côte d'Ivoire since 1980, caused by falling exports and an increasing gap in the
balance of payments and increased public spending. In January 1981 a loan for
structural adjustment was agreed with the International Monetary Fund and reduced
public spending led to the abolition of public debt over the next few years, but the fall
in coffee and cocoa prices in 1987 and 1988 damaged recovery. The author considers
the price of restructuring in deflation, lack of investment and the running down of
public services too high, and calls for a reduction of debt repayments and a new policy
of development and growth and public investment in the human resources of the

country. The author has also contributed to a report for the French Ministry of Cooperation, *Déséquilibres structurels et programmes d'adjustement en Côte d'Ivoire* (Structural imbalances and adjustment policies in the Ivory Coast) (Paris: République Française, Ministère de la Coopération, 1986. 195p.).

488   **Black Africa 1945-80. Economic decolonization and arrested development.**
      D. K. Fieldhouse.   London: Allen & Unwin, 1986. 260p. bibliog.

A discussion of the economic effects of decolonization and African attitudes to development. The first half of the book covers Black Africa generally, and its colonial inheritance; the second half considers individual countries – Chapter 7, p. 187-206, relates specifically to the Côte d'Ivoire. The country's early economic success was based on exports and dependent on foreign loans, but commodity price falls, the limits of world demands and land shortage have meant that growth could not be sustained. The state set up autonomous organizations for agricultural production, but the managing élite thus formed turned out to be inefficient or corrupt, and many organizations have been replaced by private investment. Industries to process agricultural products have been moderately successful, although not of a sufficiently large scale to make a great difference to the economy.

489   **Comparative advantage as a development model: the Ivory Coast.**
      Neil B. Ridler.   *Journal of Modern African Studies,* vol. 23, no. 3
      (Sept. 1985), p. 407-17.

A search for the causes of the economic difficulties of the late 1970s and early 1980s, which the author blames on public expenditure which was too high, and thus produced an external debt which could not be serviced.

490   **Côte d'Ivoire.**
      American Embassy, Abidjan.   Washington, DC: US Department of
      Commerce, International Trade Administration, 1987- . annual.
      (Foreign Economic Trends and their Implications for the United
      States).

A short annual survey of economic conditions and their implications for trade with the United States, with advice for those seeking business. This report is available from the Supt. of Docs, US Government Printing Office, Washington DC 20402. The Sudocs number C.61.11:C 82/last three digits of the year required, will aid its identification. Some large libraries hold complete microfiches of US official publications.

491   **Côte d'Ivoire: le roi est nu.** (The Côte d'Ivoire. The king is naked.)
      Pascal Koffi Teya.   Paris: L'Harmattan, 1985. 131p. map. bibliog.

After independence, the Côte d'Ivoire seemed to be a model of growing prosperity, harmonious development and political stability. This was apparently suddenly shattered when a world economic crisis brought national bankruptcy and a failure of basic public services. The author claims that corruption and tribalism had weakened the country's structure ever since independence, wealth being created for the élite while leaving the majority poor. He urges nationalization, with more democracy and local control in both management and political fields, and investment in small-scale industry.

121

492   **L'économie ivoirienne.** (The Ivoirian economy.)
      Paris: F.I.C. Publications, 1970- . annual.

Formerly published by Ediafric as a supplement to the *Bulletin de l'Afrique Noire*, this is a full survey of the economic life of the country, including agricultural as well as industrial production, transport, and the financial world.

493   **The economies of West Africa.**
      Douglas Rimmer.   London: Weidenfeld & Nicolson, 1984. 308p.
      map. bibliog. (International Economies Series).

An analysis of the structure and performance of the economies of West Africa in the post-colonial period, and of the contributions of their governments to their development. It covers members of ECOWAS, the Economic Community of West African States, with the main emphasis on the Côte d'Ivoire, Ghana and Nigeria. The author looks at development policies and instruments, summarizes the lessons of development and looks at future options.

494   **Etat et bourgeoisie en Côte d'Ivoire.** (The state and the bourgeoisie in the Côte d'Ivoire.)
      Edited by Y.-A. Fauré, J. F. Médard.   Paris: Karthala, 1982. 270p.
      2 maps. bibliog.

A collection of studies on the political and economic situation and foreign relations at a time of good exports and relative optimism. There is an article on the emergence of a political élite, and studies of investment in industries and in local agriculture, and the running of nationalized agricultural enterprises. The last study is on the position of peasants in the face of these nationalized industries. Louis Gouffern gives an extensive critique of the book in *Politique Africaine*, no. 6 (May 1982), p. 19-34, in which he points out the costs of government development policy, namely, too much reliance on foreign personnel and capital, high prices and a deterioration in local industry. There is further discussion of the book in *Politique Africaine*, no. 9 (March 1983), p. 118-43, with contributions by A. R. Zolberg and B. K. Campbell, and a response by Y.-A. Fauré.

495   **Etudes & Conjoncture.** (Studies and Circumstances.)
      Côte d'Ivoire. Ministère de l'Economie, des Finances et du Plan,
      Direction de la Prévision.   Abidjan: Direction de la Prévision, 1978- .
      quarterly.

A review of the planning of the Ivoirian economy, with statistical data and charts.

496   **The foreign exchange regime and growth: a comparison of Ghana and the Ivory Coast.**
      Francis Teal.   *African Affairs. The Journal of the Royal African Society*, vol. 85, no. 339 (April 1986), p. 267-82. bibliog.

A comparison of growth in the economies of the Côte d'Ivoire and Ghana from 1950 to 1981, during which years the Côte d'Ivoire outstripped Ghana. The author credits this growth to an increase in its exports and its liberal foreign exchange rate, whereas the foreign exchange rate in Ghana was controlled.

497 **A general equilibrium-based social policy model for Côte d'Ivoire.**
Ngee-Choon Chia, Sadek M. Wahba, John Whalley.   Washington,
DC: World Bank, 1992. 31p. bibliog. (Poverty and Social Policy
Series. Paper, no. 2).
A fairly technical essay on ways of tackling poverty in the Côte d'Ivoire. It includes a
chapter on taxation.

498 **Ivoirian capitalism. African entrepreneurs in Côte d'Ivoire.**
John Rapley.   Boulder, Colorado; London: Lynne Rienner, 1993.
198p. 3 maps. bibliog.
A history of capitalism during colonial days and since independence. The author
disagrees with the common view that capital is controlled by foreign interests or a
political élite. He demonstrates that a dynamic capitalist class has emerged and has
been responsible for the growth in the national economy. An appendix lists
corporations with private investors.

499 **The Ivory Coast: 1960-1985.**
Michelle Riboud.   San Francisco, California: International Center for
Economic Growth, 1987. 28p. (Country Studies, no. 4).
A brief history of the economy, comprehensible to the layman, with simple statistics
in the appendix.

500 **Ivory Coast: an adaptive centre-down approach in transition.**
M. Penouil.   In: *Development from above or below? The dialectics of
regional planning in developing countries.*   Edited by Walter B.
Stöhr, D. R. Fraser Taylor.   Chichester, England: John Wiley & Sons,
1981, p. 305-28. map. bibliog.
The Côte d'Ivoire is characterized as an economy which has been developed from
above, fuelled by a few activities aimed at increasing exports or developing substitutes
for imported goods. The author outlines a history of development strategies, from
hunter-gatherer, through balanced growth in one area, then polarized growth without
real industrial power and, finally, to a new aim of total generalized growth.

501 **The Ivory Coast: economic miracle or blocked development?
Implications for the geography of development.**
Peter Marden.   Melbourne, Australia: Department of Geography and
Environmental Science, Monash University, 1990. 68p. 3 maps.
bibliog. (Monash Publications in Geography, no. 38).
A history of the export-led development of the Côte d'Ivoire. The author evaluates
two competing models of the country's development. Samir Amin claims that the
country still has a structure of dependency, while Henrik Secher Marcussen and Jens
Erik Torp argue that the country has transcended this situation. The author puts
forward his own theories on the internationalization of capital and outlines economic
possibilities for the future.

502 **Multinationals and maldevelopment. Alternative development strategies in Argentina, the Ivory Coast and Korea.**
Lawrence R. Alschuler. London: Macmillan, 1988. 218p. bibliog.
After an introductory chapter on the role of multinationals, the author examines the three countries he has selected, pages 65-101 being devoted to a history of the economy of the Côte d'Ivoire since independence. It was at first very dependent on exports of coffee, cocoa and wood to France. Attempts at agricultural diversification were funded by foreign capital. The author examines successive state plans and concludes that the economy is still a dependent one, and that although the state actively intervenes and fosters growth, it encourages the use of foreign capital at the expense of true 'ivoirization' of capital. He also considers that the planter bourgeoisie is still dominant.

503 **Petits entrepreneurs de Côte d'Ivoire. Des professionnels en mal de développement.** (Small businessmen in Côte d'Ivoire. Professionals with development problems.)
Yves-André Fauré. Paris: Karthala, 1994. 385p. bibliog. (Hommes et Sociétés).
The results of a survey of 446 small and medium-size businesses in Abidjan, Toumodi and Daoukro. Introductory material surveys economic conditions and the climate for business, and the study ends by examining the social context of business. For a study of family enterprises in rural areas, see *Nonagricultural family enterprises in Côte d'Ivoire: a descriptive analysis* by Wim P. M. Vijverberg (Washington, DC: World Bank, 1988. 75p. bibliog.).

504 **Un plan pour sauver l'économie de la Côte d'Ivoire.** (A plan for saving the economy of the Côte d'Ivoire.)
E. Boa. Abidjan: Editions I. G. E. C., 1992. 66p.
An economist puts forward practical measures to tackle the country's economic crisis. He criticizes current reforms as being too timid, and demanding great sacrifices from the majority while protecting the party élite, whose corruption has been partly to blame for the country's huge debts. He suggests ways of cutting government expenditure and raising revenue, and also suggests financial reforms and ways of raising investment capital. He planned a second volume on ways of stimulating economic developement, but this was not available at the time of the compilation of this bibliography.

505 **The political economy of Ivory Coast.**
Edited by I. William Zartman, Christopher Delgado. New York: Praeger, 1984. 255p. map. bibliog. (A SAIS Study on Africa).
American, Ivoirian and French economists have contributed to this collection of studies on the Côte d'Ivoire. Problems of economic development and foreign policy are analysed, with a contribution on the structure of the political élite and the presidential succession in which Tessilimi Bakary names the current president, Henri Konan Bédié, as one of the favourites.

506 **Politique économique et ajustement structurel en Côte d'Ivoire.**
(Political economy and structural adjustment in Côte d'Ivoire.)
Moïse Koumoué Koffi.   Paris: L'Harmattan, 1994. 136p. (Collection
Points de Vue).

After a general introduction on the country's geography, the author traces its
economic history since 1960, ending with the period of structural adjustment from
1981 to 1993, when both public-sector salaries and agricultural export prices had to
fall. He then considers prospects for the future. Annexes discuss the devaluation of the
CFA (Communauté Financière Africaine) franc in 1994.

507 **Revue Economique et Financière Ivoirienne.** (Ivoirian Economic
and Financial Review.)
Abidjan: République de Côte d'Ivoire. Minstère de l'Economie des
Finances et du Plan, 1978- . quarterly.

This supersedes the *Etudes Economiques et Financières* published by the same
ministry from 1969 to 1976. It covers various aspects of the economy, providing
statistics.

508 **Stabilization and adjustment policies and programmes. Country
Study 16. Côte d'Ivoire.**
Jacques Pegatienan Hiey.   Helsinki: WIDER (World Institute for
Development Economics Research of the United Nations University),
1988. 49p.

An economist looks at two economic stabilization programmes supported by the
International Monetary Fund in 1981-83 and 1984. Since 1987 has brought further
debt problems, the author considers the effectiveness of such programmes. The same
author contributed an article 'The world economic system and development: the case
of the Ivory Coast' to *Interdependence and patterns of development*, edited by
Christian Comeliau (Paris: OECD, 1985, p. 134-44).

509 **La structure de la demande énergétique de la Côte d'Ivoire:
modèle et provisions.** (The structure of energy requirements in Côte
d'Ivoire; a model and the available supplies.)
Antoine Ahua.   Quebec: GREEN (Groupe de Recherche en Economie
de l'Energie et des Ressources Naturelles), Département d'Economie
de l'Université Laval, 1983. 166p. 3 maps. bibliog. (Dossier, no. 4).

A study of the country's energy requirements and projections for future demand,
together with an evaluation of the resources available to meet them and government
policy on energy supply.

510 **West Africa. Cameroon, Côte d'Ivoire, Gabon, Ghana, Nigeria,
Senegal. Economic structure and analysis.**
Economist Intelligence Unit.   London: E.I.U., 1990. 195p. 6 maps.
(E.I.U. Regional Reference Series).

The first part of this clear analysis covers regional issues, and includes problems such
as the high rate of loss of forest in the Côte d'Ivoire. The chapter on the Côte d'Ivoire

gives a brief history of the country since independence before proceeding to the economy, resources and trade, with some basic statistics. This publication is available on microfilm from World Microfilms Publications, 2-6 Foscote Mews, London W9 2HH, and on-line from Maid Systems Ltd, Maid House, 26 Baker St., London, W1M 1DF.

Taxation

511   **African tax systems.**
      Prepared at the request of UN Economic Commission for Africa, edited
      by Elizabeth de Brauw-Hay, Françoise Butzelaar-Mohr.   Amsterdam:
      International Bureau of Fiscal Documentation, 1970- . Updated
      quarterly.

This reference work issued in loose-leaf form, includes a regularly updated section on the Côte d'Ivoire. After a general section on doing business in the Côte d'Ivoire there are details of taxes payable by individuals and businesses, and a section on investment incentives and international treaties.

512   **Les conventions fiscales internationales conclues par la Côte
      d'Ivoire.** (International fiscal conventions agreed by the Côte
      d'Ivoire.)
      Zogbélémou Togba.   *Penant. Revue de Droit des Pays d'Afrique,*
      97th year, no. 795 (Oct.-Dec. 1987), p. 397-426.

An article on the fiscal conventions drawn up between the Côte d'Ivoire and other countries, and their relationship with the tax laws of the Côte d'Ivoire.

513   **Investissements privés en Côte d'Ivoire. Mesures d'incitation.**
      (Private investment in Côte d'Ivoire. Incentives.)
      Moïse Koumoué Koffi.   Abidjan: Nouvelles Editions Africaines,
      1986. 55p.

This summary of the varied tax incentives passed by the government to encourage private investment was written by the head of the government department for indirect taxation. He analyses tax laws as they concern the setting up of new enterprises.

514   **Memento de la fiscalité ivoirienne.** (A memorandum on Ivoirian
      taxation.)
      Arthur Andersen.   Abidjan: Association Interprofessionnelle des
      Employeurs de Côte d'Ivoire, 1983. 345p.

A handbook of taxation, with sample forms. The changes made in 1983-84 were noted in the 66-page *Memento de la fiscalité ivoirienne mise à jour 1984*, published by the Union Patronale de Côte d'Ivoire in 1984.

515 **La taxe sur la valeur ajoutée dans le développement économique de la Côte d'Ivoire.** (Value-added tax in the economic development of the Côte d'Ivoire.)
Moïse Koumoué Koffi.   Paris: Librairie Générale de Droit et de Jurisprudence; Dakar, Abidjan: Nouvelles Editions Africaines, 1981. 320p. bibliog. (Bibliothèque Africaine et Malgache, vol. 34).
The first part of this work covers general problems of taxation and its role in the economy. The author then moves on to tax incentives as an aid to investment and industry. The second half of the book deals with the history, structure and present application of value-added tax.

516 **Welfare dominance and the design of excise taxation in the Côte d'Ivoire.**
Shlomo Yitzhaki, Wayne Thirsk.   *Journal of Development Economics*, vol. 33, no. 1 (July 1990), p. 1-18. bibliog.
Two economists from the World Bank consider what forms of taxation would be both efficient and effective in taxing those who could most afford it. They conclude that taxation on telephones, particularly on connection charges, and on electricity, are the most desirable.

Planification et politique économique en Côte d'Ivoire. (Planning and political economy in Côte d'Ivoire.)
See item no. 471.

L'économie ivoirienne et la Communauté Economique Européenne. (The economy of the Côte d'Ivoire and the European Economic Community.)
See item no. 481.

The fiscal crisis of the state. The case of the Ivory Coast.
See item no. 529.

La Côte d'Ivoire en chiffres. (The Côte d'Ivoire in figures.)
See item no. 605.

Memento chiffre de la Côte d'Ivoire. 1986-7. (A statistical memo on the Côte d'Ivoire. 1986-7.)
See item no. 606.

Statistiques économiques ivoiriennes. (Ivoirian economic statistics.)
See item no. 607.

Finance

517 **Adjustment with a fixed exchange rate: Cameroon, Côte d'Ivoire, and Senegal.**
Shantayanan Devarajan, Jaime de Melo. *World Bank Review*, vol. 1, no. 1 (May 1987), p. 447-87. bibliog.

The economy of the Côte d'Ivoire suffered from the rise in oil prices in the 1970s, shortly after it had enjoyed a boom in commodity prices. As a member of the Communauté Financière Africaine, it could not devalue its nominal exchange rate to adjust. This article examines the different adjustment experiences of Cameroon, the Côte d'Ivoire and Senegal, all in the CFA. The Côte d'Ivoire suffered an economic crisis, leading to high debt-service payments and declining GDP (Gross Domestic Product) as it continued high public investment and expenditure, and therefore high imports.

518 **Analyse et programmation financières. Application à la Côte d'Ivoire.** (Financial analysis and planning. Application to the Côte d'Ivoire.)
Institut de FMI [International Monetary Fund]. Washington, DC: FMI, 1984. 356p. map.

A collection of practical studies of the finances of the Côte d'Ivoire, looking back at the years 1960-79, with tables and statistics.

519 **The balance-of-payments adjustment process in developing countries: the experience of the Ivory Coast.**
Alassane D. Ouattara. *World Development*, vol. 14, no. 8 (Aug. 1986), p. 1085-1105.

The author later became prime minister, and was an Executive Director of the International Monetary Fund at the time of writing this article. He describes the economic situation and the history of Côte d'Ivoire's balance of payments in the 1970s and 1980s. He also examines the government's financial policy and the prospects for the country's external debt and balance of payments up to 1990. In 1990 the president gave him wide powers to tackle the country's economic problems.

520 **La bataille des entreprises publiques en Côte d'Ivoire. L'histoire d'un ajustement interne.** (The battle of public enterprises in the Côte d'Ivoire. The history of an internal adjustment.)
Bernard Contamin, Yves-A. Fauré. Paris: ORSTOM, 1990. 369p. bibliog.

The history of the rise of state ownership and intervention in the 1970s and the investment crisis and reforms which followed. As a result of consultation and loan agreements concluded with the World Bank and the International Monetary Fund, state organs such as SODERIZ, for the production and marketing of rice, were dissolved and enterprises privatized.

521 **Brazil and the Ivory Coast: the impact of international lending, investment and aid.**
Edited by Werner Baer, John F. Due. Greenwich, Connecticut; London: JAI Press, 1987. 225p. (Contemporary Studies in Economic and Financial Analysis, vol. 58).

A collection of articles on the socio-economic impact of the policies in the Côte d'Ivoire of the World Bank, the African Development Bank, private foreign banks and the International Monetary Fund.

522 **Code des sociétés.** (Company law.)
Albert Aggrey. Abidjan: Juris Conseil, 1983. 269p. (Codes et Lois Usuelles de Côte d'Ivoire).

An anthology of legislation concerning companies.

523 **The commercial laws of the Ivory Coast.**
P. K. Allen, revised by Daniel and Paulette Veaux. In: *Digest of commercial laws of the world.* Edited by Lester Nelson. Dobbs Ferry, New York: Oceana Publications, 1968- .

This reference work is issued continuously in loose-leaf binders. The 69-page section on the Côte d'Ivoire was issued in April 1983 and covers aspects of law relevant to the businessman.

524 **Côte d'Ivoire.**
In: *Investment laws of the world.* Compiled and classified by the International Centre for the Settlement of Investment Disputes. Dobbs Ferry, New York: Oceana Publications, 1972- .

This reference work is issued and updated continuously in loose-leaf binders. The 72-page section on the Côte d'Ivoire was issued in May 1987, and provides the text of the Investment Code of 1984 in French and English, with supplementary texts. It includes conditions governing private investment in the tourist industry.

525 **The decline of the Franc Zone: monetary politics in francophone Africa.**
Nicolas Van de Walle. *African Affairs. The Journal of the Royal African Society,* vol. 90, no. 360 (July 1991), p. 383-405.

The crisis in the Franc Zone has been caused by the collapse of commodity prices and the appreciation of the French franc *vis-à-vis* the dollar. The French Treasury has had to help the two regional central banks and the de-linking of the Communauté Financière Africaine (CFA) franc was a possibility at the time. This article explains the structure of the Franc Zone and its problems, questioning its ability to aid the economic development of the region. The CFA franc has since been devalued by half.

526   **Développement économique et rôle des caisses rurales d'épargne et de prêts en milieu paysan.** (Economic development and the role of rural savings banks in the peasant environment.)
Jean-Baptiste Amethiers.   Abidjan: CEDA, 1989. 213p. bibliog.
The author urges the people of the Côte d'Ivoire to save and invest in the future of the country instead of relying on foreign investment. He introduces the subject by describing the rural environment. The main part of the work is a review of various banks and savings institutions. The cover title of this work is *Mobilisation de l'épargne en milieu rural. L'exemple ivoirien.* (Mobilizing savings in a rural environment. The Ivoirian example.)

527   **Le dirigeant de PME et son comportement financier.** (The director of small and medium-scale enterprises and his financial activities.)
Soa Djaman.   Tokyo: Institute of Developing Economies, 1984. 113p. bibliog. (JRP Series, no. 40).
The first part of this work covers the financial practices and running of small businesses, their problems, and government activities to aid businesses. The second part includes life histories of some Ivoirian entrepreneurs who are running small or medium-sized businesses. A section of the book is in English.

528   **The effectiveness of monetary policy in Côte d'Ivoire.**
Christopher E. Lane.   London: Overseas Development Institute, 1989. 84p. bibliog. (Working Paper, no. 30).
A study of the monetary system and policy of the Côte d'Ivoire and an evaluation of the country's membership of the West African Monetary Union. The cover title of this work is *Monetary policy effectiveness in Côte d'Ivoire.*

529   **The fiscal crisis of the state. The case of the Ivory Coast.**
Bonnie K. Campbell.   In: *Contradictions of accumulation in Africa. Studies in economy and state.*   Edited by Henry Bernstein, Bonnie K. Campbell.   Beverly Hills, California: Sage Publications, 1985, p. 267-310. bibliog. (Sage Series on African Modernization and Development, vol. 10).
An article on the problems of state revenue and finance, and foreign investment and loans.

530   **Introduction aux finances publiques de la Côte d'Ivoire.**
(Introduction to public finance in the Côte d'Ivoire.)
François Régis Mahieu.   Abidjan: Nouvelles Editions Africaines, 1983. 128p.
A survey of public finance, taxation and investment in the Côte d'Ivoire, in the context of the wider problems of public investment in developing countries.

531   **La notion d'établissement public à caractère financier en droit**
       ivoirien. (The notion of a financial public enterprise in Ivoirian law.)
       Zogbélémou Togba.   *Penant. Revue de Droit des Pays d'Afrique,*
       103rd year, no. 812 (May-Sept. 1993), p. 149-88.

An examination of the legal status of various categories of state enterprise, governed
by the law of 5 November 1970. Questions of financial autonomy and external control
are considered.

532   **The securities market and underdevelopment. The stock exchange**
       in the Ivory Coast, Morocco, Tunisia.
       Andrea Calamanti.   Milan, Italy: Finafrica, Giuffrè, 1983. 221p.
       bibliog. (The Credit Markets of Africa Series, no. 16).

The first part of the work deals with the general problems of establishing and
operating capital markets in developing countries, their effects on savings and
investment, on economic organization, Africanization, the shift from public to private
management and on government policy. Pages 97-132 describe the establishment of
the Abidjan Stock Exchange in 1976 and its activities.

Investissements privés en Côte d'Ivoire. Mesures d'incitation. (Private
investment in Côte d'Ivoire. Incentives.)
See item no. 513.

Trade and Business

Internal trade

533 **Crise, mobilité professionnelle, conversion identitaire. L'exemple du commerce de l'igname à Korhogo (Côte d'Ivoire).** (Crisis, occupational mobility and the conversion of identities: the yam trade in Korhogo, Côte d'Ivoire.)
Pascal Labazée. *Cahiers d'Etudes Africaines,* no. 127, vol. 32 (1992), cahier 3, p. 455-67. bibliog.

Rural incomes have collapsed in the Korhogo area, because of crisis in the cotton and rice industries. Profits in the yam trade have also dropped. The fortunes of the Diula, the traditional traders, have therefore declined, together with their sense of identity, while the Senufo have moved into the trade. The trading practices of both have changed. There is a short summary in English on pages 535-6.

534 **Négociants au long cours. Rôle moteur du commerce dans une région de Côte d'Ivoire en déclin.** (Long-distance traders. The driving force of commerce in a declining region of the Côte d'Ivoire.)
Sylvie Bredeloup. Paris: L'Harmattan, 1989. 318p. bibliog. (Ville et Entreprises).

Dimbokro, on the Nzi river, for a long time the capital of the cocoa-growing area, has been suffering a slow decline as the industry moved away. The author looks at its trading history and at the valiant struggles of its traders, particularly women, to keep the market going by trading in plantain and yams.

External trade

535 **Bäuerliche Exportproduktion in der Côte d'Ivoire. Fallstudie zu wirtschaftlichen und sozialen Auswirkungen der Kaffee- und Kakaoproduktion.** (Peasant export production in Côte d'Ivoire. A case-study of the economic and social effects of coffee and cocoa production.)
Karin Fiege. Hamburg, Germany: Institut für Afrika-Kunde, 1991. 409p. (Arbeiten aus dem Institut für Afrika-Kunde, no. 78).
A study of an export-orientated peasant economy which includes many statistics on the cultivation of coffee and cocoa and interviews with farmers. There is a summary in English.

536 **Code des douanes.** (Customs law.)
Albert Aggrey. Abidjan: Editions Juris Conseil, 1983. [pages are numbered in several sequences].
A compilation of the regulations concerning customs (in the meaning of importing and exporting goods).

537 **Consumer markets in West Africa.**
London: Euromonitor, 1984. 421p. map.
The chapter on the Côte d'Ivoire, p. 119-58, gives an introduction to the economy and provides statistics on agricultural and industrial production, imports and exports, and the consumption of goods.

538 **Francophone West Africa.**
British Overseas Trade Board. Tropical Africa Advisory Group. London: British Overseas Trade Board, [1983?]. 33p.
Britain imports twice as much from West Africa as it exports to this region. This report concludes that the Côte d'Ivoire, Cameroon and Gabon offer the best prospects for British exporters. Two pages are devoted specifically to the Côte d'Ivoire, its economic situation, French trade, and supposed barriers to British trade.

539 **Nationale Strategien und Hindernisse agro-exportorientierter Entwicklung. Kakao- und Kaffeepolitik in der Côte d'Ivoire und in Kamerun.** (National strategies and obstructions to agro-export-orientated development. Cocoa and coffee policy in the Côte d'Ivoire and Cameroon.)
Cord Jakobeit. Hamburg, Germany: Institut für Afrika-Kunde, 1988. 422p. 4 maps. bibliog. (Hamburger Beiträge zur Afrika-Kunde, vol. 34).
A thesis which analyses the factors leading to past success in rising exports. Since past increases were due to more land being taken into cultivation rather than greater intensity of cultivation, the author is not optimistic about further increases and examines strategies for development and an increase in rural incomes.

540 **Politiques maritimes et développement. Côte d'Ivoire. Corée du Sud.** (Maritime policy and development. Côte d'Ivoire. South Korea.) Elisabeth Gouvernal. Paris: Ministère de la Coopération et du Développement, 1988. 345p. bibliog.

A study of the economic development of the Côte d'Ivoire, its foreign debts, its maritime trade, and government policy on exports. The development of the port of Abidjan and the road routes leading to it are examined, together with the role of state and foreign investment and state intervention in shipping firms.

541 **La rebellion ivoirienne contre les multinationals.** (The Ivoirian rebellion against the multinationals.) Marc Zike. Abidjan: Edition Ami, 1990. 185p. bibliog.

Henri Konan Bédié, later the President of the Côte d'Ivoire, wrote the preface to this study by a young economist of the role of the Côte d'Ivoire in the international agreements reached when world producers of cocoa and coffee met in Abidjan in 1986. He examines world markets, the problems of price fluctuations and government strategy. The Côte d'Ivoire is the first producer of cocoa and the third of coffee in the world. He argues for more equity and humanization in North–South world relations.

542 **Trade and development in Economic Community of West African States (ECOWAS).** Edited by Adeyinka Orimalade, R. E. Ubogu. New Delhi: Vikas Publishing House, 1984. 589p.

The Côte d'Ivoire is a member of ECOWAS. This is a collection of articles, mostly in English, on trade, economic development and the growth of industries in the countries of West Africa. Chapter 17, in French, is by Otrou Ali and concerns foreign investment in the Côte d'Ivoire.

Business

543 **Terminal signs. Computers and social change in Africa.** Benetta Jules-Rosette. Berlin; New York: Mouton de Gruyter, 1990. 424p. bibliog.

The Côte d'Ivoire began to introduce computers in the late 1970s. By 1981 there were 275 mainframe computers in the country, the highest number in any country in Sub-Saharan Africa. Pages 107-55 deal with the computer revolution in the Côte d'Ivoire, but the rest of the book uses Kenya and the Côte d'Ivoire as the two main examples of the use of computers in Africa. The author covers training for computer specializations and the use of computer consulting firms.

Trade strategies and employment in the Ivory Coast.
See item no. 601.

Industry and Mining

Industry

544 **Deuxième journée de l'industrie. Abidjan 27 novembre 1986.**
(Second one-day conference on industry. Abidjan 27 November 1986.)
Abidjan: Ministère de l'Industrie, [1986]. 70p.
Speeches and reports from a one-day conference on the country's industries. Subjects covered included problems of the recession, the promotion of small-scale industry, and state support for industry. A review of the industrial sector and of government policy on industry was produced by the United Nations Industrial Development Organization in the same year: *Côte d'Ivoire* (Vienna: UNIDO, Regional and Country Studies Branch, 1986. 104p. Industrial Review Series, no. 6).

545 **Effets d'un investissement massif sur les déplacements de populations en Côte d'Ivoire: exemple du complexe agro-industriel de Ferkessédougou.** (The effects of massive investment on population movements in Côte d'Ivoire: the example of the agro-industrial complex of Ferkessédougou.)
Koby Assa. *Annales de l'Université d'Abidjan, Série G, Géographie*, vol. 7 (1977), p. 41-84. 4 maps.
Just south of Ferkessédougou, in the centre of the northern border of the country, the government created a sugar-production complex, with plantations, two dams and a processing factory. This article looks at the migration of workers towards the plant, integration of ethnic groups in the workforce, and the mobility, education and social conditions of the employees.

546 **Industrialization in the Economic Community of West African States (ECOWAS).**
Edited by Vremudia P. Diejomaoh, Milton A. Iyoha. Ibadan: Heinemann Educational Books (Nigeria), 1980. 551p. maps.
The Côte d'Ivoire is a member of ECOWAS. This is a collection of studies, mostly in English, on the planning of industry.

547 **L'industrie ivoirienne de 1960 à 1985. Bilan et perspectives.**
(Ivoirian industry from 1960 to 1985. A survey and prospects.)
Prepared for the VIIIth congress of the PDCI-RDA by the Ministry for Industry. Abidjan: Ministère de l'Industrie, [1985]. 24p.
Brief statistics of different sections of industry – textile, food, wood, rubber, and mechanical and electrical enterprises – are followed by an analysis of the problems of industry and plans for improvements. Local industry needs to be more productive, dynamic and efficient to compete with excessive imports. More local products need to be processed effectively, exports increased and industry developed in the regions, and more local as opposed to foreign investment and control is called for. The booklet sets out the legal and political means proposed towards these ends.

548 **Multinationals and development in Black Africa. A case study in the Ivory Coast.**
Jean Masini (et al.). Farnborough, England: Saxon House for the European Centre for Study and Information on Multinational Corporations, 1979. 181p.
The authors consider the role of the state in investing directly in industry or encouraging private investment. The economic structure of the country is analysed and there is a survey of its industries – which process foodstuffs and chemicals and produce electrical and mechanical goods – and the investment behind them. Three multinationals, Air Liquide, Carnaud and Nestlé and their Ivoirian subsidiaries are studied in detail. Originally published in French in the same year by PUF in Paris under the title *Les multinationales et le développement: trois entreprises et la Côte d'Ivoire*.

549 **Principales industries installées en Côte d'Ivoire.** (Main Ivoirian industries.)
Abidjan: Chambre d'Industrie de Côte d'Ivoire, 1966- . annual.
A directory of firms in the Côte d'Ivoire and full statistics of industrial production, salaries, investment and productivity. It was formerly entitled *Principales industries ivoiriennes*.

550 **Villes et industries en Côte d'Ivoire. Pour une géographie de l'accumulation urbaine.** (Towns and industries in the Côte d'Ivoire. Towards a geography of urban concentration.)
Alain Dubresson. Paris: Karthala, 1989. 845p. maps. bibliog.
An exhaustive study of urbanization and industrialization in the Côte d'Ivoire. The first part is a history of industrialization around Abidjan and other inland towns.

The author then examines the resultant growth in the urban population and the transition to urban salaries. The third part examines the effects of manufacturing industry on other urban activities, especially informal ones, at a time of economic hardship in the towns. The bibliography covers forty pages, but much of the material consists of theses and locally available reports.

Mining

551　West African diamonds 1919-1983: an economic history.
Peter Greenhalgh.　Manchester, England: Manchester University Press, 1985. 306p. 3 maps. bibliog.

A survey and history of the mining of diamonds in West Africa. There are short sections on the mining and marketing of diamonds in the Côte d'Ivoire in the Tortiya and Seguela fields.

L'économie ivoirienne. (The Ivoirian economy.)
See item no. 492.

Etat et bourgeoisie en Côte d'Ivoire. (The state and the bourgeoisie in Côte d'Ivoire.)
See item no. 494.

Trade and development in Economic Community of West African States.
See item no. 542.

Agriculture and Fishing

Agriculture

552   **Actors and institutions in the food chain. The case of the Ivory Coast.**
Winifred Weekes-Vagliani.   Paris: Development Centre of the OECD, 1985. 74p. 4 maps. bibliog. (Development Centre Papers).

A study in the context of the research programme 'Food for all: capacity of developing countries to ʹreach their food requirements'. The author looks at socio-cultural factors in food production and the choice of crops, and the economic impact of cash crops. She considers the value of land among various ethnic groups, migration, and government intervention. Later chapters cover the role of markets and the women who trade in them, and questions of consumption and nutrition.

553   **Agricultural ecology of savanna. A study of West Africa.**
J. M. Kowal, A. H. Kassam.   Oxford: Clarendon Press, 1978. 403p. bibliog.

A thorough study of the history, climate, soil, water resources, livestock and crops of the savannah region, which forms the northern half of the Côte d'Ivoire. Problems of soil conservation and the improvement of farming systems are discussed.

554   **L'agriculture en Côte d'Ivoire.** (Agriculture in the Côte d'Ivoire.)
Abdoulaye Sawadogo.   Paris: Presses Universitaires de France, 1977. 367p. bibliog.

This very full survey has short sections on each of the many crops grown in the Côte d'Ivoire, with statistics from the 1960s and 1970s. There is information on the climate and on the history of agriculture, and on the labour force and the marketing structures of the time. The author examines the role of state and party in agricultural development and marketing.

555 **L'agriculture ivoirienne. 20 années de développement agricole
1960-1980.** (Ivoirian agriculture. 20 years of agricultural development
1960-80.)
Compiled by Ediafric – La Documentation Africaine.   Paris: Ediafric,
1980. 186p.

A report on the agricultural economy, compactly written and consisting mainly of
statistics and information on marketing organizations, with prospects for the future.

556 **L'alimentation en Afrique: manger ce qu'on peut produire.
L'exemple de la consommation alimentaire en Côte d'Ivoire.** (Food
supply in Africa: eating what one can produce. The example of food
consumption in Côte d'Ivoire.)
Denis Requier-Desjardins.   Paris: Karthala; Abidjan: PUSAF, 1989.
180p. bibliog.

The author proposes that more research should be done on the dynamics of food
supply. Can consumption be analysed? Is there a crisis? He examines dependence on
imports and state subsidies for food production.

557 **Alleviating soil fertility. Constraints to increased crop production
in West Africa.**
Edited by A. Uzo Mokwunye.   Dordrecht, The Netherlands; Boston,
Massachusetts: Kluwer Academic, 1991. 244p. map. bibliogs.

A collection of technical essays, mostly in English, on the use of fertilizers. An article
in French, on efficient use of nitrogen fertilizers, on pages 125-9, is summarized in
English.

558 **Association agriculture–élevage en Afrique. Les Peuls
semi-transhumants de Côte d'Ivoire.** (The association of agriculture
and herding in Africa. The semi-nomadic Peuls in Côte d'Ivoire.)
Philippe Bernadet.   Paris: L'Harmattan, 1984. 235p. 3 maps. bibliog.

The Peuls migrated from Burkina Faso, Mali and Mauretania into the Niellé sub-
prefecture because of the Sahel droughts. This is an account of their agriculture, which
is a mixture of cattle herding and the cultivation of food crops.

559 **The *Caisse de Stabilisation* in the coffee sector of the Ivory Coast.**
Neil B. Ridler.   *World Development*, vol. 16, no. 12 (Dec. 1988),
p. 1521-6. bibliog.

A paper which examines the role of the marketing board, the Caisse de Stabilisation,
and in particular its role in stimulating technological development. Comparisons are
made with Colombia.

560   **The cocoa conundrum: Côte d'Ivoire.**
Gerald Bourke.   *Africa Report,* vol. 33, no. 5 (Sept.-Oct. 1988), p. 29-34.
The Côte d'Ivoire is the world's biggest producer of cocoa, yet it imports nearly half
the food its population requires. Falling world prices have caused economic worries
and exposed the risk of relying so largely on a single cash crop.

561   **Coffee and the Ivory Coast. An econometric study.**
Theophilos Priovolos.   Lexington, Massachusetts: Lexington Books,
1981. 218p. bibliog.
A technical study which includes mathematical models, with an introduction on the
economic development of the country.

562   **Contribution à l'étude des races bovines autochtones en Côte
d'Ivoire, les boeufs 'baoulé' et 'lagunes'.** (A contribution to the study
of the distinct bovine races of the Côte d'Ivoire, the 'Baule' and
'Lagoon' cattle.)
Pierre-Louis Verly.   *Annales de l'Université d'Abidjan, Série E,
Ecologie,* vol. 2, fasc. 1 (1969), p. 149-234. 3 maps. bibliog.
A detailed zoological study with many photographs and diagrams. The conclusion
traces the origins of these species.

563   **Les crises cacaoyères. La malédiction des âges d'or?** (Cocoa crises.
The curse of the golden age?)
François Ruf.   *Cahiers d'Etudes Africaines,* no. 121-2, vol. 31 (1991),
cahier 1-2, p. 83-134. bibliog.
After the drastic fall in cocoa prices and the resultant loss of national revenue in the
late 1980s, the author examines the history of cocoa production and prices. He looks
at other producers across the world and evaluates the effect of falling prices on the
incomes of producers, and the economics of production and land use.

564   **The economics of rainfed rice cultivation in West Africa. The case
of the Ivory Coast.**
Harald Lang.   Saarbrücken, Germany; Fort Lauderdale, Florida:
Verlag Breitenbach, 1979. 236p. 5 maps. bibliog. (Socio-Economic
Studies on Rural Development, no. 35).
Rice is mainly grown in the west of the Côte d'Ivoire where various varieties of
upland, non-irrigated rice are grown. This is a study of the economics of rice
production in the Côte d'Ivoire.

565   **L'économie de l'espace rural de la région de Bouaké.** (The economy
of the rural area of Bouaké.)
G. Ancey, J. Chevassu, J. Michotte.   Paris: ORSTOM, 1974. 251p.
maps. (Travaux et Documents de l'ORSTOM, no. 38).
A study of the agriculture, trade, markets and the migration of population in this area.
The relationship of rural to urban areas is considered.

566 **L'économie de plantation en Côte d'Ivoire forestière.**
(The plantation economy in the forest regions of Côte d'Ivoire.)
Dian Boni. Abidjan: Nouvelles Editions Africaines, 1985. 458p.
bibliog.
A detailed study of the forest region with a history of crop production. The author covers climate, agricultural methods, the formation of great industrial plantations, state intervention, and the commercializaton and distribution of the region's products: cocoa, coffee, bananas and pineapples.

567 **Export-led rural development: the Ivory Coast.**
Eddy Lee. In: *Agrarian policies and rural poverty in Africa.* Edited by Dharam Ghai, Samir Radwan. Geneva: International Labour Office, 1983, p. 99-127. (A WEP Study).
Before the introduction of cash crops, peasants grew root crops in the south and mainly cereals in the north as subsistence crops. The author describes the introduction of cash crops, the resulting immigration of labour, and yields, which are rather low for coffee, but good for cocoa, though not as high as those in Latin America. Workers in the south can earn as much as seven times those in the north and there are also great inequalities between the incomes of unskilled immigrants and high-earning Europeans, Syrians and Lebanese. The nationalized agricultural production enterprises extract agricultural surpluses, leaving the peasant producers poor.

568 **Fertiliser distribution in Ivory Coast.**
Harald Stier. Paris: Development Centre of the Organization for Economic Cooperation and Development, 1972. 91p. (OECD Technical Papers).
A study of the import, distribution, requirements, consumption and costs of fertilizers for different crops.

569 **Impasses et contradictions d'une société de développement: l'exemple de l'opération 'riziculture irriguée' en Côte d'Ivoire.**
(Impasses and contradictions in a development society: the example of 'irrigated rice-culture' in the Côte d'Ivoire.)
Jean-Pierre Dozon. *Cahiers ORSTOM. Série Sciences Humaines,* vol. 16, nos 1-2, p. 37-558. bibliog.
This article describes the activities of the government development body SODERIZ, set up to develop rice-growing, its efforts to create a workforce, and the economic problems which led to its being wound up. The whole issue is devoted to rural migration and the social changes caused by the development of agriculture. On pages 59-82 is an article by Jean-Pierre Chauveau 'Economie de plantation et nouveaux milieux sociaux' (Plantation economy and new social conditions) on the forest areas of the Gagou and Baule, and two articles by Alfred Schwartz and Colette Vallat on immigration into the Bakwe region to undertake new agriculture – details of these are given in the Population section of this bibliography (see item no. 197).

570 **Innovation et transformation du milieu rural en Côte d'Ivoire: la diffusion du coton Allen dans la zone dense à l'ouest de Bouaké.**
(Innovation and transformation of the rural environment in the Côte d'Ivoire: the diffusion of Allen cotton in the dense zone to the west of Bouaké.)
Jean Michotte. *Cahiers ORSTOM. Série Sciences Humaines,* vol. 8, no. 4 (1970), p. 7-19. map.
A study of the introduction and culture of cotton, a crop which was forced on the peasant farmers, and was still, at the time of writing, less profitable and popular than coffee and cocoa.

571 **Inside the miracle. Cotton in the Ivory Coast.**
Bonnie K. Campbell. In: *The politics of agriculture in tropical Africa.* Edited by Jonathan Barker. Beverly Hills, California: Sage Publications, 1984, p. 143-71. bibliog. (Sage Series on African Modernization and Development, vol. 9).
Cotton was introduced as a cash crop in the central and northern savannah region in an effort to redress regional imbalances, since other cash crops were grown in the tropical south of the country. This is a history of the introduction, financing, marketing and state subsidy of cotton production. The cotton industry needs to be protected and subsidized and the production of cotton is shown to increase women's labour and take time from the production of food crops.

572 **The Ivory Coast economic 'miracle': what benefits for peasant farmers?**
Robert M. Hecht. *Journal of Modern African Studies,* vol. 21, no. 1 (March 1983), p. 25-53.
An examination of reasons why peasant farmers have not benefited from the Ivoirian economic 'miracle'. The government has held down prices paid to producers and siphoned off a large share of export earnings. Cocoa and coffee are farmed by an élite, sometimes absentee farmers living in the towns. Most peasant farmers are heavily taxed, economically frustrated and not organized into a effective political bloc.

573 **Motorisation et plantations en zone forestière ivoirienne: quelques données globales.** (Mechanization and plantations in the Côte d'Ivoire forest region: some general data.)
Philippe Bonnefond. *Cahiers ORSTOM. Série Sciences Humaines,* vol. 15, no. 3 (1978), p. 245-59. 3 maps. bibliog.
The mechanization of agriculture consists mainly of the use of tractors in forestry and in the cultivation of cash crops. J. A. Luogo has written a wider study of changes in plantation structures and systems in West and East Africa: *The socio-economic implications of structural change in plantations in African countries* (Geneva: International Labour Organization, 1986. 170p.).

574 **La mutation d'une économie de plantation en basse Côte d'Ivoire.**
(Changes in a plantation economy in the lower Côte d'Ivoire.)
Jean-Philippe Colin.   Paris: Editions de l'ORSTOM, 1990. 284p.
6 maps. bibliog.
An in-depth study of the agriculture of the village of Djimini-Koffikro, in the Adiaké
sub-prefecture of Aboisso département. Aboisso is on the coast and Ghana borders it
on the east. Products include palm oil, coconut products and pineapples, sold through
state-owned enterprises, as well as food crops. Coffee and cocoa plantations are in
decline. The author looks at recent changes in agricultural practice and problems of
food self-sufficiency. An English summary is provided on pages 259-70.

575 **Un plan Marshall pour l'Afrique?** (A Marshall plan for Africa?)
Abdoulaye Sawadogo.   Paris: L'Harmattan, 1987. 119p. bibliog.
The author, a former Minister of Agriculture and now a lecturer in geography at
Abidjan University, considers current economic problems and plans to diversify crops
in the Côte d'Ivoire. He also debates future possibilities for aid and development and
ways in which Africa can make the best use of its resources to feed its own people.

576 **Les planteurs absentéistes de Côte d'Ivoire.** (Absentee planters of
the Côte d'Ivoire.)
Yapi Simplice Affou.   Paris: ORSTOM, 1987. 95p. bibliog. (Travaux
et Documents de l'ORSTOM, no. 210).
A survey of coffee and cocoa plantations in the south-east of the country with
absentee landlords, a situation which leads to lower efficiency.

577 **The political economy of West African agriculture.**
Keith Hart.   Cambridge: Cambridge University Press, 1982. 226p.
bibliog.
A survey of the rise of commercial (as opposed to subsistence) farming and its social
impact. The author looks at commercial crops and the role of the state as employer,
and goes on to consider future developments. Thirty-three pages of bibliography
include a select annotated bibliography and a supplementary list without annotations.

578 **Politics, the cocoa crisis, and administration in Côte d'Ivoire.**
Richard C. Crook.   *Journal of Modern African Studies,* vol. 28, no. 4
(Dec. 1990), p. 649-69.
The state paid a fixed price to its cocoa producers, making a profit when prices were
high, but subsidizing production when prices fell dramatically. When the marketing
board, the Caisse de Stabilisation et de Soutien des Prix des Produits Agricoles was
facing bankruptcy in 1989, prices paid to producers had to be lowered. Government
efforts to remedy the situation and make agriculture more efficient, have been
hampered by administrative difficulties, and the loss of confidence in the government.
Taxes on the informal economy and fees for residence permits for foreigners have
been introduced to raise revenue. The author looks forward to political change which
may improve the economic situation.

579 **Politics, the state and agrarian development: a comparative study of Nigeria and the Ivory Coast.**
Michael J. Watts, Thomas J. Bassett. *Political Geography Quarterly*, vol. 5, no. 2 (April 1986), p. 103-25. bibliog.

A comparison of the political and economic systems of the two countries and the effects of those systems and philosophies on food production. At the time of writing, food self-sufficiency was declining in the Côte d'Ivoire, despite state intervention. The authors examine the development policies of the state, with its aims of export-led agro-industrial development, and the results of state enterprise and intervention. One example was a disastrous sugar production programme, another is the cotton industry. Food crops have been neglected in favour of the development of industrial crops, so that rural resources are subsidizing industrial expansion.

580 **La problématique de l'autosuffisance alimentaire en Côte d'Ivoire.**
(The problem of food self-sufficiency in Côte d'Ivoire.)
A. Traoré. *Annales de l' Université d'Abidjan, Série K, Sciences Economiques,* vol. 6 (1983), p. 51-127. bibliog.

A look at the problems of the food-production side of agriculture, as opposed to cash crops. The author calls for productivity improvements through the industrialization of agriculture, while taking account of traditional agricultural practices and the tastes of the consumer.

581 **Le programme sucrier ivoirien. Une industrialisation régional volontariste.** (The Ivoirian sugar programme. A voluntarist regional industrialization.)
Catherine Aubertin. Paris: ORSTOM, 1983. 191p. bibliog. (Travaux et Documents de l'ORSTOM, no. 169).

The government made considerable efforts to develop the sugar industry in the north of the country, and through SODESUCRE established a plant at Borotou-Koro, with adjoining cane fields and villages. The author examines the development, its accounts and the pay of its personnel. She concludes that the project has had a negligible effect on exports and has shown little return on investment as the sugar costs at least 200F per kilo while the world price is less than 100F.

582 **La relève paysanne en Côte d'Ivoire. Etude d'expériences vivrières.** (The peasant relief [new generation] in Côte d'Ivoire. A study of food supply experiments.)
Yapi Simplice Affou. Paris: ORSTOM and Karthala, 1990. 231p. bibliog.

A look at the current problems of agriculture. Poor storage and traditional methods of production are preventing the achievement of food self-sufficiency in Côte d'Ivoire. The state is running projects at various centres to train and educate young people in better methods, and the author evaluates their success.

583 **Riches paysans de Côte d'Ivoire.** (Rich peasants of the Côte
d'Ivoire.)
Jean-Marc Gastellu. Paris: L'Harmattan, 1989. 178p. 2 maps.
bibliog. (Collection Alternatives Rurales).
A study of large agricultural plantations which have been built up by the Morounou,
or Agni-Moronou, a sub-group of the Agni, in the areas around the towns of
Bongouanou and M'batto in the south-east of the country.

584 **Rubber in West Africa.**
Jas Edington. Lagos, London: Rex Collings, 1991. 267p.
Rubber was introduced into the Côte d'Ivoire in 1953, but production was initially
low. The first government-supported project began in 1973 and there are now
extensive plantations. This is a handbook on the planting, culture, tapping and
processing of rubber.

585 **Les 'soubresauts' de la politique rizicole en Côte d'Ivoire.** (The 'fits
and starts' of policy on rice cultivation in Côte d'Ivoire.)
Placide Zoungrana. *CIRES. Cahiers Ivoiriens de Recherche
Economique et Sociale*, no. spécial (1990), p. 7-28. bibliog.
In a special number devoted to self-sufficiency in food, the author describes the over-
optimistic government policy of the 1970s to dramatically increase rice production
through a state production unit. It was difficult to change traditional methods,
however. Production faltered, and when the government dramatically increased
imports, prices fell and investment was undermined.

586 **Trypanotolerant cattle and livestock development in West and
Central Africa.**
A. P. M. Shaw, C. H. Hoste. Rome: Food and Agriculture
Organization of the United Nations, 1987. 2 vols. bibliogs. (FAO
Animal Production and Health, Papers 67/1, 67/2).
Report of a regional study by the FAO during which nineteen countries were visited in
1985. The economic aspects of livestock production, trade and transport are
considered. Volume 2, p. 135-56 are specifically on the Côte d'Ivoire. There is
information on trade and the legal background, and a short bibliography.

587 **Vache de la houe, vache de la dot. Elevage bovin et rapports de
production en Moyenne et Haute Côte d'Ivoire.** (Cows for hoeing,
cows for dowry. The raising of cattle and production links in Middle
and Upper Côte d'Ivoire.)
Philippe Bernadet. Paris: CNRS, 1988. 228p. 13 maps. bibliog.
On the ownership and raising of cattle in the north and centre of the country. Some
cattle entered the country with the Peul migrating from desert areas in the 1960s and
1970s after the Sahel droughts.

588   **Yam cultivation and socio-ecological ideas in Aouan society, Ivory Coast. A contribution to crop sociology.**
Hans van den Breemer.   *Sociologia Ruralis*, vol. 29 (1989), no. 3/4, p. 265-79. bibliog.
Yams are the staple food crop of the Aouan, or Ahouan, as they are referred to in French-language reference sources. The Ahouan are a sub-group of the Amantian, an Agni group, and they live in the Prikro sub-prefecture. The author looks at the cultivation of the yam, and its significance in Ahouan society.

Fishing

589   **Du pouvoir des génies au savoir scientifique. Les métamorphoses de la lagune Ebrié (Côte d'Ivoire).** (From the power of genies to scientific knowledge. The metamorphoses of the Ebrié lagoon.)
François Verdeaux.   *Cahiers d'Etudes Africaines,* no. 101-2, vol. 26 (1986), cahier 1-2, p. 145-71. 2 maps. bibliog.
A history of the exploitation of the lagoon. Modern research and scientific exploitation of the fishing stocks conflict with traditional practices and beliefs.

Le pays akyé (Côte d'Ivoire). Etude de l'économie agricole. (The Akyé region. A study of the agricultural economy.)
See item no. 235.

Anthropologie économique des Gouro de Côte d'Ivoire. (Economic anthropology of the Guro of Côte d'Ivoire.)
See item no. 287.

L'économie ivoirienne. (The Ivoirian economy.)
See item no. 492.

Etat et bourgeoisie en Côte d'Ivoire. (The state and the bourgeoisie in the Côte d'Ivoire.)
See item no. 494.

Bäuerliche Exportproduktion in der Côte d'Ivoire. (Peasant export production in Côte d'Ivoire.)
See item no. 535.

Nationale Strategien und Hindernisse agro-exportorientierter Entwicklung. Kakao- und Kaffeepolitik in der Côte d'Ivoire und in Kamerun. (National strategies and obstructions to agro-export-orientated development. Cocoa and coffee policy and the Côte d'Ivoire and Cameroon.)
See item no. 539.

Ländlicher Wegebau – Ein Beitrag zur Agrarentwicklung? Eine empirische Untersuchung aus der Elfenbeinküste (Côte d'Ivoire). (Rural roadbuilding – a contribution to agricultural development? An empirical study from the Côte d'Ivoire.)
See item no. 590.

CIRES. Cahiers Ivoiriens de Recherche Economique et Sociale. (Ivoirian Notes on Economic and Social Research.)
See item no. 779.

Transport

590 **Ländlicher Wegebau – Ein Beitrag zur Agrarentwicklung? Eine empirische Untersuchung aus der Elfenbeinküste (Côte d'Ivoire).**
(Rural roadbuilding – a contribution to agricultural development? An empirical study from the Côte d'Ivoire.)
Gudrun Kochendörfer-Lucius. Munich, Germany: Weltforum Verlag, 1989. 237p. 5 maps. bibliog. (Ifo-Institut für Wirtschaftsforschung München, Afrika-Studien, no. 114).

A study of farming systems in a marginal region in the western Côte d'Ivoire demonstrates the impact of rural roads on local smallholders. Products can be sold on national and international markets, but the effects of accessibility can be social, economic and ecological degradation.

591 **Port Autonome d'Abidjan. Réalités et perspectives.**
(The Autonomous Port of Abidjan. Facts and perspectives.)
Service Commercial et des Relations Publiques, Port Autonome d'Abidjan. Abidjan: SAPEPS, 1982. 24p. map.

A short illustrated guide to the port, with statistics of goods handled between 1951 and 1981. There is a detailed map of the Ebrié lagoon and the Vridi Canal which was cut across the lagoon spit to allow access from the sea.

592 **Les transports urbains en Afrique à l'heure de l'ajustement. Redéfinir le service public.** (Urban transport in Africa at a time of adjustment. A redefinition of public service.)
Xavier Godard, Pierre Teurnier. Paris: Karthala, 1992. 243p. bibliog.

A survey of public transport, in reality bus services, in Black Africa at a difficult time of great urban growth, with an emphasis on francophone countries. The work includes information on the bus services of Abidjan, run by SOTRA, and a map of the Abidjan network.

Les investissements publics dans les villes africaines (1930-1985). Habitat et transports. (Public investment in African towns (1930-85). Housing and transport.)
See item no. 608.

Employment

General

593 **Abidjan. Urban development and employment in the Ivory Coast.**
Heather Joshi, Harold Lubell, Jean Mouly. Geneva: International
Labour Office, 1976. 115p. 2 maps. (A WEP Study).

A picture of employment and labour supply in the capital and in the rest of the
country. Many immigrants from other African countries take unskilled jobs, and
migration and employment prospects for migrants are studied in detail. There are also
sections on the informal employment sector, employment prospects in urban
construction, and the social problems of population pressure. The study is backed by
plentiful statistics. A statistical survey of the rural and urban employment of Ivoirian
women was published by K. Akadiri as *L'emploi des femmes en Côte d'Ivoire. Une
étude comparative du PECTA. Rapport soumis au Gouvernement de la République de
Côte d'Ivoire* (The employment of women in the Ivory Coast. A comparative study of
the Jobs and Skills Program. Report submitted to the government of the Republic of
Ivory Coast) (Addis Ababa: International Labour Organization, 1985. 60p.).

594 **Code du travail.** (Employment code.)
Albert Aggrey. Abidjan: Juris Conseil, 1983. 413p.

The full texts of legislation on every aspect of employment have been assembled by
Albert Aggrey. Sections include contracts, working conditions, and the government
organizations concerned with labour.

595 **Droit du travail et de la prévoyance social en Côte d'Ivoire.**
(Labour and social security law in the Côte d'Ivoire.)
Paul Akoi Ahizi. Abidjan: CEDA, 1979. 301p.

An exposition of the laws concerning employment, salaries and conditions. The
second part deals with the operations and difficulties of the Caisse Nationale de
Prévoyance Sociale which offers social security.

596 **Les formes d'importation de technologies et leurs effets sur l'emploi et la formation. Le cas de la Côte d'Ivoire.** (Forms of technological imports and their effects on employment and training. The case of the Côte d'Ivoire.)
Kone Zobila. Paris: Institut International de Planification de l'Education (UNESCO), 1983. (Document de Travail. IIEP/S92/19).
A report on the importation of technology and its impact on employment and training. The author considers perspectives for education and urges realistic plans for an education system and syllabus appropiate to the needs of the country.

597 **Législation du travail.** (Employment law.)
Ministère de l'Enseignement Technique et de la Formation Professionelle. Abidjan: CEDA, 1978. 123p.
A short summary of employment law, but not providing the actual texts of the law. Chapters include government responsibilities for employment, trade unions, employment contracts, training, and conditions of work and problems of health.

598 **Occupational safety and health problems in Côte d'Ivoire.**
Dongo Rémi Kouabenan. *International Labour Review*, vol. 129, no. 1 (1990), p. 109-19.
The author outlines several causes for a high industrial accident rate in the country, including unfamiliarity with new technology, lack of instructions and training, and fear of unemployment, but he concentrates on the failure to observe safety regulations. He found dirt, ignorance and fatalism on the part of the workers, and unwillingness to spend time and money on safety on the part of employers. He recommends more training and government inspection.

599 **Oui patron! Boys cuisiniers en Abidjan.** (Yes boss! Boy cooks in Abidjan.)
Raymond Deniel. Abidjan: INADES; Paris: Karthala, 1991. 162p. map.
Interviews with twelve cooks in Abidjan, working for Westerners. Only one came from the Côte d'Ivoire. The rest came from Burkina Faso, Mali and Benin. They talk of their origins, education, feelings and hopes, and conflicts with the police and the authorities. High youth unemployment leads to insecurity.

600 **La situation de l'emploi dans une ville moyenne africaine. Le cas de Bouaké.** (The employment situation in an average African town. The case of Bouaké.)
Atta Koffi. *Annales de l'Université d'Abidjan, Série G, Géographie*, vol. 10 (1981), p. 131-49. map. bibliog.
Bouaké is the second-largest town in the country, situated at its centre, and the only provincial industrial centre, drawing many immigrants from the savannah region. This large-scale immigration has caused rapid growth, though many people do not stay in the town. Employment has not kept pace with growth, and the author looks at changes in patterns of employment over the last twenty years.

601 **Trade strategies and employment in the Ivory Coast.**
Terry Monson. In: *Trade and employment in developing countries.*
Edited by Anne O. Krueger (et al.). Chicago, Illinois: University of
Chicago Press, 1981, vol. 1, p. 239-90. bibliog.
A survey of the effect of trade on the labour market in the 1970s. In the early
seventies there was considerable immigration into the Côte d'Ivoire to supply
shortages in the labour market, and it was government policy to attract foreign
investment. Exports have on the whole created more employment, but some
government policies have reduced opportunities.

602 **The working behaviour of young people in rural Côte d'Ivoire.**
Rob Alessie (et al.). *World Bank Economic Review*, vol. 6, no. 1
(Jan. 1992), p. 139-54. bibliog.
The Côte d'Ivoire is undergoing a period of structural adjustment, during which
attempts are being made to re-allocate labour through changes in relative prices. The
authors use mathematical models to assess how price changes affect the working
patterns of young people in rural areas. The data come from the living standards
survey of 1985 and 1986.

Trade unions

603 **L'UGTCI et le 'développement harmonieux'.** (The UGTCI and
'harmonious development'.)
Ismaïla Touré. *Politique Africaine*, no. 24 (Dec. 1986), p. 79-90.
The Union Générale des Travailleurs de Côte d'Ivoire (General Union of Côte
d'Ivoire Workers), linked to the PDCI, until recently the only permitted party, is a
union which follows government policy and urges its members to work harmoniously
for social concord and the fulfilment of government plans. The author notes some
short-lived conflicts and strikes, at the end of which the workers soon submitted to
national policy.

**Etude des conséquences sociales de la politique de développement en
Côte d'Ivoire.** (A study of the social consequences of development policy in
Côte d'Ivoire.)
See item no. 646.

Gender, education and employment in Côte d'Ivoire.
See item no. 647.

**Les programmes spéciaux d'emploi et de formation de la jeunesse en
République de Côte d'Ivoire.** (Special youth employment and training
programmes in the Côte d'Ivoire.)
See item no. 656.

Statistics

604 **Black Africa. A comparative handbook.**
Donald George Morrison, Robert Cameron Mitchell, John Naber
Paden.   London: Macmillan Reference Books, 1989. 2nd ed. 716p.
maps.

Comparative statistics from all the countries of Africa in the fields of social
conditions, politics and education. There is also a section specifically on the Côte
d'Ivoire, with a map and a short bibliography.

605 **La Côte d'Ivoire en chiffres.** (The Côte d'Ivoire in figures.)
Côte d'Ivoire. Ministère du Plan.   Paris: Société Africaine d'Edition,
1975- . maps.

This compilation of statistics for popular consumption is a fairly weighty volume, but
comprehensible for the layman. There is a general section on the country and its
administration, but the main part consists of statistics on the economy and industry,
exports, prices and transport. The latest editions, 1982 and 1988, were published by
Inter Afrique Press of Abidjan.

606 **Memento chiffre de la Côte d'Ivoire. 1986-7.** (A statistical memo on
the Côte d'Ivoire. 1986-87.)
Direction de la Statistique et de la Comptabilité Nationale.   Abidjan:
La Direction, 1988. 5th ed. 205p.

This duplicated work provides statistical information on all aspects of the economic
and social life of the country.

607 **Statistiques économiques ivoiriennes.** (Ivory Coast economic
statistics.)
Abidjan: Chambre d'Industrie de Côte d'Ivoire, 1976- . annual.

A brief summary of statistics concerned with trade, agriculture and industry.

Enquête démographique à passages répétés. Agglomération d'Abidjan.
(Demographic survey with repeated presentations. Abidjan area.)
See item no. 201.

Enquête ivoirienne sur la fécondité 1980-81. Rapport principal. (Ivoirian survey of fecundity 1980-81. Main report.)
See item no. 202.

La nuptialité en Côte d'Ivoire. (Marriage in the Côte d'Ivoire.)
See item no. 207.

Etudes & Conjoncture. (Studies and Circumstances.)
See item no. 495.

Environment

Town planning

608   **Les investissements publics dans les villes africaines (1930-1985).**
Habitat et transports. (Public investment in African towns (1930-85).
Housing and transport.)
Edited by Sophie Dulucq, Odile Goerg.   Paris: L'Harmattan, 1989.
222p. (Villes et Entreprises).

The first part of this work is a history of public investment in the towns of colonial
French Africa, and includes facts and statistics from the Côte d'Ivoire. The second
part deals with the same countries after independence and includes chapters on
investment in housing and transport in Abidjan up to 1985.

Environmental protection

609   **Appropriation et gestion de la rente forestière en Côte d'Ivoire.**
(Appropriation and management of forest income in the Côte d'Ivoire.)
Eric Léonard, Jonas-Guéhi Ibo.   *Politique Africaine,* no. 53 (March
1994), p. 25-36.

A survey of the history of the exploitation of forest crops, including cocoa, and the
role of the state in their management. SODEFOR, the Sociéte d'Etat pour le
Développement des Plantations Forestières (State Organization for Forest
Development), has attempted to conserve forests and replace them in designated areas.
SODEFOR has set up a Commission Paysans–Forêt (Peasant–Forest Commission), to
encourage re-afforestation and to evict illegal settlers in designated forests. In 1991,
the Ministry for the Environment published a report on the environment and on
recommendations made to halt environmental damage. It is entitled *Rapport national*

sur l'état de l'environnement en Côte d'Ivoire (National report on the state of the environment in Côte d'Ivoire) (Abidjan: Ministère de l'Environnement, de la Construction, et de l'Urbanisme, 1991. 116p. maps).

610 **Les fôrets en Côte d'Ivoire, une richesse naturelle en voie de disparition.** (Forests in Côte d'Ivoire, natural riches in the course of destruction.)
C. Arnaud, J. Sournia. *Cahiers d'Outre-Mer*, no. 127 (July-Sept. 1979), p. 281-301. map. bibliog.

The Côte d'Ivoire is a naturally wooded country, but the export of wood and the growth of agriculture have destroyed its forests. This is an account of the destruction of forests, with the export of more timber since the opening of the port of San Pedro. Only three to four million hectares of forest remain, mostly in the west and south-west. There is a summary in English.

611 **La problématique de la reconstitution du couvert arbore dans la zone dense de Korhogo.** (The problem of the reconstitution of forest cover in a dense [densely populated] zone of Korhogo.)
Sinali Coulibaly. *Annales de l'Université d'Abidjan, Série G, Géographie*, vol. 7 (1977), p. 5-39. 2 maps.

The area around Korhogo, in the north-central Senufo part of the country, is exceptionally densely populated, at about 60-80 inhabitants per square kilometre, compared with between 5 and 20 in the rest of the region. This has lead to a destruction of forest cover in order to create agricultural land. The author looks in particular at the growth of mango orchards, and at efforts to re-introduce forest trees.

612 **La reconstitution de la forêt tropicale humide. Sud-ouest de la Côte d'Ivoire.** (The reconstitution of tropical humid forest. The south-west of the Côte d'Ivoire.)
Francis Kahn. Paris: ORSTOM, 1982. 148p. 4 maps. bibliog.

The report of a project to restore tropical forest which has been cut down for agriculture. An appendix lists species found at various stages of regrowth.

Health

613 AIDS – the leading cause of adult death in the West African city of Abidjan, Ivory Coast.
K. M. Decock (et al.). *Science*, vol. 249, no. 4970 (17 Aug. 1990), p. 793-6.

A survey conducted in 1988/9 of 698 corpses in Abidjan's two largest morgues, representing 7 per cent of the city's annual deaths, found that 41 per cent of male and 32 per cent of female corpses were infected with the HIV virus. AIDS was considered to be the leading cause of death in men, and the second cause in women after complications of pregnancy or abortion. It was calculated that 15 per cent of adult male deaths and 13 per cent of adult female deaths were due to AIDS.

614 Contribution à la prise en charge des enfants malnutris. Cas de l'Hôpital Protestant de Dabou. (The management of malnourished children. Cases from the Protestant Hospital of Dabou.)
T. Mutombo. *Médecine Tropicale*, vol. 52, no. 4 (Oct.-Dec. 1992), p. 407-14.

An investigation into the most effective treatment of malnutrition with limited resources, and the subsequent education and rehabilitation of children. Benefits of treatment sometimes disappear when the child returns to a poor environment.

615 Cost-effectiveness of the Expanded Programme on Immunization in the Ivory Coast: a preliminary assessment.
Donald S. Shepard, Layes Sanoh, Emmou Coffi. *Social Science & Medicine*, vol. 22, no. 3 (1986), p. 369-77. bibliog.

A calculation of the cost-effectiveness of the measles component of the Expanded Programme on Immunization in the Côte d'Ivoire. The researchers concluded that the measles component is highly effective in preventing deaths compared to many alternative health programmes in developing countries. An earlier version of the paper was presented at the National Council for International Health Conference, Washington, DC, in June 1982.

616 **Difficultés de la surveillance epidémiologique de la rougeole en Afrique: exemple de la Côte d'Ivoire.** (Difficulties in the epidemiological surveillance of measles in Africa: the example of Côte d'Ivoire.)
J. L. Rey (et al.). *Annales de la Société Belge de Médecine Tropicale*, vol. 71, no. 1-2 (June 1991), p. 115-21.

Two epidemics were first considered to be measles, and then turned out not to be. The authors conclude that measles may be over-reported because it is a target disease in the Expanded Programme of Immunization.

617 **L'épidemiologie de la fièvre jaune en Afrique de l'Ouest.** (The epidemiology of yellow fever in West Africa.)
R. Cordellier. *Bulletin. World Health Organization,* vol. 69, no. 1 (1991), p. 73-84.

Observations were made during the epidemics in Côte d'Ivoire in 1982, in Burkina Faso in 1983, in Nigeria in 1986 and 1987, and in Mali in 1987, in order to re-define the dynamics of yellow fever virus circulation in time and space.

618 **Equipes mobiles ou agents de santé: quelle stratégie contre la maladie de sommeil?** (Mobile teams or health workers: which strategy against sleeping sickness?)
C. Laveissière, H. Meda. *Annales de la Société Belge de Médecine Tropicale,* vol. 73, no. 1 (March 1993), p. 1-6.

In the face of a resurgence of sleeping sickness, the authors evaluate the most economic methods of control. They recommend a surveillance network of local community health workers who could also be used in other health programmes. There is a summary in English.

619 **Les facteurs de risque de la trypanosomiase humaine africaine dans les foyers endémiques de Côte d'Ivoire.** (Risk factors for human African trypanosomiasis in the endemic foci of Côte d'Ivoire.)
A. H. Meda (et al.). *Médecine Tropicale*, vol. 53, no. 1 (Jan.-March 1993), p. 83-92. bibliog.

A study of the risk factors for catching sleeping sickness. The risk is greater for coffee and cocoa farmers who sleep on their farms, and for people fetching water from natural holes and pools. A summary in English is included.

620 **The failure of falciparum malaria prophylaxis by mefloquine in travellers from West Africa.**
C. P. Raccurt (et al.). *American Journal of Tropical Medicine and Hygiene,* vol. 45, no. 3 (Sept. 1991), p. 319-24.

Due to the spread of chloroquine-resistant strains of *Plasmodium falciparum*, doctors at the vaccination centre at Bordeaux found it necessary to prescribe mefloquine for travellers. In spite of this, sixteen cases of falciparum malaria have been recorded in Bordeaux since October 1988, fifteen of which were in patients who had returned from West Africa. The researchers therefore suspect that mefloquine-resistant falciparum malaria is present in Côte d'Ivoire, Burkina Faso and Sierra Leone.

621 **Gestalt-therapie, culture africaine, changement. Du Père-Ancêtre au Fils Créateur.** (Gestalt therapy, African culture, change. From the Father-Ancestor to the Creator Son.)
Jean-Marie Delacroix. Paris: L'Harmattan, 1994. 268p. bibliog.

The author spent six years leading personal development groups in Abidjan. He formed a culturally mixed group which used Gestalt therapy in their dicussions. He offers insights into the psychological exchange in a mixed-cultural situation, and looks at a father's status and the role of aggressivity. He compares the role of traditional healers and modern psychotherapists in the search for a healer for the modern African.

622 **Un guérisseur de la basse Côte d'Ivoire: Josué Edjro.** (A healer from the lower Côte d'Ivoire: Josué Edjro.)
Harris Memel-Fotê. *Cahiers d'Etudes Africaines*, no. 28, vol. 7 (1967), cahier 4, p. 547-605. bibliog.

In 1965 a Christian healer appeared in the village of Akradjo, sixty-five kilometres west of Abidjan. The author visited him many times, and describes his activities and their social significance. He transcribes testimonies of patients and categorizes types of illness and cures. He records the reactions of Church and medical authorities. The latter were not able to confirm any cures, but made some improvements in the standards of hygiene among patients.

623 **Healing is as healing does: pragmatic resolution of misfortune among the Senufo (Ivory Coast).**
Nicole Sindzingre. *History and Anthropology,* vol. 2, part 1 (Sept. 1985), p. 33-57. bibliog.

A sociologist explains attitudes to illness and healing among the Senufo.

624 **Households, communities, and preschool childen's nutrition outcomes: evidence from rural Côte d'Ivoire.**
John Strauss. *Economic Development and Cultural Change*, vol. 38, no. 2 (Jan. 1990), p. 231-61.

A study of child nutrition funded by the Living Standards Measurement Study of the World Bank and by the National Institute of Child Health and Human Development. A total of 1,600 households were surveyed and 504 children under 6 and their mothers were weighed and measured in order to assess factors which may affect nutrition. Although, in general, domestic calorie availability exceeds estimated requirements by 15 per cent in the Côte d'Ivoire, in rural areas 10.5 per cent of children under 6 are too short for their age, and 4.4 per cent are too light given their stature. Improvements to drinking-water supply in rural areas would also reduce malnutrition.

625 **Human trypanosomiasis in the Ivory Coast. Therapy and problems.**
F. Doua, F. B.Yapo. *Acta Tropica,* vol. 54, no. 3-4 (Sept. 1993), p. 163-8.

A recent alarming growth in cases of sleeping sickness was thought to be due to the neglect of prevention and control measures. The authors were examining the treatment of cases in the Bouaflé district.

626 **Malnutrition in the Côte d'Ivoire. Prevalence and determinants.**
David E. Sahn. · Washington, DC: World Bank, 1990. 30p. bibliog.
(Social Dimensions of Adjustment in Sub-Saharan Africa. Working
Paper, no. 4).

Malnutrition is most serious in the savannah region where 23 per cent of the children
studied were stunted, indicating long-term malnutrition, while for urban children the
figure was 11 per cent. Causes are studied, with plentiful statistics, and are shown to
depend on family income, the education of the mother and access to medical facilities.

627 **The perception of AIDS in the Bété and Baoulé of the Ivory Coast.**
Andrea Caprara (et al.). *Social Science and Medicine,* vol. 36, no. 9
(May 1993), p. 1229-35. bibliog.

Structured interviews were conducted in 1990 to understand the socio-cultural aspects
of the disease. People holding traditional beliefs blamed infection on sorcery or on
having urinated in the same place as an AIDS patient. The need for health education
on the risks of AIDS transmission was obvious. The Bété had a greater knowledge of
condoms than the Baule.

628 **The present and future course of the AIDS epidemic in Côte
d'Ivoire.**
B. N. Soro and others from the Surveillance Unit, National AIDS
Programme, Abidjan. *Bulletin. World Health Organization,* vol. 70,
no. 1 (1992), p. 117-23.

An assessment of future mortality based on a survey in 1989. In 1989 there were an
estimated 25,000 sufferers. By 1994 the researchers estimated that the number of
cases would reach 89,000 adults and 41,000 infants and children. It was also estimated
that there would be 371,000 uninfected children born to HIV-infected mothers, and in
consequence they would probably become orphaned.

629 **Prévalence de l'asthme et des maladies respiratoires en milieu
scolaire à Bouaké (C.I.): résultats préliminaires.** (Prevalence of
asthma and repiratory illnesses in a school environment at Bouaké,
C.I.: preliminary results.)
M. Roudaut (et al.). *Médecine Tropicale,* vol. 52, no. 3 (July-Sept.
1992), p. 279-83.

Bouaké is the second-largest town in Côte d'Ivoire, in the centre of the country, with a
small industrial zone. The article is a survey of children's health in that town.

630 **Prophétisme et thérapeutique. Albert Atcho et la communauté de
Bregbo.** (Prophecy and healing. Albert Atcho and the Bregbo
community.)
Colette Piault (et al.). Paris: Hermann, 1975. 328p. map. bibliog.
(Collection 'Savoir').

A study of Albert Atcho, a popular healer, and the people who come to consult him in
the Ebrié village of Bregbo, 30 kilometres from Abidjan.

631 Santé de l'enfant d'âge scolaire en Côte d'Ivoire. Aspects de santé publique, de croissance et de nutrition en relation avec les infections parasitaires. (Health of schoolchildren in the Côte d'Ivoire. Public health aspects: nutrition and growth in connection with parasitic diseases.)
L. Haller, E. Lauber.   Basel, Switzerland: Schwaber, 1980. 132p. map. (*Acta Tropica. Supplementum* 11 and vol. 37 (1980), no. 4).
A study of 430 schoolchildren in four villages of the forest region. It was shown that 30 per cent of the children studied suffered from moderate malnutrition, with vitamin deficiencies and health problems such as parasites, malaria and tuberculosis. The French text is accompanied by a short summary in English.

632 Syndrome d'immunodéficience acquise (SIDA) en milieu rural. Cas de Dabou et environs. (Acquired immuno-deficiency syndrome [AIDS] in a rural environment. Dabou and its surroundings.)
T. Gneragbe, T. Mutombo.   *Médecine Tropicale,* vol. 53, no. 3 (July-Sept. 1993), p. 309-13.
In the early 1980s rates of HIV infection ranged from 1 to 7 per cent in this rural area. Infection rates of 15 to 21.9 per cent were found in the late 1980s and in the face of this catastrophic growth the authors argue the need for social and health care provision.

633 Utilisation des systèmes de santé modernes et traditionnels en zone rurale ivoirienne. (The use of modern and traditional systems of health in an Ivoirian rural zone.)
A. Coulibaly (et al.).   *Annales de la Société Belge de Médecine Tropicale*, vol. 69, no. 4 (Dec. 1989), p. 331-6.
A survey was carried out by means of a questionnaire to establish the use of a local rural health centre and traditional medicinal herbalists. Many people consulted both. There is a summary in English. A study of the resources devoted to health care in rural areas which shows the need for increased services is *The demand for medical care in developing countries: quantity rationing in rural Côte d'Ivoire* by Avi Dor and Jacques van der Gaag (Washington, DC: World Bank, 1988. 66p. bibliog. LSMS Working Paper, no. 35). Avi Dor also contributed to 'Non-price rationing and the choice of medical care providers in rural Côte d'Ivoire', *Journal of Health Economics*, vol. 6 (1987), no. 4, p. 291-304.

Medicinal plants in tropical West Africa.
See item no. 81.

Medicinal plants of West Africa.
See item no. 82.

Plantes médicinales de la Côte d'Ivoire. (Medicinal plants of Côte d'Ivoire.)
See item no. 84.

Occupational safety and health problems in Côte d'Ivoire.
See item no. 598.

Education

General

634 **Une aventure ambiguë. Le programme d'éducation télévisuelle (1971-1982).** (An ambiguous adventure. The programme of education television, 1971-82.)
Paul Désalmand. *Politique Africaine*, no. 24 (Dec. 1986), p. 91-103.
Concerned at the failure of traditional methods to achieve full literacy among the population an ambitious programme of educational television was launched in 1971, and abandoned as a failure in 1982. The author doubts if 100 per cent literacy is achievable.

635 **Avoir 20 ans en Afrique. Reportage.** (20 years old in Africa. A report.)
Pierre-André Krol. Paris: L'Harmattan, 1994. 249p. map.
The author spent three months talking to students in the final year at a school with 4,000 pupils in Gagnoa, south-west of the centre of Côte d'Ivoire. Classes have up to a hundred pupils, and pupils talk of their feelings on every subject, from their studies to politics and their health. They still form part of traditional village life while studying in a Western tradition, and their prospects are not bright in times of recession and rapidly growing population.

636 **Les bâtisseurs de l'enseignement en Côte d'Ivoire (1942-1958). Témoignage.** (The pioneers of education in the Côte d'Ivoire, 1942-58. Witness.)
Abdoulaye Jabali Touré. Abidjan: CEDA, 1983. 151p.
Sketches of teachers active in the period 1942-58, written in a conversational style which seeks to capture the pioneering spirit of the early teachers.

637 **Les collégiens de Côte d'Ivoire en famille.** (Students of the Côte d'Ivoire at home.)
Jean-Marie Gibbal. *Cahiers d'Etudes Africaines*, nos 73-6, vol. 19, cahiers 1-4, p. 87-100.

A study of conflicts facing secondary school students on their return to their villages in three areas: Issia (Bété), Sakasso (Baule) and Ferkessédougou (Senufo). The students' manners, morals and extravagance cause offence and are punished by traditional magical sanctions. Scholastic failures can be blamed on malign magical influences. An example of the conflicts of traditional and Western capitalist ideology.

638 **Convergence and divergence in educational development in Ghana and the Ivory Coast.**
Remi Clignet, Philip Foster. In: *Ghana and the Ivory Coast. Perspectives on modernization.* Edited by Philip Foster, Aristide R. Zolberg. Chicago, Illinois: Chicago University Press, 1971, p. 265-91.

A comparison of colonial education in Ghana and the Côte d'Ivoire. In the Côte d'Ivoire education expanded more slowly as the government distrusted mission schools and insisted on employing French teachers who demanded high standards in the use of the French language, whereas in Ghana African teachers were used and mission schools encouraged. The French also emphasized the teaching of agricultural studies. The authors consider the access of all classes to education in the 1960s and the concern for 'Africanization', in spite of which the Côte d'Ivoire system mirrors the French one.

639 **Côte d'Ivoire: system of education.**
P. Kokora. In: *The international encyclopedia of education,* 2nd ed. Edited by Torsten Husén, T. Neville Postlethwaite. Oxford; New York: Elsevier Science, 1994, vol. 2, p. 1152-61. bibliog.

A concise account of the educational system at all levels, including adult and vocational training, examinations, research, and the training of teachers.

640 **Croissance démographique et prévisions des effectifs scolaires et de la population active en Côte d'Ivoire 1980, 1985, 1990.**
(Demographic growth and forecasts of educational facilities and of the active population of the Côte d'Ivoire.)
Paul Koffi Koffi, Aboumédiane Touré. Abidjan: Ecole de Statistique d'Abidjan, 1980. 102p. bibliog. (Etudes et Recherches, no. 2 [Dec. 1980]).

A short introduction on the school system of the Côte d'Ivoire precedes a statistical survey of school age and numbers in the educational system in the late 1970s and projections of numbers up to 1990.

641 **L'enseignement en Côte d'Ivoire depuis les origines jusqu'en 1954.**
(Education in the Côte d'Ivoire from the beginnings until 1954.)
Leonard Sosoo.   Abidjan: Imprimerie Nationale, [ca. 1985]. 82p.
bibliog.

This short history of education begins with the traditional education of children within
the family, and continues with the establishment of formal schools in colonial times.

642 **L'enseignement en Côte d'Ivoire de 1954 à 1984.** (Education in Côte
d'Ivoire from 1954 to 1984.)
Leonard Sosoo.   [Abidjan]: [the author?], [ca. 1986]. 303p. bibliog.

A detailed examination of education since independence. Most of the work is
concerned with the creation of educational institutions and the successive ministries of
education, with legislation and government policy on education, and with the work of
various commissions.

643 **Enseignement et langues maternelles en Côte d'Ivoire.** (Teaching
and maternal languages in Côte d'Ivoire.)
Pascal Kokora.   *Annales de l'Université d'Abidjan, Série D, Lettres,*
vol. 10 (1977), p. 233-46.

An argument for the use of native languages in education. The author summarizes the
arguments which have been advanced for the national use of French, and then
discusses problems of the introduction of national languages, dealing first with
university-level and then with primary-level education. An additional problematic
factor is when to teach one of the four regional languages designated by the
government.

644 **Enseignement primaire. Statistiques. Année scolaire 1991-1992.**
(Primary education. Statistics. Academic year 1991-92.)
République de Côte d'Ivoire. Ministère de l'Education Nationale.
Direction de la Planification, de l'Evaluation et des Statistiques.
[Abidjan]: [La Ministère], [1992?]. 107 leaves. map.

An extremely detailed statistical analysis of pupils and teachers in primary education.
A brief look back at achievements over the last twenty years is included at the end of
the volume. In the current year 1,459,002 pupils were enrolled, with about 41 per cent
of them being girls.

645 **Enseignement secondaire général. Statistiques. Année scolaire
1991-1992.** (Secondary general education. Statistics. Academic year
1991-92.)
République de Côte d'Ivoire. Ministère de l'Education Nationale.
Direction de la Planification, de l'Evaluation et des Statistiques.
[Abidjan]: [Le Ministère], 1992. 28 leaves.

A compilation of statistics on secondary education, with a brief introduction. In this
year 396,606 pupils were engaged in secondary education, of which 128,778 were
girls. This showed an increase in total numbers of nearly 10 per cent over the previous
year.

646 **Etude des conséquences sociales de la politique de développement en Côte d'Ivoire.** (A study of the social consequences of development policy in Côte d'Ivoire.)
INADES. Abidjan: INADES Documentation, 1986. 36p. bibliog.

This study considers statistics on income and employment which show that the growth in population has not been matched by a growth in jobs. The numbers of children receiving education has grown, but this education has increased the drift to the towns, thus increasing unemployment, instead of encouraging young people to stay in the country. Girls have fewer educational opportunities; technical education is not sufficiently developed, and is too concentrated in Abidjan. The report concludes that the educational system is not tailored to the job market.

647 **Gender, education and employment in Côte d'Ivoire.**
Simon Appleton, Paul Collier, Paul Horsnell. Washington, DC: World Bank, 1990. 63p. 3 maps. bibliog. (Social Dimensions of Adjustment in Sub-Saharan Africa. Working Paper, no. 8. Policy Analysis).

An investigation of gender differences in employment and education. Girls have less access to education than boys, and are also less likely to work for wages. They face discrimination from employers in the private sector. There is less discrimination in the public sector, but since women have lower aspirations, and, on average, lower levels of formal education, they are less qualified to enter the public service.

648 **Histoire de l'éducation en Côte d'Ivoire.** (The history of education in the Côte d'Ivoire.)
Paul Désalmand. Abidjan: CEDA, 1983- . vol. 1. 456p. maps. bibliog.

Volume one begins with traditional education within the family and covers early educational efforts by missionaries and state education under the French colonial powers up to 1944. The second volume, planned to cover the years from 1944 to the present, had not appeared at the time of writing.

649 **Les jouets des enfants baoulé. Essais sur la créativité enfantine dans une société rurale africaine.** (The toys of Baule children. Essays on the creativity of children in a rural African society.)
Chantal Lombard. Paris: Quatre Vents, 1978. 236p. map. bibliog.

The results of a study undertaken under the auspices of Unesco in 1972. Toys and games are described and the feelings of children explored. A few texts from singing games are recorded.

650 **The management of educational crises in Côte d'Ivoire.**
Cyril Kofie Daddieh. *Journal of Modern African Studies*, vol. 26, no. 4 (Dec. 1988), p. 639-59.

The crises of this article are the strikes by school and university teachers and the riots among students caused by political dissent in 1982 and 1983. The author recounts how these were managed by the President and how tension was defused by a mixture of coercion and conciliation so that presidential power was undiminished.

651 **School attainment, parental education and gender in Côte d'Ivoire and Ghana.**
Aysit Tansel and Economic Growth Center, Yale University. New Haven, Connecticut: Yale University, 1993. 40p. bibliog. (Center Discussion Paper, no. 692).

The results of a survey, conducted from 1985 to 1987 in the Côte d'Ivoire, of factors which influence a household's decision to send children to school. Costs, distance to school and parental education are studied in relation to male and female schooling at primary, middle and higher education levels.

652 **L'utilisation de la télévision scolaire au Niger, en Côte d'Ivoire et au Sénégal.** (The use of educational television in Niger, the Côte d'Ivoire and Senegal.)
Max Egly. *International Review of Education*, vol. 32, no. 3 (1986), p. 338-46.

This article, in a journal published by the Unesco Institute for Education, gives a brief and concise account of the programme for educational television in the Côte d'Ivoire which was launched in 1971 and wound up in 1983. The reasons for its demise were cultural: public opinion was always against it, and, in a way, it was too successful in educating pupils at the primary level, who then had little chance of using that education in employment or of continuing their education at a secondary level where there were few places.

Higher education and technical training

653 **Accès et succès à l'université. Enquête exploratoire, analyses typologiques, profils et résultats des étudiants de 1ère année de la Faculté des Sciences Economiques pour l'année 1983/4.** (Access and success at university. An exploratory study, typological analyses, profiles and results of first-year students at the Economic Science Faculty for the year 1983/4).
Bernard Barrère, Claude Coulibaly, Dominique Desbois, Georges Vidal. Abidjan: Ministère de l'Education National Chargé de l'Enseignement Secondaire et Supérieure, 1986. 368p. bibliog.

A detailed analysis of the student population, their backgrounds, their studies and way of life, their finances, the way they spend their time and their examination results.

654 **L'enseignement supérieur en Afrique noire francophone.**
La catastrophe? (Higher education in francophone Black Africa.
Catastrophe?)
Paul John Marc Tedga.   Abidjan: PUSAF; Paris: l'Harmattan, 1988.
223p.

A study of the problems faced by university students in the francophone areas of
Africa. There is a survey of courses offered, research done, the finances of
universities, and their future. The author also looks at how students support
themselves, and gives details of fees, grants and (on page 73) the cost of living in the
University of Abidjan. Those who go to France to study find it as difficult as other
graduates to find suitable employment. A useful description of the country's higher
education institutes is to be found in the article 'Education: la priorité' (Education: the
priority), *Jeune Afrique Economie* (Paris), no. 129 (March 1990), p. 179-273.

655 **Institut National Supérieur de l'Enseignement Technique. Une**
école de formation d'hommes. 10 ans après. (The National Higher
Institute of Technical Training. A training institute for men. 10 years
later.)
Abidjan: Ministère de l'Education Nationale et de la Recherche
Scientifique, [1985]. 40p.

An illustrated history of this national institution for training in engineering and
technology. Opened in Abidjan in 1975, it moved to a futuristic new building in
Yamoussoukro in 1983.

656 **Les programmes spéciaux d'emploi et de formation de la jeunesse**
en République de Côte d'Ivoire. (Special youth employment and
training programmes in the Côte d'Ivoire.)
PECTA.   Addis Ababa: Bureau International du Travail, Programme
des Emplois et des Compétences Techniques pour l'Afrique (PECTA),
1985. 69p. 2 maps. bibliog. (Etude Comparative du PECTA).

A report by the Programme for Employment and Technical Training in Africa of the
International Labour Office. The introduction covers the economic situation of the
country, and employment, or lack of it. Special services to train young people are then
described, and something of their history. In rural areas there are programmes in
agriculture, crafts and fishing. In urban areas courses take place in 'Production
Jeunesse' centres. Many specific programmes are described.

657 **L'Université ivoirienne et le développement de la nation.**
(The Ivoirian University and the development of the nation.)
Valy Charles Diarrassouba.   Abidjan: Nouvelles Editions Africaines,
1979. 214p. bibliog.

The Rector of the University reflects on its role in the development of the country. He
considers the problems of running costs and of the unsuitability of traditional
university structures in a development situation. He covers the organization of the
University, its research, its teaching structures and its cultural role.

658   **Vocational and technical education in Côte d'Ivoire. An economic assessment.**
Christiaan Grootaert.   Coventry, England: University of Warwick, 1987. 144p. (University of Warwick, Development Economics Research Centre. Discussion Paper, no. 87).
The author emphasizes that this paper, a fairly technical economic study of the funding and costs of vocational education, is a basis for discussion, rather than a formal paper. There is an excess of students with qualifications in the area of business studies or secretarial skills, but a shortage in some technical and scientific fields and in those taking up apprenticeships.

Dynamique de population et stratégies de développement en Côte d'Ivoire. (Population dynamics and development strategies in Côte d'Ivoire.) *See* item no. 200.

Les formes d'importation de technologies et leurs effets sur l'emploi et la formation. Le cas de la Côte d'Ivoire. (Forms of technological imports and their effects on employment and training. The case of the Côte d'Ivoire.) *See* item no. 596.

Santé de l'enfant d'âge scolaire en Côte d'Ivoire. Aspects de santé publique, de croissance et de nutrition en relation avec les infections parasitaires. (Health of schoolchildren in the Côte d'Ivoire. Public health aspects: nutrition and growth in connection with parasitic diseases.) *See* item no. 631.

Scientific research

659   **Register of development research projects in Africa.**
International Development Information Network.   Paris: Organization for Economic Cooperation and Development, 1992. 346p.
Seven pages of this directory summarize, in English or French, the activities of research projects being conducted in the Côte d'Ivoire, and give the names of the researchers working on them.

660   **The world of learning.**
London: Europa Publications, 1947- . annual.
A standard reference work, which lists under the heading 'Côte d'Ivoire', the research institutes, libraries and colleges of the Côte d'Ivoire, and details, including a list of staff, of the University of Abidjan.

Literature

General history and criticism

661 **25 romans clés de la littérature négro-africaine.** (25 key novels of
Black African literature.)
Paul Désalmand.   Paris: Hatier, 1988. 80p. bibliog.

The introduction to this short work gives a chronology of 'négritude', that is, African culture and literature in Western forms. The author then summarizes one novel from each of three Côte d'Ivoire writers, Bernard Dadié, Amadou Koné and Ahmadou Kourouma, and from Amadou Hampaté Ba, a writer from Mali who lives in the Côte d'Ivoire. Short biographical details are provided for each.

662 **Annales de l'Université d'Abidjan. Série D. Lettres.** (Annals of the
University of Abidjan. Series D. Literature.)
Abidjan: University of Abidjan, 1965- . annual (with gaps).

A majority of articles in this review are on African themes, with West Africa and the Côte d'Ivoire predominating, but many more general contributions are included. The sub-series J, Traditions Orales, contains records of traditional tales and poetry.

663 **Les anneés littéraires en Afrique (1912-1987).** (The years of
literature in Africa, 1912-87.)
Pius Ngandu Nkashama.   Paris: L'Harmattan, 1993. 455p.

A bibliography in chronological order of African literature in Western languages and oral literature which has been transcribed into Western languages. It also includes essays, bibliographies and criticism, and, for each year, a summary of political and cultural events. The country of origin is given for each author of original literature. The works cited are also listed alphabetically by title and author. It is intended to update this work every five years.

664   **Anthologie de la littérature ivoirienne.** (Anthology of Ivoirian literature.)
Amadou Koné, Gérard D. Lezou, Joseph Mlanhoro.   [Abidjan]: CEDA, 1983. 307p. bibliog.
An anthology to illustrate the history of Côte d'Ivoire literature, from folk-tales up to 1980. It includes an alphabetical list of authors and their works.

665   **Aperçu du théâtre ivoirien d'expression française avant l'indépendance.** (A study of Ivoirian francophone theatre before independence.)
Richard Bonneau.   *Annales de l' Université d' Abidjan, Série D, Lettres*, vol. 5 (1972), p. 31-113.
A look at the beginnings of French-language theatre, and studies of some plays, including synopses and extracts. Immediately following this article, in the same issue, are studies by the same author of the plays 'La colère de Baba' by Mamadou Berté, on pages 115-25 and 'Monsieur Thôgô-gnini' by Bernard Dadié, on pages 127-44.

666   **La création romanesque devant les transformations actuelles en Côte d'Ivoire.** (Novel writing in the face of current changes in Côte d'Ivoire.)
Gérard Dago Lezou.   Abidjan: Nouvelles Editions Africaines, 1977. 259p. bibliog.
A survey of themes in Ivoirian fiction, and a consideration of how they reflect social problems. The main writers considered are Bernard Dadié, Ahmadou Kourouma and Charles Nokan. The author also surveyed the tastes of the reading public.

667   **Dictionnaire des oeuvres littéraires négro-africaines de langue française des origines à 1978.** (Dictionary of Black African literature from its origins to 1978.)
Edited by Ambroise Kom.   Sherbrooke, Quebec: Naaman; Paris: ACCT, 1983. 671p.
An encyclopaedia of signed articles of up to a thousand or more words on significant literary works in French up to 1978. The entries for novels summarize the plots, and for poetry they provide a literary analysis. A number of authors from the Côte d'Ivoire are included. The works are entered alphabetically by title, but an index groups them under author.

668   **Littérature africaine. Histoire et grands thèmes.** (African literature. History and great themes.)
Jacques Chevrier, Amadou Tidiane Traore.   Paris: Hatier, 1987. 447p. bibliog.
A text-book on the history of African literature, illustrated with extracts. A number of Côte d'Ivoire authors are included.

669 **Littératures africaines à la Bibliothèque Nationale 1920-1972.**
(African literatures in the Bibliothèque Nationale 1920-72.)
Paulette Lordereau, assisted by Luadia L. Ntambwe.   Paris:
Bibliothèque Nationale, 1991. 234p.
In this bibliography of African literature and literary criticism acquired by the
Bibliothèque Nationale between 1920 and 1972, pages 66-72 are devoted to the Côte
d'Ivoire. Bernard Dadié is the most prolific author.

670 **Littératures africaines à la Bibliothèque Nationale 1973-1983.**
(African literatures at the Bibliothèque Nationale 1973-83.)
Paulette Lordereau.   Paris: Bibliothèque Nationale, 1984. 199p.
This bibliography of more recent African literature and criticism was the first
compiled by Paulette Lordereau, the specialist in African literature at the Bibliothèque
Nationale. Pages 73-80 cover the Côte d'Ivoire.

671 **Littératures africaines de 1930 à nos jours.** (African literatures from
1930 to today.)
Pius Ngandu Nkashama.   Paris: Silex, 1984. 672p.
This is an anthology of short extracts from the fiction and poetry of French-language
African literature, with a short introduction. The first two parts group extracts in
chronological sections, and include writers from the Côte d'Ivoire. The third section,
from 1970 to 1982, groups the writers by countries, and there are chapters on the Côte
d'Ivoire under the sections for poetry and fiction.

672 **Littératures nationales d'écriture française.** (African French-
language literatures.)
Alain Rouch, Gérard Clavreuil.   Paris: Bordas, 1986. 511p. bibliogs.
One chapter of this work (p. 134-64) gives a brief survey of the French-language
literature of the Côte d'Ivoire, together with extracts from the works of major authors.
For each of the eight authors there is also a short biography, a survey of their whole
work, and a bibliography.

Authors

673 **Ecrivains, cinéastes et artistes ivoiriens. Aperçu
bio-bibliographique.** (Ivoirian writers, film-makers and artists.
A bio-bibliographical sketch.)
Richard Bonneau.   Abidjan: Nouvelles Editions Africaines, 1973.
175p. bibliog.
A directory of writers, musicians and visual artists, although writers predominate. For
each subject there is a biography, a photograph and a bibliography which includes
critical works as well as the artist's publications or recordings. There is an index of
persons and titles.

674 **Romancières africaines d'expression française. Le sud du Sahara.**
(French-language African women novelists. South of the Sahara.)
Beverly Ormerod, Jean-Marie Volet.   Paris: L'Harmattan, 1994. 159p.

A directory of women novelists which gives a short biography, a portrait photograph in some cases, a record of interviews given, and summaries of novels or short stories written, with bibliographical details, and sometimes a photograph of the cover. Côte d'Ivoire writers included are Assamala Amoi, Anne-Marie Adiaffi, Tanella Boni, Jeanne de Cavally, Flore Hazoumé, Simone Kaya, Akissi Kouadio, Kakou Oklomin, Véronique Tadjo, Regina Yaou, and Mary-Lee Martin Koné who is of American origin but lives in the Côte d'Ivoire as the wife of the writer Amadou Koné.

Jean-Marie Adiaffi

675 **The identity card.**
Jean-Marie Adiaffi, translated by Brigitte Katiyo.   Harare: Zimbabwe Publishing House, 1983. 114p. (Writers, no. 17).

First published in French in 1980 as *La carte d'identité,* by Hatier, Paris, in the Monde Noir Poche Series, no. 7. It won first prize for Black Literature in Paris in 1981. Adiaffi is Professor of Philosophy at Abidjan University. The novel is about Mélédouman, an Ashanti prince, who is arrested by the French commandant Kakatika on mysterious charges, tortured and blinded. He is given seven days to find his missing identity card. His search and his discussions with Kakatika reveal the theme of the search for personal and national identity. Adiaffi's second novel was *Une vie hypothéquée* (A mortgaged life) published by Les Nouvelles Editions Africaines in Abidjan, in 1984. He also published a collection of poetry, *D'éclairs et de foudres. Chant de braise pour une liberté en flammes* (Lightning and thunder. A song of glowing embers for a liberty in flames) in 1982, at CEDA Editions in Abidjan.

Bernard Dadié

676 **Bernard Dadié. Ecrivain ivoirien.** (Bernard Dadié. Ivoirian writer.)
Presented by Roger Mercier, M. Battestini, S. Battestini.   Paris: Fernand Nathan, 1978. 63p. (Classiques du Monde. Littérature Africaine).

Dadié is the best known and oldest of the Côte d'Ivoire's writers. This is a collection of extracts from Dadié's work, introduced by a short biographical note. Dadié was born in 1916 in Assinie, of an Agni sub-group, brought up as a Catholic, and educated with other promising possible future administrators from the whole of French West Africa at the Ecole Normale William-Ponty on Gorée Island. His first work was *Afrique debout* (Stand up, Africa) a collection of poems published by Seghers in 1950. He went on to write folk-tales, fiction, some of it autobiographical, and pieces for the theatre. An earlier edition, also published by Nathan, appeared in 1964.

677 **The black cloth. A collection of African folk-tales.**
Bernard Binlin Dadié, translated by Karen C. Hatch. [Amhurst]:
University of Massachusetts Press, 1987. 140p.

A translation of 'Le pagne noir: contes africaines' published in 1955 by Présence
Africaine in Paris. A transcription of folk-tales in which he became interested during
his work at the Institut Français (later diplomatically renamed Fondamental) d'Afrique
Noir at Dakar from 1936 to 1947.

678 **Climbié.**
Bernard B. Dadié, translated by Karen C. Chapman. London:
Heinemann Educational, 1971. 157p. (African Writers, no. 87).

In this autobiographical novel, Dadié recounts his childhood, his struggles against the
French colonialists, and his experiences in prison. As Press representative for the Parti
Démocratique de Côte d'Ivoire, Dadié was imprisoned after political disturbances in
1949. *Climbié* was first published in French by Seghers, Paris, in 1953.

679 **Comprendre l'oeuvre de Bernard B. Dadié.** (Understanding the
work of Bernard B. Dadié.)
Nicole Vincileoni. Paris: Editions Saint-Paul, 1986. 319p. bibliog.
(Les Classiques Africains, no. 860).

A study of Bernard Dadié's work. His publications included drama, poetry and
traditional tales, but he is perhaps best known for his 'Carnet de prison' (Prison
notebook), published in 1981 (thirty years after it was written) by CEDA in Abidjan,
and his semi-autobiographical 'Un nègre à Paris' (A negro in Paris) published in Paris
in 1959 by Présence Africaine, and re-issued in 1976 and 1984.

680 **La critique sociale dans l'oeuvre théâtrale de Bernard Dadié.**
(Social criticism in the theatrical work of Bernard Dadié.)
Barthélémy Kotchy. Paris: L'Harmattan, 1984. 247p. map. bibliog.

A critical survey of Dadié's plays, with an introduction about the Côte d'Ivoire and
the historical and social context of Dadié's work.

Amadou Koné

681 **Jusqu'au seuil de l'irréel. Chronique.** (To the threshold of the
unreal. A chronicle.)
Amadou Koné. Abidjan, Dakar: Nouvelles Editions Africaines, 1980.
143p.

Amadou Koné was born in 1953, and studied at the University of Abidjan and in
Limoges, France. His first novel, a passionate love story, *Les frasques d'Ebinto* (The
escapades of Ebinto) was written when he was 18. It was published in Paris in 1975,
by La Pensée Universelle; in 1980 it appeared again under two imprints: CEDA in
Abidjan and Hatier in Paris. *Jusqu'au seuil de l'irréel* is the story of Karfa and his son
Lamine and their encounters with sorcerers, which lead to the death of Lamine and the
girl he loves. Karfa and the girl's father unite to kill the sorcerers. An earlier edition
by the same publisher appeared in 1976.

173

Ahmadou Kourouma

682 **Kourouma et le mythe. Une lecture de 'Les soleils des indépendances'.** (Kourouma and myth. A reading of 'The suns of independence'.)
Pius Ngandu Nkashama. Paris: Silex, 1985. 204p.

Ahmadou Kourouma was born in about 1927 in Boundiali, of a Malinké father, but spent his childhood in Guinea, where some of his first novel, *Les soleils des indépendances*, is set. A student at Bamako, he was arrested after disturbances. He joined a native army unit, but was imprisoned and reduced to the ranks for refusing to take part in the suppression of political disturbances. He spent some of his later army service in the Far East. He later worked in banking and was a distinguished sportsman.

683 **The suns of independence.**
Ahmadou Kourouma, translated by Adrian Adams. London: Heinemann, 1981. 136p. (African Writers Series, no. 239).

Kourouma sent this, his first novel, to be published in Montréal, Québec, by the University of Montréal in 1968. Seuil, in Paris, brought out an edition in 1970. It is the epic of Fama, the heir to a Malinké dynasty, displaced by the changes caused by independence, and forced to live on hand-outs. His wife Salimata is sterile, and when he takes a second wife, strife ensues. Imprisoned after a political disturbance, and abandoned by his wives, he dies trying to return to his homeland.

Bernard Zadi Zaourou

684 **Les Sofas; suivi de L'oeil. Théâtre.** (Two plays: 'The Sofas'; followed by 'The eye'.)
Bernard Zadi Zaourou. Paris: Pierre Jean Oswald, 1975. 122p. (Théâtre Africain, no. 26).

Bernard Zadi Zaourou, a Bété, was born in 1938, and after studies in Abidjan, and imprisonment for political reasons, pursued his literary studies at Strasbourg. He returned to Côte d'Ivoire to teach literature at Abidjan University, and wrote poetry and plays as well as literary criticism. The play 'Les Sofas' was first put on in Strasbourg in 1969, and staged in Abidjan in 1972. The 'Sofas' were the warriors of Samori, and the main protagonist is Samori himself, who created an empire at the end of the nineteenth century and defied the French for many years. 'L'oeil' concerns attempts to persuade someone who is out of work to sell his wife's eye for 5 million francs, to replace the damaged eye of the wife of a local administrator. The eye becomes a symbol of the people's conscience, which will detect abuses of power. L'Harmattan brought out a later edition in Paris in 1979.

Oral literature

685 **Bheteh-nini. Contes bété.** (Bété tales.)
Texts collected and translated by G. Zogbo, transcribed by L. Gouzou.
Abidjan: CEDA, 1980. 91p.
Transcriptions and translations of folk-tales with illustrations by Philippe Prochazka.

686 **Contes de Côte d'Ivoire.** (Tales of the Côte d'Ivoire.)
Joseph Mondah.   Paris: Clé International; Abidjan: Nouvelles
Editions Africaines, 1983. 111p. (Collection Contes du Monde Entier).
The first volume of a re-telling of tales for schools.

687 **Les contes du soir chez le Godié de Côte d'Ivoire.** (Evening tales of
the Godié of Côte d'Ivoire.)
P. D. Kokora.   Abidjan: Université d'Abidjan, Institut de Linguistique
Appliquée, [1985?]. 144p. map.
The Godié are a small group on the coast east of the Sassandra, surrounded by Kru,
and probably of Kru origin, with Akan strands. This is a transcription and translation
of fifteen of their tales, with musical notation of the parts which are sung.

688 **La mare aux crocodiles. Contes et légendes populaires de Côte
d'Ivoire.** (The crocodile lake. Tales and popular legends from the Côte
d'Ivoire.)
F.-J. Amon d'Aby.   Abidjan: Nouvelles Editions Africaines, 1973.
122p.
Forty tales from across the country in French translations.

689 **Le murmure du roi. Recueil de dix contes.** (The murmur of the king.
A collection of ten stories.)
F.-J. Amon d'Aby.   Abidjan: CEDA, 1984. 62p.
A re-telling of popular tales.

690 **Ntalen jula. Contes dioula.** (Diula tales.)
Texts collected by J. Derive, M. J. Derive.   Abidjan: CEDA, 1980.
185p.
Ten tales collected in Kong are transcribed and translated.

691 **Proverbes populaires de Côte d'Ivoire.** (Popular proverbs from the
Côte d'Ivoire.)
F. J. Amon D'Aby.   Abidjan: CEDA, 1984. 102p
An anthology in French, with explanatory notes and indexes by subject and ethnic
origin. The majority of the proverbs are either Akan or Guéré.

175

692   **Le roman de l'araignée chez les Baoulé de Côte d'Ivoire.** (The story of the spider among the Baule of Côte d'Ivoire.)
Maurice Delafosse.   *Annales de l'Université d'Abidjan, Série F, Ethnosociologie*, vol. 2, fasc. 2 (1970), p. 13-31.
A collection of tales concerning the spider, who represents among the Baule, and other African groups, the triumph of intelligence and trickery over brute force.

693   **Two themes on the origin of death in West Africa.**
Denise Paulme.   *Man. The Journal of the Royal Anthropological Society*, new series, vol. 2, no. 1 (March 1967), p. 48-61. bibliog.
The text of the Frazer Lecture given at Oxford in 1966. The author explores a theme she felt was omitted from H. Abrahamsson's book *The origin of death: studies in African mythology* (1951. Stud. Ethnogr. Upsal., no. 3). The theme concerns exchange with death, or death as a price to be paid for life. The hunter trades with death by killing animals and must pay by dying himself or giving up a member of his family. She tells tales from the Dan and Bété of the Côte d'Ivoire and compares them with tales from Togo and from other parts of the world.

Arts

Visual arts

694 **African art in transit.**
Christopher B. Steiner.   Cambridge: Cambridge University Press,
1994. 220p. bibliog.
A study of the commercialization of African art and the circulation of African art
objects in the international art market, based on field research among art traders in
Côte d'Ivoire. The author analyses the role of the African middleman and discusses
the question of 'authenticity'. The same author has contributed an article on the art
trade in Abidjan to *African Arts*, vol. 24, no. 1 (Jan. 1991), p. 38-43, in which he
describes the search for or faking of desirable 'colonial' antiquities.

695 **Animaux dans l'art ivoirien.** (Animals in Ivoirian art.)
B. Holas.   Paris: Paul Geuthner, 1969. 331p.
Photographs of animal sculptures, masks and paintings from many ethnic groups, with
a short, explanatory paragraph accompanying each picture.

696 **Art de la Côte d'Ivoire et de ses voisins. Catalogue des objets
extraits de la collection Guenneguez.** (Art from the Côte d'Ivoire and
neighbouring countries. Catalogue of objects from the Guenneguez
collection.)
André Guenneguez, Afo Guenneguez.   Paris: L'Harmattan, 1991.
256p. 2 maps.
The largest published collection of illustrations of Ivoirian art. The photographs are
arranged by ethnic group, with explanatory notes on the group and its art.

697   **L'artisanat.** (Crafts.)
Ministère de l'Education Nationale. Sous-Direction de la Pédagogie,
under the direction of Abdoulaye Ouattara.   Abidjan: Nouvelles
Editions Africaines, 1985. 126p. (Ecole et Développement).

An illustrated book for schools on the crafts of the Côte d'Ivoire, with emphasis on the
production methods. The crafts featured are sculpture, pottery, basketry, metal-
working, the lost-wax method of producing metal objects, the weaving and dying of
cloth, and hairdressing.

698   **Arts de la Côte d'Ivoire dans les collections du Musée
Barbier-Mueller.** (Arts of the Côte d'Ivoire in the collections of the
Barbier-Mueller Museum.)
Edited by Jean-Paul Barbier.   Geneva, Switzerland: Musée
Barbier-Mueller. 2 vols. 10 maps. bibliog.

A sumptuously illustrated work. The first volume, 422 pages in length, consists of
articles on the arts of most of the peoples of the Côte d'Ivoire, with many colour
photographs of objects and ceremonies. The longest articles are on the Senufo, the
Guro and the Baule. The second volume is a catalogue of the museum's holdings from
the Côte d'Ivoire, and include masks, sculpture, carvings and metal-work. There are
eight detailed maps to indicate the origins of the works, and a glossary of artistic
terms in the major languages.

699   **Christian Lattier. Le sculpteur aux mains nues.** (Christian Lattier.
The bare-handed sculptor.)
Yacouba Konaté.   Saint-Maur, France: Editions Sépia, 1993. bibliog.

A biography of Christian Lattier (1925-78), who studied and exhibited in France,
before returning to exhibit and teach in the Côte d'Ivoire. Many of his sculptures
consisted of complex iron shapes, often derived from animals or traditional masks,
covered in tightly wound string.

700   **Colons. Statuettes habillées d'Afrique de l'Ouest.** (Colonials.
Clothed statues from West Africa.)
Eliane Girard, Brigitte Kernel.   Paris: Syros Alternatives, 1993. 136p.

A large proportion of this book illustrates statuettes from the Baule, Guro, Lobi and
Senufo of the Côte d'Ivoire. These statuettes of people wearing European clothes,
carved in the 1940s and 1950s are still copied today and the authors show how to
distinguish copies from genuiune colonial work.

701   **Côte d'Ivoire. Artisanats traditionnels.** (Côte d'Ivoire. Traditional
crafts.)
Jocelyne Etienne-Nugue, Elisabeth Laget.   Paris: L'Harmattan;
Dakar: Institut Culturel Africain, 1985. 287p. 8 maps. bibliog.
(Collection Artisanats Traditionnels en Afrique Noire).

An introduction surveys craft markets throughout the country. The main part of the
work describes the crafts of basketry, pottery, painted and woven textiles, metal- and
wood-working, and traditional house construction. There are numerous photographs,
some of them in colour.

702 **Gold of Africa. Jewellery and ornaments from Ghana, Côte d'Ivoire, Mali and Senegal in the collection of the Barbier-Mueller Museum.**
Timothy F. Garrard, photographs by Pierre-Alain Ferrazzini. Munich, Germany: Prestel, 1989. 247p. map.

A catalogue, with stunning photographs, of items in the Barbier-Mueller Museum, Geneva, collected in the last fifty years, which were exhibited in a touring exhibition. The main part of the work is an illustrated text on the techniques of goldsmiths, based on research in West Africa, including contacts with a Baule caster at Bouaké. There are many colour photographs of gold objects being produced and worn.

703 **Masques et danses de Côte d'Ivoire.** (Masks and dances of the Côte d'Ivoire.)
Georges Courrèges. [Clermont-Ferrand, France]: L'Instant Durable, 1989. 96p. bibliog.

A short history of masks and dancing, with reflections on their meaning for today. The many colour photographs included were taken by the author.

704 **Le Musée de Dakar. Arts et traditions artisanales en Afrique de l'Ouest.** (The Dakar Museum. Arts and traditional crafts in West Africa.)
Francine Ndiaye. [La Celle-Saint-Cloud, France]: Sépia, 1994. 194p. bibliog.

An illustrated catalogue of the holdings of the Musée d'Art Africain in Dakar, which houses the collections of the Institut Fondamental (formerly Français) d'Afrique Noire, founded in 1936. The Institute was established to study and preserve the heritage of French West Africa of which the Côte d'Ivoire was a part. About a third of the items in this catalogue are from the Côte d'Ivoire, and include wooden and metal masks, furniture, sculpture, jewellery and textiles.

705 **Suivez la mode.** (Follow the fashion.)
Emmanuel von Kirchendorf. Geneva, Switzerland: Les Editions du Temps, 1976. 111p.

An album of photographs of hand-painted shop signs.

706 **West African weaving.**
Venice Lamb. London: Duckworth, 1975. 228p. bibliog.

Much of this book is devoted to the woven textiles of the Asante and Ewe in Ghana and Togo, but the first part of the work covers the history of narrow-strip weaving and the trade in textiles. Kong in the Côte d'Ivoire was a centre for the trade. There is information on the Baule, who tie-dye some of their cloths after weaving, and the Senufo who also paint their cloths. Lamb includes pictures of some of the pulleys and beaters used in weaving.

Ethnic arts

Akan

707   **Akan weights and the gold trade.**
Timothy F. Garrard.   London: Longman, 1980. 393p. 3 maps. bibliog.
A detailed and scholarly volume, illustrated with many black-and-white photographs, on the history of the goldweights produced by the Akan. The first part of the work deals with the history of the gold trade, which was conducted in both Ghana, formerly the Gold Coast, and the Côte d'Ivoire. Kong was one trading centre. The history of the Guinea trade and relations between the Dutch and the Akan on the coast are investigated, as is the history of the production of goldweights, and the evolution of the weighing system. The work concludes with chapters on the names and dating of goldweights.

708   **Portraiture among the Lagoon peoples of Côte d'Ivoire.**
Monica Blackmun Visonà.   *African Arts,* vol. 23, no. 4 (Oct. 1990), p. 54-61, 94-5. bibliog.
An illustrated survey of carved portrait statues, some of which are carved as portraits of the deceased to honour them.

709   **Grave monuments in Ivory Coast.**
Susan Domowitz, Renzo Mandirola.   *African Arts*, vol. 7, no. 4 (Aug. 1984), p. 46-52.
An article, with colourful illustrations, on the elaborately sculpted grave monuments which have been erected by the roadside in recent years by the Anyi and Brong, who are part of the Akan group. Figures include portraits, and accompanying mourners, angels, policemen, musicians and animals.

Northern Mande

710   **Manding art and civilisation.**
Edited by Guy Atkins.   London: Studio International, 1972. 47p. 2 maps. bibliog.
A booklet, consisting mainly of photographs, produced to accompany the exhibition 'Manding: Focus on an African civilization', held in 1972 at the Department of Ethnography of the British Museum. At the same time a conference on the Manding was held at the School of Oriental and African Studies. There are photographs of statues, masks, musical instruments and musicians, and short articles on masks, marionettes and music.

711 **Shared masking traditions in the Northeastern Ivory Coast.**
Kathryn L. Green. *African Arts*, vol. 20, no. 4 (Aug. 1987),
p. 62-9, 92. bibliog.

The author considers the masking traditions of the mainly Muslim populations of the Kong sub-prefecture.

Southern Mande

712 **Classification stylistique du masque dan et guéré de la Côte
d'Ivoire occidentale (A. O. F.).** (Stylistic classification of Dan and
Guéré masks in west Côte d'Ivoire (A. O. F.)).
P. J. L. Vandenhoute.   Leiden, The Netherlands: E. J. Brill, 1948.
48p. map. bibliog. (Mededelingen van het Rijksmuseum voor
Volkekunde, Leiden, no. 4).

The descriptions of Dan and Guéré masks are accompanied by a discussion of common features and grouping into types, and illustrated by photographs.

713 **The arts of the Dan in West Africa.**
Eberhard Fischer, Hans Himmelheber.   Zurich, Switzerland: Museum
Rietberg, 1984. 192p. bibliog.

The revised and translated version of an exhibition catalogue first published in 1976 to accompany an exhition of Dan arts at the Rietberg Museum, Zurich. The works of art shown were drawn from collections in Switzerland and South Germany, and the authors regret not being able to include masterpieces in American, French or Belgian collections. As well as numerous photographs of masks and wood-carvings from the Dan, and a few from neighbouring cultures, the authors have photographed and described ceremonies in which the masks are used.

714 **Die Kunst der Guro, Elfenbeinküste.** (The art of the Guro, Côte
d'Ivoire.)
Eberhard Fischer, Lorenz Homberger.   Zurich, Switzerland: Museum
Rietberg, 1985. 312p. map. bibliog.

A well-illustrated survey of Guro carved masks and sculptures, based on an exhibition held at the museum. More than a catalogue, it includes the results of field-studies of ceremonies and the Guro way of life.

715 **La poterie wan et mona dans la région de Mankono: une
contribution à l'étude de la céramique ivoirienne.** (Wan and Mona
pottery from the Mankono region: a contribution ot the study of
Ivoirian ceramics.)
Bernadine Biot.   *Annales de l'Université d'Abidjan, Série I, Histoire,*
vol. 17 (1989), p. 31-32. map. bibliog.

The Mona, also known as the Mouan or Mwa, and the Wan or Ouan, are small Southern Mande ethnic groups in the Mankono département in the east-centre of the country. Their traditional pottery industry goes back to the sixteenth century. This is an illustrated description of production methods of a craft which is in decline.

716 **Women and masks among the Western Wè of Ivory Coast.**
Monni Adams. *African Arts,* vol. 19, no. 2 (Feb. 1986), p. 46-55, 90. bibliog.

A report of research conducted among the Boo sub-group of the Wè in western Côte d'Ivoire where, although preparing and performing with masks is restricted to men, the women take an active part in the mask festivals and dance in headdresses similar to male masks and costumes. The role of women in the festivals and dances is described and illustrated with colour photographs.

Voltaic

Senufo

717 **Art and death in a Senufo village.**
Anita J. Glaze. Bloomington, Indiana: Indiana University Press, 1981. 267p. map. bibliog.

A study of the meaning, nature and purpose of art in a typical Senufo village, based on field research carried out in the Kufolo region, in a cluster of villages around Dikodougou, in 1969-70. There is an introductory chapter on the seven distinct Senufo artisan and farmer goups of the region. The author then looks at the 'sandogo' and 'poro', the women's and men's organizations, and their roles in the arts.

718 **L'art sacré sénoufo. Ses différentes expressions dans la vie sociale.**
(Sacred Senufo art. Its different expressions in social life.)
B. Holas. Abidjan: Nouvelles Editions Africaines, 1978. 332p.

After an introduction on Senufo beliefs, the main part of the work consists of photographs of sculptures and masks, with accompanying explanatory texts. There are also pictures of people performing ceremonies and playing musical instruments.

719 **Bestiaire et génies. Dessins sur tissus des Sénoufo.** (Bestiaries and spirits. Senufo drawings on cloth.)
Elisabeth Laget. Paris: Quintette, 1984. 112. map. bibliog. (Linéales).

An anthology of designs drawn by the Senufo, with an introduction on the Senufo way of life and methods of producing textiles.

720 **Dialectics of gender in Senufo masquerades.**
Anita J. Glaze. *African Arts,* vol. 19, no. 3 (May 1986), p. 30-9, 82. bibliog.

A study of the male and female elements of Senufo masquerades, with photographs (some in colour) of masks, staffs and ceremonies.

721 **Le double monstrueux. Les masques-hyène des Sénoufo.**
(The double monster. Hyena-masks of the Senufo.)
Jean Jamin. *Cahiers d'Etudes Africaines*, no. 73-6, vol. 19 (1979),
cahier 1-4, p. 125-42. bibliog.

In this Festschrift volume for Denise Paulme, Jean Jamin studies the masks from their anthropological point of view, and includes drawings of some masks.

722 **Glänzend wie Gold: Gelbguss bei den Senufo, Elfenbeinküste.**
(Glitters like gold: brass casting among the Senufo of the Côte
d'Ivoire.)
Till Foerster. Berlin: Reimer, 1987. 252p. map. bibliog.

Written to accompany an exhibition at the Berliner Musuem für Völkerkunde, this work not only lists the museum's holdings, but also provides a study of a range of objects: masks, figures, rings and bracelets. Background information is given on the Senufo, and the author has studied the use of brass objects in healing and divination. There is also a study of the history of the casting of brass in West Africa, with archaeological evidence.

723 **Kreenbele Senufo potters.**
Carol Spindel. *African Arts*, vol. 22, no. 2 (Feb. 1989), p. 66-73, 103.
bibliog.

The author worked for a year with Kreenbele potters, an artisan sub-group of the Central Senufo group, in the village of Katiali, about 60 kilometres north of Korhogo, in the north of the country. Artisan groups live among the farming majority who belong to a different sub-group. The author describes the creation of pottery, and the craftsmen's way of life.

724 **Senufo ornament and decorative arts.**
Anita Glaze. *African Arts*, vol. 12, no. 1 (Nov. 1978), p. 63-71, 107.

This introduction to cultural themes in Senufo art is illustrated with cast brass ornament, mudcloth painting and architectural bas-relief. Images of bush spirits, pythons, chameleons and hunters are considered.

Lobi

725 **L'art traditionnel lobi. Lobi traditional art.**
Giovanni Franco Scanzi. [Milan, Italy?]: Ed. Milanos, 1993. 416p.
bibliog.

The Lobi are usually omitted from books on Ivoirian art, since most of this group live in Burkina Faso; but a significant proportion live in the Côte d'Ivoire. Most of the objects illustrated (mainly in colour) in this book were collected in Burkina Faso between 1955 and 1968 and are in private collections. They include statues and jewellery. The text is in both French and English.

726 **Kunst und Religion der Lobi.** (Art and religion of the Lobi.)
Piet Meyer. Zurich, Switzerland: Museum Rietberg, 1981. 184p.
2 maps. bibliog.
A well-illustrated study of carved figures and their use in religious ceremonies.

Kunst und Religion bei den Gbato-Senufo, Elfenbeinküste. (Art and religion among the Gbato-Senufo, Côte d'Ivoire.)
See item no. 298.

Woman power and art in a Senufo village.
See item no. 303.

Architecture

727 **Architecture coloniale en Côte d'Ivoire.** (Colonial architecture in Côte d'Ivoire.)
Ministère des Affaires Culturelles. Abidjan: Ministère des Affaires Culturelles, 1985. 319p. maps. bibliog. (Inventaire des Sites et Monuments de Côte d'Ivoire, vol. 1).
An exhaustive collection of pictures and plans of colonial buildings, civic, military, domestic and commercial, often now in ruins or disappeared. A map dates the creation of various colonial settlements, and the texts relate the history of major centres and of the three successive capitals, Grand-Bassam, Bingerville and Abidjan.

728 **Architecture soudanaise. Vitalité d'une tradition urbaine et monumentale. Mali, Côte d'Ivoire, Burkina Faso, Ghana.**
(Soudanese architecture. The vitality of an urban and monumental tradition. Mali, Côte d'Ivoire, Burkina Faso, Ghana.)
Sergio Domain. Paris: L'Harmattan, 1989. 5 maps. bibliog.
The French Soudan was established in the West African desert area formerly covered by the great Mali and Songhay empires, and this Muslim desert culture was extended to the north of the Côte d'Ivoire, strengthened by the conquests of Samori at the end of the last century. The traditional, decorated mud-brick buildings with their cone-like turrets are notable at Kong, and the author also includes photographs of modern mosques.

729 **La Côte d'Ivoire.**
Françoise Doutreuwe. In: *Rives coloniales. Architectures, de Saint-Louis à Douala.* Edited by Jacques Soulillou. Marseille, France: Parenthèses, 1993, p. 105-34. map.
A survey, with photographs, of the colonial buildings of the Côte d'Ivoire from the earliest days.

Music and dance

Music

730 **La chanson populaire en Côte d'Ivoire. Essai sur l'art de Gabriel Srolou.** (Popular song in the Côte d'Ivoire. Essay on the art of Gabriel Srolou.)
Edited by Ch. Wondji. Paris: Présence Africaine, 1986. 342p. bibliog.
A tribute to the popular 'tohourou' singer Gabriel Srolou, who died at the age of 38. Included are essays on the singer and on popular music, in particular on the tohourou tradition. Tohourou arose among the Bété, has no set forms or known composers, and is associated with the use of masks in dances and ceremonies.

731 **Contribution à l'étude de quelques instruments de musique baoulé – région de Béoumi.** (A contribution to the study of some Baule musical instruments from the region of Beoumi.)
Réné Ménard. *Jahrbuch für musikalische Volks- und Völkerkunde,* vol. 1 (1963), p. 48-99. 2 maps.
A detailed description of musical instruments, mostly percussion, and the way they are played. The author also lists the dances they accompany and the regions in which they are used. Although a sequel is indicated at the end of the article, none appears in succeeding issues.

732 **Introduction à la drummologie.** (Introduction to the study of drums.)
G. Niangoran-Bouah. Abidjan: G.N.B., 1981. 199p. bibliog.
The author has pioneered and even invented the term for the study of drums and their language, and has collected texts, mostly from the Abron, transmitted by talking drums. Parallel translations into French are included.

733 **Ivory Coast.**
Hugo Zemp. In: *The new Grove dictionary of music and musicians.* Edited by Stanley Sadie. London: Macmillan, 1980, vol. 9, p. 431-4. map. bibliog.
A description of music and musical instruments among the Dan, Guéré, Baule and Senufo.

734 **La légende des griots malinkés.** (The legend of the Malinké griots.)
Hugo Zemp. *Cahiers d'Etudes Africaines,* no. 24, vol. 6, cahier 4 (1966), p. 611-42. bibliog.
Griots are singers who usually recount historical traditions. The author collected Malinké legends concerning their origins during three excursions to the Côte d'Ivoire between 1961 and 1966. He includes two photographs of griots playing a xylophone and a lute-harp, respectively.

735 **Les musiciens du beat africain.** (African beat musicians.)
Nago Seck, Sylvie Clerfeuille. Paris: Bordas, 1993. 256p.
(Les Compacts).

A general introduction to popular commercialized music in Africa ends with a brief
description of music in the Côte d'Ivoire. The popular Ziglibithy rhythm has
traditional Bété origins, and other traditional rhythms have also been modernized as
part of the commercial industry. The main part of the work consists of biographies of
popular musicians, and includes seven from the Côte d'Ivoire.

736 **Musique dan. La musique dans la pensée et vie sociale d'une
société africaine.** (Dan music. Music in the thought and social life of
an African society.)
Hugo Zemp. Paris; The Hague: Mouton, 1971. 320p. maps. bibliog.
(Cahiers de l'Homme. Nouvelle Série, no. 11).

A study of Dan music and musicians. The first part deals with musical instruments, the
second with the relationship between music and language, and the third with the social
context of music-making.

737 **Musique et excision chez les Djimini (Côte d'Ivoire).** (Music and
excision among the Djimini.)
Mamadou Coulibaly. *Cahiers de Musiques Traditionnelles,* vol. 5
(1992), p. 37-52. bibliog.

An account of the music and dances related to funeral and excision ceremonies
performed by the Djimini. They are part of the Senufo group and live in the north of
the Côte d'Ivoire, the south of Mali and the west of Burkina Faso. Some songs are
transcribed and translated.

738 **Trompes sénoufo.** (Senufo horns.)
Hugo Zemp. *Annales de l'Université d'Abidjan, Série F, Ethnosociologie,*
vol. 1, fasc. 1 (1969), p. 25-50. bibliog.

An illustrated study of transverse horns in wood, metal or animal horn.

Dance

739 **L'avenir des danses traditionelles en Côte d'Ivoire.** (The future of
traditional dances in Côte d'Ivoire.)
Christian Valbert. *Arts d'Afrique Noire,* vol. 29 (Spring 1979),
p. 7-23.

A survey of people's knowledge of, and attitudes to, traditional and modern dances,
conducted in 1970-71, while the author was working at Abidjan University.
Consideration is given to the role of the Ministry of Culture in the preservation of
traditional dances. Photographs of dancers and instrumentalists are included.

740 **La danse.** (Dance.)
Ministère de l'Education Nationale, Enseignement du Premier Degré,
under the editorship of Abdoulaye Ouattara. Abidjan: Nouvelles
Editions Africaines, 1985. 126p. 7 maps. (Ecole et Culture).

A text-book for primary school-children on eight types of dance from the different
regions of the country, with many black-and-white photographs. Movements,
costumes and musical instruments are described, and a little information on the ethnic
background of the dancers is included.

741 **La danse africaine c'est la vie.** (African dance is life.)
Alphonse Tiérou. Paris: Maisonneuve et Larose, 1983. 142p.

The author, who is from the Guéré in the west of the Côte d'Ivoire, is a propagandist
for African dance in France, having founded the Bloa Nam dance school at Nîmes. He
expounds the ethos of African dance, its place in social life, its relationship to the
percussion music which accompanies it, and its future. He is enthusiastic about the
physical and spiritual benefits of dance.

742 **Dooplé: the eternal law of African dance.**
Alphonse Tiérou. Chur, Switzerland; Philadelphia, Pennsylvania:
Harwood Academic Publishers, 1992. xii, 88p. (Choreography and
Dance Studies, vol. 2).

Originally published in French in 1989 by Maisonneuve and Larose as *Dooplé. Loi
éternelle de la danse africaine.* In this second book on dance, the author begins with
observations on the attitudes embodied in African dance and explains for Westerners
the influence of the dancer's perception of the natural world and his social world on
the forms of his dance. He sets out African ideals of human proportions and postures
(curved bellies, long necks, bow-legs and turned-in feet) and illustrates them with
photographs of wooden statues. The second part of the book is a manual of dances and
movements with some illustrative photographs.

Cinema

743 **Le cinéma en Côte d'Ivoire.** (Cinema in Côte d'Ivoire.)
A collective work of the Centre d'Enseignement et de Recherche
Audiovisuels, edited by Antoine Kakou. Abidjan: Centre
d'Enseignement et de Recherche Audiovisuels, 1986. 232p. bibliog.
(Communication Audiovisuelle, no. 6).

A history of the Ivoirian cinema industry from early film shows in the 1930s. Topics
also covered are the use of documentary films in education, the economics of the
industry and its support by the government, the cinema audience and the conservation
of film.

744 **Dictionnaire du cinéma africain.** (Dictionary of the African cinema.)
L'Association des Trois Mondes.   Paris: Karthala, 1991- . 1 vol. to
date. 398p.

Volume 1 of this work in progress gives details of films made by directors from the
Côte d'Ivoire, including documentaries and vidoes. For feature films a summary of the
plot is included, and details of casts, distribution and showings at festivals.

Vers une définition de l'art bété: le mythe de Srele. (Towards a definition
of Bété art: the myth of Srele.)
See item no. 262.

Ecrivains, cinéastes et artistes ivoiriens. (Ivoirian writers, film-makers and
artists.)
See item no. 673.

Sports

745 **Le sport comme loisir et/ou moyen de diversion en Afrique: l'exemple du foot-ball en Côte d'Ivoire.** (Sport as leisure and/or a means of diversion in Africa: the example of football in Côte d'Ivoire.) Moriba Touré. *Kasa Bya Kasa. Revue Ivoirienne d'Anthropologie et de Sociologie*, no. 6 (April-June 1985), p. 36-52.

An account of the role of professional football in the social life of the country, with details of media coverage and international matches.

Mass Media

746 **The African book world and press: a directory.**
Edited by Hans M. Zell.   London: Hans Zell, 1989. 4th ed. 306p.
Pages 32-5 of this publication list the libraries, reseach institutes, publishers, printers
and some of the periodicals of the Côte d'Ivoire, together with their addresses.

747 **L'Afrique noire et ses télévisions.** (Black Africa and its television
services.)
André-Jean Tudesq.   Paris: Anthropos / Institut National de
l'Audiovisuel, 1992. 340p. map. bibliog.
A survey of television services in Black Africa, with numerous references to the Côte
d'Ivoire and its Télévision Ivoirienne, with a chart of statistics. In the late 1970s much
of the transmission time was taken up with educational programmes, but this was
dramatically scaled down in the 1980s and recent television shows a great increase in
imported entertainment programmes.

748 **De la publicité en Côte d'Ivoire.** (On advertising in Côte d'Ivoire.)
Ousmane Sy Savane.   Abidjan: CEDA, 1987. 122p. bibliog.
A look at the world of advertising and its effectiveness and the organization of the
industry. Advertising is concentrated in newspapers and journals, but television
advertising is getting off the ground.

749 **L'influence des Américains noirs sur les Ivoiriens dans la région
d'Abidjan (à travers les mass-média) de 1981 à 1984.** (The influence
of Black Americans on Ivorians in the Abidjan region, through the
mass media, from 1981 to 1984.)
Aminata Ouattara.   *Kasa Bya Kasa*, no. 7 (July-Sept. 1985), p. 70-97.
A survey of the reception by adults and young people of American music on the radio,
and American programmes and films seen on television and in the cinema. The author
found that people had an unrealistic view of the position of Black people in America,

assuming they enjoyed material benefits which they do not, and aspiring to such a Westernized life-style for themselves, turning their backs on traditional African values.

750 **Periodicals from Africa. A bibliography and union list of periodicals published in Africa.**
Standing Conference on Library Materials on Africa, compiled by Carole Travis, Miriam Alman. Boston, Massachusetts: G. K. Hall & Co., 1977. 619p. (Bibliographies and Guides in African Studies).

Pages 103-8 of this publication lists periodicals and serials from the Côte d'Ivoire, many of which are still being produced. A supplement was added in 1984, and the relevant pages are 32-5.

751 **Presse et information en Côte d'Ivoire.** (Press and information in the Côte d'Ivoire.)
Section Ivoirienne, UIJPLF (Union Internationale des Journalistes et de la Presse de la Langue Française). Abidjan: UIJPLF, 1983. 132p. 2 maps.

A handbook to the media in the Côte d'Ivoire. The introduction explains the language situation and the position of French. There follows a chapter on the laws of the press, a bibliography of newspapers published from 1893 to 1958, a directory of current newspapers, and chapters on radio and television and on press agencies and journalists' associations.

752 **Presse francophone d'Afrique; vers le pluralisme. Actes de colloque Panos/UJAO. UNESCO – Paris, les 24 et 25 janvier 1991.**
(The French-language press of Africa; towards pluralism. proceedings of the Panos/UJAO colloquium, UNESCO – Paris, 24 and 25 January 1991.)
Institut Panos. Union des Journalistes de l'Afrique de l'Ouest. Société des Editeurs de Presse. Paris: L'Harmattan, 1991. 278p.

The Institut Panos is an independent and international network of journalists specializing in the environment and in development. It has four centres, and the Paris centre covers francophone Africa. It is aimed at developing sources of information. The Union des Journalistes de l'Afrique de l'Ouest is established at Dakar, Senegal, but includes members from the Côte d'Ivoire. Members delivered papers at this conference on democratization and the growing freedom of the press, on sources of information, and on the future of African newspapers. On pages 190-2 Méma Soumahoro reviews some of the newspapers of the Côte d'Ivoire, mentions their financial difficulties and looks forward to new legislation.

753   **La radio en Afrique noire.** (Radio in Black Africa.)
A.-J. Tudesq.   Paris: A. Pedone, 1983. 312p. map. bibliog. (Afrique Noire, vol. 12).

A thorough survey of radio services in Black Africa. The author examines their role in the diffusion of information, the radio audience, radio diffusion and reception, and the range of programmes. The index entry for the Côte d'Ivoire leads to numerous references, including references to major towns within the country.

Bibliographies, Research Guides and Periodicals

Bibliographies

754 **Africa bibliography.**
Edinburgh: Edinburgh University Press, 1985- . annual.
This bibliography, which was published by Manchester University Press until 1988, lists books, articles and essays in English or other languages. There is a general section on West Africa, and a section specific to the Côte d'Ivoire, with subject subdivisions. There are also author and subject indexes. It appears about two years in arrears.

755 **Africa index: selected articles on socio-economic development.**
Addis Ababa: Library of the United Nations Economic Commission for Africa, 1971- . 3 issues a year. (Code E/ECA/LIB/SER/E).
Lists and indexes periodical articles, papers and chapters in books. The lack of a country index limits its usefulness.

756 **Africa south of the Sahara. Index to periodical literature.**
Compiled in the African Section, African and Middle Eastern Division, Library of Congress. Boston, Massachusetts: G. K. Hall, 1971. 4 vols. 1st supplement, 1973. 1 vol.; 2nd supplement, 1982, 3 vols.
These are photocopies of entries on index cards of items relating to Africa which are not included in the standard periodical indexes, such as the Social Sciences and Humanities indexes. The four main volumes cover the years 1900-70, the first supplement covers 1971-72 and the second supplement, which has the benefit of author and periodical indexes, covers 1972-76. Some of the entries are almost too small to read with the naked eye.

757 **African book publishing record.**
Oxford: Hans Zell, 1975- . quarterly.
An acquisitions tool for the librarian, this publication contains book reviews, a directory of African publishers, and a listing of current publications arranged by subject, by country, and by author.

758 **Bibliographie de la Côte d'Ivoire.** (Bibliography of the Côte d'Ivoire.)
Abidjan: Bibliothèque Nationale, 1969- . annual.
Includes items published in or about the Côte d'Ivoire.

759 **Bibliographie de la Côte d'Ivoire.** (Bibliography of the Côte d'Ivoire.)
Geneviève Janvier. Abidjan: Université d'Abidjan, 1972- .
(Unnumbered supplements of the *Annales de l'Université d'Abidjan*).
A series of volumes which has recently re-started. Volumes one to three cover material from the whole of the twentieth century. Volume 1, *Sciences de la vie* (Natural sciences), was published in 1972. Volume 2, *Sciences de l'Homme* (Humanities), appeared in 1973, and Volume 3, written in collaboration with Guy Peron, *Sciences physiques et de la terre* (Physical and earth sciences) was published in 1975. Volume 4, published in 1978, *Sciences de la terre, Sciences de la vie* covered items from 1970 to 1976. The latest publication, volume 5, part 1 (1985), *Sciences de l'homme exceptée l'économie,* covers 1970-82, and is by T. Ayé-Pimanova.

760 **Bibliographie de l'Afrique sud-saharienne. Sciences humaines et sociales.** (Bibliography of South-Saharan Africa. Humanities and social sciences.)
Tervuren, Belgium: Musée Royal de l'Afrique Centrale, 1932- .
This bibliography lists books and periodical articles, mainly in French, and uses appropriate subject headings which give some idea of content. A country and subject index is provided, and it lists periodicals on Africa, with addresses. Unfortunately it appears four or five years in arrears.

761 **Bibliographie des travaux en langue française sur l'Afrique au sud du Sahara. Sciences sociales et humaines.** (Bibliography of French-language works on Africa south of the Sahara. Social sciences and humanities.)
Paris: Ecole des Hautes Etudes en Sciences Sociales, Centre d'Etudes Africaines (CARDAN), 1979-92. annual.
A bibliography covering the years 1977-88, based on the acquisitions of the library of the Centre d'Etudes Africaines and other African-interest libraries in Paris.

762 **Le ficher Afrique.** (The Africa fiche.)
Abidjan: INADES Documentation, 1970- .
A computerized bibliographical bulletin on fiches. It has sections on politics and history, economy, society and the rural world, citing items from 120 journals.

763 **International African bibliography.**
Compiled and edited by David Hall, in association with the Centre of African Studies at the Library, School of Oriental and African Studies, University of London. London: Mansell Publishing, 1971- . quarterly.

Originally published by the International African Institute, this publication lists books, articles and essays in edited books, mainly in English and from fairly widely available periodicals. There is a section on West Africa and one specifically on Côte d'Ivoire.

764 **Repertoire des thèses africanistes françaises.** (Listing of Africanist theses in French.)
Paris: Centre d'Etudes Africaines, Ecole des Hautes Etudes en Sciences Sociales, 1977-91. annual, later bi-annual.

This publication began with theses on the whole of Africa, then limited itself to Sub-Saharan Africa. For earlier theses, the same organization published from 1966 to 1977 two annual series, *Inventaire de thèses et mémoires africanistes de langue française soutenus* and *Inventaire de thèses africanistes de langue française en cours* in its *Bulletin d'information et liaison.* Since the *Répertoire* has ceased publication, its editors refer readers to the Fichier (card-index) national des thèses, 200 av. de la République, 92 Nanterre, France.

765 **US imprints on Sub-Saharan Africa: a guide to publications catalogued at the Library of Congress.**
Washington, DC: Library of Congress, African Section, 1986- .

An annual listing of titles catalogued the previous year, with title and subject indexes. The Library of Congress catalogue is available through computer network services and a search from such a service probably provides the fullest bibliography of complete books (not periodical articles or essays) available.

766 **A world bibliography of African bibliographies.**
Theodore Besterman, revised by J. D. Pearson. Oxford: Basil Blackwell, 1975. 241 columns.

The first section guides the reader to general bibliographies and catalogues. The second section is arranged by country.

Research guides

767 **Africa: a guide to reference material.**
John McIlwaine. London: Hans Zell, 1993. 507p. (Regional Reference Guides, no. 1).

A helpful guide to reference material. In the first general part there are sections on directories of organizations, atlases, yearbooks and statistical compilations. After a section on West Africa there is a chapter specifically on Côte d'Ivoire.

768 **The African studies companion: a resource guide and directory.**
Hans M. Zell.   London: Hans Zell, 1989. 165p. (Hans Zell Resource
Guides, no. 1).

A guide to reference books, bibliographies, journals and major libraries for African
studies, with details of special features, facilities and access. Also included are
publishers with African Studies lists, and notes on the objectives and addresses of
organizations and donor agencies concerned with Africa.

769 **French colonial Africa. Guide to official sources.**
Gloria D. Westfall.   London: Hans Zell, 1992. 226p.

A description of the guides and bibliographies for the colonial period in French
Africa, and a guide to the archives of France and the former colonies, and their
inventories. There is also an annotated bibliography of the official publications of the
countries.

770 **International guide to African studies research.**
Edited by the International African Institute, compiled by Philip Baker.
London: Hans Zell, 1987. 2nd ed. 264p.

A world-wide directory of research institutions concerned with Africa. Details are
provided of the personnel, resources and publications of each institution, and there are
indexes of themes, periodicals and researchers.

771 **The national archives of the Ivory Coast.**
Ashton W. Welch.   *History in Africa*, vol. 9 (1982), p. 377-80.

A discussion of problems of access and use of the National Archives (Archives de
Côte d'Ivoire). They contain documents and official publications from the earliest
colonial days.

772 **The SCOLMA directory of libraries and special collections on
Africa in the United Kingdom and in Europe.**
Edited by Tom French.   London: Hans Zell, 1993. 5th ed. viii, 355p.

A guide to libraries with materials on Africa, giving their opening hours, and details
of access and services, and describing the collections.

Periodicals

773 **Africa International.**
Paris: Paris International, 1958- . monthly.

A news magazine mainly concerned with francophone Africa, and including items on
the Côte d'Ivoire. The largest section of each issue embraces politics, followed by a
section on economic questions, and one on society and culture.

774   **Afrique Contemporaine.** (Contemporary Africa.)
       Paris: La Documentation Française, 1962- . quarterly.
The first part of this journal contains articles on the politics, economics and social conditions of Africa, but with a strong bias towards francophone Africa. The middle section is a chronology of the events of the previous quarter, listed by country. The last part is a bibliography, with one section grouped according to countries and the other grouped by themes common to the whole of Africa.

775   **Année Africaine. 1963 etc.** (African year.)
       Paris: A. Pedone, 1965- . annual.
Between 1963 and 1976 half of each volume contained articles on the political and economic problems of Africa as a whole, while the second half consisted of chronologies of the year's events in individual countries. From 1977 the whole volume contained articles on general topics and on individual countries, and from 1977 to 1980 it also included an annotated bibliography. Since the 1987-88 issue (published in 1990), *Année Africaine* has been published by the Centre d'Étude d'Afrique Noire, Université de Bordeaux 1, France.

776   **Bulletin de l'Afrique Noire. Hebdomadaire confidentiel d'informations macroéconomiques et sectorielles.** (Bulletin of Black Africa. Weekly confidential report of macroeconomic and sectoral information.)
       Paris: FIC Publications, 1956- . weekly.
An up-to-date record of financial information and statistics from Sub-Saharan Africa.

777   **Cadres Magazine. Mensuel Africain d'Informations Economiques.** (Outlines Magazine. African Monthly of Economic Information.)
       Abidjan: A. P. E., 1983- . monthly.
A magazine on economic affairs, with the main emphasis on the Côte d'Ivoire and Africa.

778   **Cahiers d'Etudes Africaines.** (Notes on African Studies.)
       Paris: Ecole des Hautes Etudes en Sciences Sociales, 1960- . quarterly.
The most well-known French academic journal on Africa, with most of its material on the former French colonies. Articles cover ethnography, history, social sciences and literature. Some of them are in English.

779   **CIRES. Cahiers Ivoiriens de Recherche Economique et Sociale.** (Ivoirian Notes on Economic and Social Research.)
       Abidjan: Université Nationale de Côte d'Ivoire, 1974- . quarterly.
Articles on trade and the economy, agriculture, and social questions.

780   **Entente Africaine.** (African Cooperation.)
       Abidjan: Inter Afrique Press, 1969- quarterly.
A popular, illustrated magazine, reporting on the countries of the Conseil de l'Entente: Côte d'Ivoire, Benin, Burkina Faso, Niger and Togo.

781 **Fraternité Matin.** (Morning Brotherhood.)
Abidjan: Société de Presse et d'Edition de la Côte d'Ivoire, 1964- .
daily.
The main daily paper of the Côte d'Ivoire, issued by the PDCI, until recently the only permitted political party. It contains national and regional news, and limited international news.

782 **Ivoire Dimanche.**
Abidjan: Société de Presse et d'Edition de la Côte d'Ivoire, 1971- .
weekly.
A weekly magazine with in-depth articles, film and book reviews and comic strips.

783 **Journal des Africanistes.** (Africanists Journal.)
Paris: Société des Africanistes, 1931- . semi-annual.
Formerly entitled *Journal des la Société des Africanistes*, this periodical includes extensive bibliographies on the ethnography, history, geography and prehistory of the Côte d'Ivoire, as well as book reviews.

784 **Kasa Bya Kasa. Revue Ivoirienne d'Anthropologie et de Sociologie.**
(The Ivoirian Review of Anthropology and Sociology.)
Abidjan: Université d'Abidjan, Institut d'Ethno-Sociologie, 1982- .
Averages two issues a year.
Publishes articles by the sociologists and anthropologists of the University of Abidjan. The main themes are the Côte d'Ivoire and West Africa.

785 **Présence Africaine.** (African Presence.)
Paris: Présence Africaine, 1947- . quarterly.
The journal, founded by Alioune Diop, contains articles on literature, culture, history and social questions. It comes from a publishing house which pioneered the publication of works by African writers. An English edition was also published to begin with, but lasted only a few issues, and articles in English are now included in the main serial.

786 **West Africa.**
Camberwell, London: West Africa Publishers, 1917- . weekly.
A lively illustrated weekly news magazine with items on the Côte d'Ivoire.

Indexes

There follow three separate indexes: authors (individual or corporate); titles; and subjects. Title entries are italicized and refer either to the main titles, or to other works cited in the annotations. The numbers refer to bibliographical entry rather than page numbers. Individual entries are arranged in alphabetical sequence.

Index of Authors

A

Abrahamsson, H. 693
Adebayo, A. G. 122
Adiaffi, Jean-Marie 675
Adjobi, Jacob 190
Adloff, Richard 183
Aggrey, Albert 439, 454-5, 522, 536, 594
Ahikpa, Lohou Abby 237
Ahonzo, Etienne 209
Ahua, Antoine 509
Aiko Zike, Marc 484
Ajayi, J. F. A. 120-1
Akadiri, K. 593
Akoi Ahizi, Paul 595
Alessie, Rob 602
Alland, Alexander 222
Allen, P. K. 523
Alman, Miriam 750
Alschuler, Lawrence R. 502
Amethiers, Jean-Baptiste 526
Amin, Samir 194
Amon D'Aby, F. J. 228, 688-9, 691
Amondji, Marcel 179, 186, 433
Amselle, Jean-Loup 293
Ancey, A. 565
Andersen, Arthur 514
Angoulvent, G. 172
Antoine, Philippe 201, 401

Appleton, Simon, 647
Arens, W. 382
Arnaud, C. 610
Arvel, Anne 57
Asare Opoku, Kofi 381
Ascani, Maurice 9
Assa, Koby 545
Atkins, Guy 274, 710
Aubertin, Catherine 581
Augé, Marc 379-80, 427, 459
Avenard, J. M. 30
Aye-Pimanove T. 759
Ayensu, Edward S. 82

B

Baba Kake, Ibrahima 215
Baer, Werner 521
Baesjou, René 135
Bagarre, E. 37
Bakary, Tessy D. 436
Baker, Philip 770
Bamba, Moussa 348
Barbier, Jean-Paul 698
Barker, Jonathan 571
Barrère, Bernard 209, 653
Barrère, Monique 207
Bassett, Thomas J. 143
Battestini, M. 670
Battestini, S. 676
Baulin, Jacques 445, 448

Bayle des Hermens R. de 117
Bearth, T. 333
Benoist, Joseph-Roger de 180
Bentinck, J. 330
Bernadet, Philippe 558, 587
Bernstein, Henry 529
Bernus, Edmond 28
Berron, Henri 428
Bertrand, J. 32
Besterman, Theodore 766
Bharati, Agehananda 265
Bianco, A. 358
Bie, Sde 112
Binger, Gustave 338
Binger, Louis-Gustave 71, 77
Biot, Bernardine 715
Blackmun Visonà, Monica 708
Blanc-Pamard, Chantal 413
Blaustein, Albert P. 451
Boa, E. 504
Bolli, Margrit 308
Bond, George 384
Bondonneau, Henry 43
Boni, Dian 235, 566
Bonnassieux, Alain 404
Bonneau, Georges-Auguste 160

Index of Titles

205

D

Index of Subjects

223

Map of Côte d'Ivoire

This map shows the more important towns and other features.

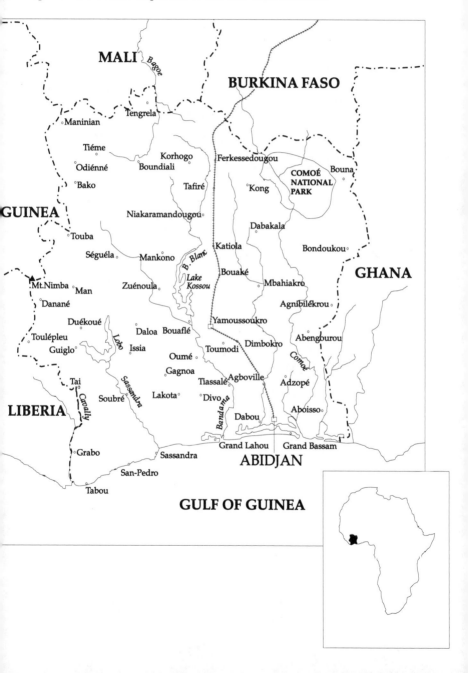

ALSO FROM CLIO PRESS

INTERNATIONAL ORGANIZATIONS SERIES

Each volume in the International Organizations Series is either devoted to one specific organization, or to a number of different organizations operating in a particular region, or engaged in a specific field of activity. The scope of the series is wide-ranging and includes intergovernmental organizations, international non-governmental organizations, and national bodies dealing with international issues. The series is aimed mainly at the English-speaker and each volume provides a selective, annotated, critical bibliography of the organization, or organizations, concerned. The bibliographies cover books, articles, pamphlets, directories, databases and theses and, wherever possible, attention is focused on material about the organizations rather than on the organizations' own publications. Notwithstanding this, the most important official publications, and guides to those publications, will be included. The views expressed in individual volumes, however, are not necessarily those of the publishers.

VOLUMES IN THE SERIES

1 *European Communities*,
   John Paxton
2 *Arab Regional Organizations*,
   Frank A. Clements
3 *Comecon: The Rise and Fall of an
   International Socialist
   Organization*, Jenny Brine
4 *International Monetary Fund*,
   Anne C. M. Salda
5 *The Commonwealth*, Patricia M.
   Larby and Harry Hannam
6 *The French Secret Services*, Martyn
   Cornick and Peter Morris

7 *Organization of African Unity*,
   Gordon Harris
8 *North Atlantic Treaty Organization*,
   Phil Williams
9 *World Bank*, Anne C. M. Salda
10 *United Nations System*, Joseph P.
   Baratta
11 *Organization of American States*,
   David Sheinin
12 *British Secret Services*, Philip H. J.
   Davies

TITLE IN PREPARATION

Israeli Secret Services, Frank A. Clements

Please renew/return items by last date
shown. Please call the number below:

Renewals and enquiries: 0300 123 4049

Textphone for hearing or
speech impaired users: 0300 123 4041

www.hertsdirect.org/librarycatalogue
L32

Hertfordshire